Decade Of Dissent

How 1960s Bob Dylan
Changed the World

Sean Egan

Decade Of Dissent
How 1960s Bob Dylan Changed The World
Sean Egan

A Jawbone book
First edition 2025
Published in the UK and the USA by
Jawbone Press
Office G1
141–157 Acre Lane
London SW2 5UA
England
www.jawbonepress.com

ISBN 978-1-916829-20-6

Printed by Short Run Press, Exeter, Devon

1 2 3 4 5 29 28 27 26 25

Table Of Contents

BOB DYLAN

PERSONAL MANAGEMENT: A B C / M INC./ALBERT B. GROSSMAN/JOHN COURT/75 E. 55 ST., N.Y.C.

Introduction

'The closest I ever got to the sound I hear in my mind was on individual bands in the *Blonde On Blonde* album. It's that thin, that wild mercury sound. It's metallic and bright gold, with whatever that conjures up. That's my particular sound.'

Bob Dylan, 1978

At the beginning of 1965, Bob Dylan was only a few months but a world-shattering change away from achieving what he considered his particular sound.

At the time, there was no reason to think that he wasn't purveying precisely the sound he wanted to with the format of one man, one guitar, and a singular ability to exquisitely articulate his peers' grievances about the conduct of their supposed elders and betters. Over the last three years, it had earned him the sobriquet 'Voice Of A Generation'. His opening four acoustic albums (1962–1964) shook up folk music by injecting into it youth, vitality, and, above all, relevance. He captured the 60s' burgeoning libertarian zeitgeist with protest songs like 'Blowin' In The Wind' and 'The Times They Are A-Changin'' that were not just notable sociopolitically but intoxicating linguistically. This beautifully articulated barrier-smashing would characterise him and his music for the next several years. Dylan would be a poetic voice of dissent for the rest of the 1960s. However, his dissent would not always be directed at the expected targets: he set his face against both political and musical foes, and against both those who were assumed to be his enemies and people whom it might be imagined were his allies. His iconoclasm was all-encompassing: he was perennially determined to not go the established way, regardless of who it might surprise or offend.

Yet despite the ego-gratification of adoring audiences, the artistic fulfilment of writing great songs, and the financial rewards that resulted from the fact of many of those songs—especially 'Blowin' In The Wind'—being the subject of cover versions, Dylan wasn't fulfilled by folk. However, it wasn't that easy for him to do what he really wanted to do. It is difficult to convey to today's audiences the chasm that in the first half of the 1960s yawned between popular music and folk, culturally, demographically, intellectually, and financially. Nonetheless, when Dylan booked into Columbia Studio A in New York in January 1965, he was accompanied by a full band, and furthermore not one made up of folk musicians. Tellingly, though, they would not appear on all the tracks on the resultant album. The LP, *Bringing It All Back Home*, was divided neatly down the middle, only the first side featuring tracks with band accompaniment, with the second cleaving to Dylan's familiar voice/guitar/harmonica format. Although in truth side two was aesthetically more successful than the first side, the latter bequeathed 'Subterranean Homesick Blues', which took the proletarian grievances, unapologetic irritability, and Kalashnikov delivery of Chuck Berry's 'Too Much Monkey Business' and added a New York hipster sensibility and political tinge. It was a type of rock music never heard before—one that retained its fun and sweat but added to it intellect.

Bringing It All Back Home came out in March 1965. Although there were grumbles from some of Dylan's followers about naked commerciality, they were as relatively muted as the mutterings about the way the subject matter of Dylan's previous album, *Another Side Of Bob Dylan* (August 1964), had favoured the personal over the political. The real storm of disapproval would begin at the Newport Folk Festival on July 25, 1965, when Dylan came out wrapped in a leather jacket and an electric guitar and played songs backed by a raucous band. He was loudly booed, and his reputation as a fame-seeking, money-grubbing betrayer of the pure and anti-mercenary folk idiom started to snowball. There was far worse to come.

The week before Newport had seen the release of his new 45, 'Like A Rolling Stone'. An apparent denunciation of a former lover, the single was revolutionary in its six-minutes-plus length, its gritty, streetwise lyrics, and its ostentatious tearing asunder of moon-in-June pop conventions. In the opinion of many, it remains the greatest single ever released.

During the period from March 1965 to June 1966, Dylan released no fewer than three long-players, one of them a double. Two of them—*Highway 61 Revisited* and *Blonde On Blonde*—are by common consensus among the finest albums ever made. All these artistic achievements become even more staggering when one reflects on the fact that Dylan wrote them in isolation: there was no McCartney to his Lennon, no Richards to his Jagger—a collaborator to pick up the slack if the muse wasn't within reach.

Some of his long-term followers, however, were not going to be mollified over his new direction by anything so trivial as classic recordings. That Dylan was now less interested in deploying denunciatory rhetoric to address the persecution of James Meredith or the killing of Hattie Carroll than he was in examining society through the type of distance, wryness, surrealism, and metaphor heard in *Highway 61*'s 'Desolation Row' was unforgivable. So too was his new beat-group-like format, associated by folkies with pompadoured chumps wailing platitudes at doe-eyed teenagers. Accordingly, when Dylan went on a world tour in 1966, the enthusiastic reception to the solo acoustic set with which he opened each gig was in stark contrast to the venom that resulted when he returned from the wings for a second set backed by his new permanent band, The Hawks. He was consistently booed to the rafters, and this despite the fact that he happened to be providing audiences with some of the greatest music ever heard on a concert stage.

The naysayers were wasting their breath. This was Bob Dylan's time. Nobody's influence was more pervasive at that or any other juncture in music history. It was a point that was not merely his peak as a creative artist but one when his sound and style were absolutely everywhere.

Any apprehension Dylan may have had that he might lose his folk audience with his new sound but simultaneously discover that the pop purchasers could not respond to music filtered through his particular prism was soothed, to say the least, by the commercial successes of his own releases and a veritable tidal wave of covers by other artists. He also had a legion of imitators, from lightweights like Donovan and Sonny & Cher to already prominent titans like The Beatles and The Rolling Stones. Meanwhile, his scathing, hipster persona (very unusual in a celebrity at that point, even in rock) and the surreal humour evident at his press conferences only added to the impression of an entertainer of singular poise and unprecedented intellectual gravitas.

However, while Dylan could—just about—cope with city-to-city booing, his own hyperactive creativity was playing havoc with his well-being. He was being worked well beyond the limits of his constitution by his rapacious manager, Albert Grossman. In July 1966, Dylan had a minor motorcycle accident. He exploited it to flee his predicament, begging off all professional activity for nearly a year and a half. It was then an unthinkable span of time for a musical artist to be absent from a market felt to be intrinsically fickle.

In the time that Dylan spent hidden away from the world, he seemed to undergo an almost complete personality change. The icon of cool became a family man living a quiet life with his wife and children. He also seems to have effectively gone on strike, for several months writing no songs, or at least none he was prepared to show to Grossman. However, whatever else he was, Dylan was a music-maker to his core. The Hawks—in the process of restyling themselves as The Band—were at the time in the vicinity of his upstate New York home, and, although Dylan had no particular inclination to make a new album, there seemed no reason for him not to drive over to the house that they were renting nearby and jam. At some point, this turned into recording new Dylan songs. His compositional drought was transformed into a deluge as he ran through three dozen new creations that were extraordinary

8

not only in their number but in their tone. The likes of 'Down In The Flood', 'Nothing Was Delivered', 'Too Much Of Nothing', Tears Of Rage', 'Sign On The Cross', and 'This Wheel's On Fire' implied a man going through a crisis, both about how others had treated him and how he had hitherto conducted himself. There again, there were also comedy numbers and merrily obscene ditties. The songs also had for some undefinable reason related to setting, mood, whimsy, and alchemy a peculiarly olde-worlde feel, all musty acoustics and antediluvian phraseology, which only served to make them all the more delightful.

None of these recordings would obtain an official release by Dylan until 1975, but the songs themselves began to circulate in the music industry as publishing demos, originally supplied by the ever-canny Grossman in the hope of attracting cover versions. The recordings—which became colloquially known as 'The Basement Tapes'—proved that Dylan was influential when he wasn't even trying. They became the subject of the first ever rock bootleg, thus creating an entire industry, but long before that, they inspired a new wave of copycat behaviour among Dylan's peers as the rock aristocracy abandoned the latest fads of psychedelia and big production to make similarly rootsy, low-key music.

Meanwhile, Dylan's next official album was *John Wesley Harding*, released in December 1967. It took Dylan all the way back to folk, albeit with a couple of accompanists and a new brooding set of obsessions. Its haunted, even eerie, ambience is exemplified by 'The Wicked Messenger'. A relentlessly intense and unsettling track, it finds the titular messenger—clearly the artist—being informed by his multitudinous naysayers and enemies that if he cannot bring good news, he shouldn't bring any. Following which, the album's last two tracks are love songs—as though this was Dylan's way of conveying to the world that he was finally, definitively resigning from his position as voice of a generation.

It didn't work. The unprecedentedly long eighteen-month gap between albums had created a mystique around him that only made the reception to the record even more reverential than it would have been in the ordinary course of events. Even putting out *Nashville Skyline* (April 1969) didn't work. This album confirmed the philosophical retrenchment of *John Wesley Harding*'s last two cuts, and its country stylings seemed almost a gesture of contempt to the rock audience, who despised 'redneck' music. Artistically, it was lazy and slender and boasted no songs into whose lyrics deep meaning could be read. For all that, though, Dylan couldn't stop his craftsmanship leaking out: its music was at the very least slick, and the album even boasted a brace of classics in 'Lay Lady Lay' and 'Tonight I'll Be Staying Here With You'. Nor could he prevent himself from being influential: he had given permission by example for rock fans to admit to liking country music, and—as with folk and rock—his pioneering meant that the two genres would never be separated by a Berlin Wall again.

From there, Dylan would have a long career, one quality-wise of mountains and valleys, but the focus of *Decade Of Dissent* is the full circle constituted in the journey from his eponymous 1962 debut album to *Nashville Skyline*—a journey in which he went from the status of an ambitious nobody to a cultural icon to a man who tried to turn his back on idolatry. With the help of friends and collaborators, it telescopes in on this small but crucial part of his recording career to explore one of the most extraordinary and fascinating story arcs in the history of recorded music.

Chapter one

CHAPTER ONE

Voice Without Restraint

'[I spent] about three-quarters of my life around the Midwest and one quarter around the southwest—New Mexico. But then I lived in Kansas—Marysville, Kansas, and, uh, Sioux Falls, South Dakota. I bounced around a lot as a kid . . . I ran away a lot . . . I took off when I was in New Mexico . . . [I was] seven—eight—something like that . . . I was with a carnival when I was about thirteen, and I used to travel with a carnival—all kinds of shows . . . I learned a lot of songs in the carnival. That's why I know all these songs they do now and I'm only twenty.'

A version of the above comments were, for many people, the first biographical details to which they were exposed about a new musical artist named Bob Dylan. They were generated by an interview with Billy James, Manager Of Talent Acquisition And Development for Columbia Records. Included in a late-1961 Columbia press release, they were duly reprinted by the media as Dylan began to make a name for himself. Around the same time, he said similar things to journalist Robert Shelton in his first press interview. The life story they told intriguingly depicted a young man whose rambunctiousness stemmed from the grievances of material underprivilege. Unfortunately, they were all untrue.

The mundane reality was that Dylan—born on May 24, 1941—seems to have ever wanted for little. In 1952, his family became the first in their small town to obtain a television set. He had a motorcycle by the age of fifteen and soon graduated to cars. After he got into an automobile accident, his father had to settle a claim out of court for $4,000, a substantial sum of money in those days. Meanwhile, although there is some evidence that Dylan may have spent some time in a detention centre for troubled teens, if he did it was the only time before he left for university that he lived outside of his home state of Minnesota.

What sounds like a recipe for lifelong parochialism and conservativism turned out to be anything but. Echo Star Helstrom was Dylan's first proper girlfriend. She told author Toby Thompson that Dylan's father would make him do odd jobs around the furniture shop of which he was proprietor: 'He and this other fellow sometimes would have to go out on a truck and repossess stuff. I think that's where Bob first started feeling sorry for poor people. . . . Bob hated that; used to dread it worse than anything.'

Dylan also detested his father Abraham's starchy rigidity. It was certainly an authoritarian worldview that hardly looked benignly on his son's penchant for the nascent and rule-bucking musical form called rock'n'roll. Dylan seems to have had a normal relationship with his mother and five-years-younger brother, David, and to have been doted on by a grandmother, but the anguish his relationship with his dad caused him is made explicit in a poem Dylan wrote at school, aged ten, in which he stated, 'Though it's hard for him to believe / That I try each day to please him in every little way.' His ambivalence about his social caste may be manifested both in his speaking voice—full of double negatives and 'ain'ts'—and his singing style, which mangles words so that body becomes 'baddy', book becomes 'buck', and mirror 'me'er'.

Dylan didn't just disdain his class and at least one of his parents, he also hated the place from which he originated. Minnesota is a state in a region of the US that, even though it's right up in the north on the border with Canada, is confusingly known as the Midwest. His birthplace was Duluth, but Hibbing—also in Minnesota—is his true hometown, one to which his family relocated from the dying ore-mining Duluth when he was around six years old. Hibbing was very insular in Dylan's childhood and adolescence (its grand total of nil Black residents must have felt odd for someone who loved the blues and R&B from an early age). He later described it as a 'vacuum'. It had a climatic bleakness to it to match the chill that often descended on Dylan's home. (Dylan later wryly noted that he wasn't a rebel teenager because 'it was too cold'.) The low esteem in which he held the place was reciprocated. In 1968, local paper the *Hibbing Tribune* published a seventy-fifth-anniversary issue celebrating the town's history and its residents and ex-residents of achievement. Dylan—easily by now Hibbing's most famous and celebrated son—was not mentioned in it once.

Dylan also seems to have had a problem with another aspect of his hinterland: his Jewishness. His family name is Zimmerman. At the time, Jewish people entering showbusiness often adopted new names: stage legend Ethel Merman was actually another Zimmerman. Young Bob had decided on a stage name even before he left home to go to college. It may be the case that when Merman said she dropped the 'Zim' part of her surname because it would have been too long for a marquee, she was telling the truth, and it may be that the man born Robert Allen Zimmerman changed his name to Bob Dylan purely because it seemed more showbiz. With such a convoluted personality as Dylan's, though, insecurity, disingenuousness, ambiguity, and playfulness complicate the picture and any reason he gives needs to be taken with a pinch of salt.

Helstrom told Shelton in *No Direction Home*, 'The first time I met him, I asked if he was Jewish. He just changed the subject.' In 1965, Harvey Goldstein would play on Dylan's sixth album, though at that point he was going by 'Harvey Brooks'. Goldstein observes, 'For me, my name change was brought on by a couple of incidents. One was an anti-Semitic incident in Detroit, Michigan, where I had to fight some people over being Jewish, which is an absurd thing. I was working in the Catskills in upstate New York. I had a gig at a hotel, and I was sitting in the diner, and I had just gotten back and I was thinking about all this, and I looked up and I saw this big billboard that said Nat Brooks Orchestra. I said, That guy's name is *not* Nat Brooks. But that's good. That's like a name that nobody will associate anything with. It's like a bland name. I went and did that. But if I had it to do over again, I wouldn't do it. Everybody had stage names, but the reason we were doing it was to get out of the light of being Jewish.'

Goldstein—who never discussed with Dylan why the latter changed his name—would later complete the embracing of his Jewishness by moving to Israel, but he doesn't condemn Dylan's actions. 'The idea was to have a name that was just easy. Showbiz. Bernie Schwartz became Tony Curtis. It's that kind of thing. [Dylan] was changing his identity to fit into the mainstream, and part of it was taking his favourite poet, which is smart.'

Like Goldstein, many assumed that in his name change, Dylan was deliberately alluding to the romantically hedonistic lifestyle and simpatico poetic bent of Welsh verse writer Dylan Thomas (1914–1953), but for decades he consistently denied it in interviews and press conferences with comments like, 'I've read some of Dylan Thomas's stuff, and it's not the same as mine. We're different.' Helstrom recalled Dylan telling her as far back as 1958 that he was going to go by 'Dillon'. It was by this spelling that he was frequently billed in his pre-fame public appearances. His biographer Robert Shelton hypothesised that *Gunsmoke* TV series character Matt Dillon and/or a pioneer Hibbing family named Dillion (sic) may have inspired the choice. Dylan claimed he had an uncle named Dillon and changed the spelling because it looked better, but family members have disputed this. Some might assume that the matter was finally settled by Dylan's memoir *Chronicles* (2004), in which he admitted he'd named himself after the Welshman, but considering that doubts have been cast on the veracity of the contents of that book, we can't be sure this isn't more Dylan playfulness. Either way, Robert Zimmerman changed his legal name to Bob Dylan in August 1962, between the release of his first and second albums, and he felt strongly enough about it that he took his proudly Jewish dad with him to St. Louis County Court, Hibbing, to witness the necessary document.

Dylan's childhood may have been materially comfortable, but it seems safe to say that his formative experiences created a seething psychological stew. It also seems safe to say that this was a good thing. The simmering worldview ultimately engendered provided the impetus for 'Blowin' In The Wind', 'Masters Of War', 'Ballad Of Hollis Brown', 'The Lonesome Death Of Hattie Carroll', 'The Times They Are A-Changin'', and many other early compositions in which he inveighed against poverty, racism, warmongering, and social authoritarianism. It also informed many songs on *Bringing It All Back Home* and *Highway 61 Revisited*, which, though less didactic, were infused with compassion for the put-upon.

Surprisingly, one thing Dylan doesn't seem to have had a complex about is his height. Although he is only five foot seven, this posed him no apparent problems in terms of either attractiveness to the opposite sex (he is a strikingly good-looking man with twinkling blue eyes) or being able to look after himself (as uber-fan/stalker A.J. Weberman found out to his cost in the early 70s—witnesses attest to a confrontation in which Dylan pounded Weberman's head on the pavement).

Significantly, Dylan was probably a poet before he was a songwriter, by the age of eleven or twelve composing reams of verse and indicating professional poetry-writing ambitions that exasperated a father who felt he should study architecture. That poem by young Dylan about Abraham is astoundingly precocious in its facility with language and its apparently deliberate ambiguity. This is a testament to how sophisticated and well-read he was from an early age. His parents claimed that even his taste in comic books was elevated, veering more toward *Classics Illustrated* than *Superman*. Meanwhile, respected Dylan fanzine *The Telegraph* once claimed it was impossible to fully understand Dylan's canon without an acquaintanceship with Shakespeare. Moreover, Dylan has an incredible memory—one testified to by the fact of his ability to effortlessly recite from stages his repertoire of often long and complicated lyrics, and to repeatedly overhaul those lyrics.

We can therefore probably attribute the fact that he was never an A-grade student to him perceiving education as intertwined with an authoritarianism that uncomfortably reminded him of his home life. Or perhaps that he was cognisant that nobody needs to pass their SATs to be a rock star. Of course, one doesn't need academic qualifications to take over the family business either, but Dylan wasn't about to do that. 'I was never going to be anything else, never,' Dylan later said. 'I was playing when I was twelve years old, and all I wanted to do was play my guitar.' Anthony Scaduto—who spoke to both Dylan and his friends and family for his groundbreaking 1971 biography *Bob Dylan*—stated that Dylan was playing the family piano when he was eight or nine and guitar by the time he was ten, with harmonica introduced into the mix at some point, all without formal lessons.

Particularly important to Dylan's apprehension of his special destiny were Johnny Ray (whose voice and style were the first with which he totally fell in love), Hank Williams ('my first idol', as he later described him), Gatemouth Page (not a musician but an Arkansas DJ who specialised in blues and R&B), Bill Haley (insofar as, like so many others of the period, Dylan liked at least one of his songs, 'Rock Around The Clock', before moving onto the harder rock'n'roll stuff), Elvis Presley (of whom he has said, 'When I first heard Elvis's voice, I just knew that I wasn't going to work for anybody and nobody was going to be my boss'), and Little Richard (his stated ambition in a high school yearbook was 'to join Little Richard'). Some will be surprised at how mainstream most of his tastes were: although happy to exalt the first-wave rockers in interviews, Dylan has also long cultivated an image of a musical purist who subsists on obscure and long-deleted folk and blues records.

Motion pictures were also important to the young Bobby Zimmerman. Courtesy of an uncle who owned four local movie houses, he could see an unlimited number of pictures. Beautiful, doomed rebel icon James Dean was a huge influence, similarly naturalistic and iconoclasm-associated thespian Marlon Brando another, but so was a third, very different screen star. In that previously mentioned Columbia press release/first ever interview, Dylan cited Charlie Chaplin as his hero, and he spoke in a later interview of imitating his movements. (With typical Dylan contrariness, he has also vehemently denied in interviews that he was ever enamoured with Chaplin. One learns to disregard such Dylan bluffs and double-bluffs and determine the truth by what seems most plausible in the particular circumstances.) It's certainly not a huge leap to imagine Chaplin's 'Little Tramp' character as influencing Dylan's unkempt, underprivileged early 60s image, which his lover Joan Baez once likened to a 'poverty-stricken little Welsh schoolboy'. Generally, his love of moving media (TV possibly played a bigger part in his formative years than it did for most of his contemporaries) may have caused a sense of dramatic pacing to seep into him and inform his writing.

In his early teens, Dylan graduated from solo bedroom strumming to playing in bands, at which point he began to focus his writing more on song words than poetry. His prolificness in this department amazed and impressed his bandmates. The same awe was never inspired by his musicianship. Dylan knows how to play piano but, like many guitarists, he can make it sound like he's wearing boxing gloves when he does. Guitar-wise, his knowledge of chords and tunings is vast but his technique utilitarian to unremarkable. The sole instrument on which he is a virtuoso is the harmonica, but even this one instance of out-of-the-ordinary musical facility is not widely acknowledged. It seems to be down to the simple matter that though he wrests pleasing and sometimes amazing sounds from the 'mouth harp', his technique is all wrong. Just as many people disdain as mere 'shouters' vocalists who don't sing from the diaphragm, regardless of the impressive noises they might make (for example, The Animals' Eric Burdon), so many harmonica players have a problem with the fact that Dylan plays chords on the instrument, the consequence of blowing, rather than executing single notes or bent notes, which require skilful shaping of tongue and lips. Al Kooper, a famed multi-instrumentalist musician and sometime Dylan collaborator, says, 'He's a unique harmonica player. He invented a style of playing the harmonica.' Charlie McCoy is another multi-instrumentalist and sometime Dylan collaborator, one of whose specialities is harmonica.* He says of Dylan's technique, 'I'll tell you what, it's harder than it sounds. Because I've been asked to imitate it on sessions before. As a harmonica player, when you first hear it, it's like, Oh, yeah, I could remember when I was a kid picking up a harmonica…

---

* Probably his most famous piece of work is his blowing on 'Stone Fox Chase' by Area Code 615, which became the memorable theme tune to the BBC's long-running music magazine TV show *The Old Grey Whistle Test*.

but it's a little more involved than that. And it fits his vocal, it fits his songs, and that's the important thing. It doesn't matter how technically good it is. What does it do with the music, and what does it do *for* the music? I think history's proven that he's right on the money.'

Dylan's early ensembles, like The Golden Chords and The Satin Tones, were the usual salad-days propositions of performing at school shows, talent contents, local hops, and any other public gathering that would indulge them, often doing so for free or, at most, pennies. One of his first professional gigs was as piano player for Bobby Vee, just before the latter acquired fame. (Vee remembered it as constituting two dances in Fargo and that Dylan played great but wasn't retained because his band couldn't afford an extra member; Dylan, though, told his—politely sceptical—mates that he appeared on Vee's 1959 single 'Suzie Baby'.) Ironically, the reason the boy who had always been known as 'Bobby' decided to go by 'Bob' at the same time as he adopted 'Dylan' is because he wanted to differentiate himself from pompadoured, clean-cut crooners like Vee and Bobby Darin.

While music was Dylan's ideal escape route from the insularity and eventlessness of Hibbing, it of course wasn't in his gift to magic up stardom: a high public profile and a recording contract were things at the end of a long yellow brick road. The break from home he could effect in the here and now—and despite his mediocre grades—was the expedient of going off to college. In the autumn of 1959, he enrolled at the University Of Minnesota in Minneapolis. His father would no doubt have been able to pay for his education, but in fact, it came free, courtesy of his being awarded a state scholarship. There, he studied liberal arts, majoring in music, while, naturally, continuing his musical pursuits. The latter took a new turn—one that astonished some of his old childhood friends—when the boy steeped in rock'n'roll abandoned its flash, modernism, and electricity for down-home, traditionalist, and acoustic folk music. Dylan effectively dropped out of university after around six months and made Dinkytown, Minneapolis's bustling and slightly bohemian commercial district, his college. In its clubs, he astounded observers with both how much and how quickly he learnt folk history and technique and the way he could seamlessly incorporate such new knowledge into his stage act.

Dylan's switch of genres wasn't an irrational choice from a careerist point of view. Rock at that point seemed to be petering out and proving to be the fad that the parents of every teenager who'd loved the form had disdainfully predicted it would. Folk, however, was experiencing a revival. It was something he discussed with Helstrom in March 1962. The two ex-sweethearts had split up in the early summer of 1958. Clues as to why seemed to later be provided by Dylan's 1974 song 'Hazel', in which a protagonist expresses his love for a girl in the face of outside disapproval, only to find their paths diverging as he makes a reach for the metaphorical stars of which she's incapable ('I'm up on a hill and still you're not there'). Where Dylan had his sights set on being a recording artist, Helstrom's plan was to be an actress, and they had a pact that whoever became a star first would help the other one in their career. When Dylan made contact with her four years later, he gave her his brand new first album. Of his new direction, she was so appalled and surprised that she couldn't even be bothered to be diplomatic. 'You mean that hillbilly garbage?' she exclaimed. 'What the hell are you doing that stuff for?' She recalled his unblushing reply as 'That's the coming thing. That's how I'm going to make it.'

It might be assumed that Dylan was messing with her but, if so, he was also messing with the *Chicago Daily News* journo whom in November 1965 he told, 'I was playing rock'n'roll when I was thirteen or fourteen and fifteen, but I had to quit when I was sixteen or seventeen because I just couldn't make it that way.' There is also a feeling of real candour in his comments to Robert Shelton, to whom he said about his switch to folk, 'I hate to say this because I don't want it to be taken the wrong way, but I latched on ... because I saw a huge audience was there ... I knew I wasn't going to stay there. I knew it wasn't my thing.'

Either way, one could certainly understand Helstrom's bewilderment. Not only was folk often sombre, downbeat, and staid where rock was mostly irreverent, fast-paced, and glamorous, but the visual images of the more commercial recording artists most prominently associated with it, such as The Weavers and The Kingston Trio, were somewhat conformist: there weren't exactly many blow waves and gold lamé suits on their album jackets. In short, folk was precisely the sort of thing Dylan was supposed—and had even previously seemed—to despise. Friends from his early folk period remembered him sneering at rock'n'roll and having no intimation that he had ever been into it, unless Leadbelly (arguably more a bluesman) counts. Those who were cognisant of Dylan's hinterland with the likes of The Golden Chords gravitated to the assumption of insincerity and shameless mercenaryism. It wasn't to be the last time Dylan faced such suspicions.

Yet Dylan's love of folk seems to have been genuine. Not only did he learn traditional songs and tunings at a rate of knots but he seems never to have betrayed any disdain for the musicians, aficionados, and venue owners he began circulating among. Not least of his new acquaintances was someone who might be termed the King Of The Folkies, as well as a social conscience: Woody Guthrie, the author of the classic picaresque autobiography *Bound For Glory* and composer of leftist anthems like 'This Land Is Your Land' and 'Tear The Fascists Down'. Guthrie was now stricken with Parkinson's Disease and largely reduced to a nursing home, where Dylan repeatedly made pilgrimages. After a period when Dylan blatantly imitated the style of Ramblin' Jack Elliott, a Guthrie copyist, he went for the real thing, adopting an Oklahoma twang in tribute to Guthrie and for the same reason self-consciously turning what friends and observers recall as a mellow singing voice into something significantly more abrasive.

The Guthrie pilgrimages occurred from January 1961 onward, shortly after Dylan hitchhiked his way to New York, the city in which he made his name. After two months of hustling (Dylan's word—make of it what you will, and some have) he interpolated himself into its bustling, coffeehouse-based folk scene. There, he began acquiring a reputation as something different and special because, as he later put it, 'I played all the folk songs with a rock'n'roll attitude.' Coffeehouses did not then mean gleaming corporate chains like Starbucks and Costas but independent establishments like the Café Wha?, the Commons, the Folklore Center, the Gaslight, and Gerde's Folk City—places that were the breeding grounds of what was then called the Movement but would soon come to be termed the counterculture. The vibe in such places was informal-cum-alternative, the politics libertarian-cum-leftist, and the music folk and blues, much of it as old as the hills—albeit sometimes tweaked to include topical references—partly because such music was steeped in proletarianism and authenticity, intertwined in which was a leftist contempt for flashy, obvious, and consumerist pop and rock. The pay was derisory or non-existent, although 'passing the basket' would yield coins from appreciative and/or pitying audiences.

Dylan's Hibbing bandmates recalled him as having an easy facility for original melody, but in making the switch to folk, Dylan subsumed that talent into the genre's traditions of updating tunes so old as to be out of copyright. The public-domain route was a free-for-all: as long as they could hold a tune, any musician could make a living riding on other people's ideas without fear of being sued and without even necessarily having much talent. The more imaginative musicians and singers gave oldies a retooling, stamping their mark on a familiar song with a distinctive new arrangement, an example being Dave Van Ronk's makeover of the old bordello lament 'House Of The Risin' Sun', which saw him altering the chords and deploying a jazzy bass line. Others strapped new lyrics to established melodies, although they had to be careful of sounding contradictorily *too* contemporary. (How could it be folk if it sounded new?) One of the reasons that Dylan sounded so fresh and cutting edge in the coffeehouses and folk clubs in and around Greenwich Village at the start of the 1960s is that he clearly didn't give a damn about such concerns, and this is perhaps where his exploitation of folk for his own purposes benefitted both him and the genre in general. Dressing himself in scruffy beatnik clothing, incorporating the latest street/youth slang and delivering songs with a rock'n'roll attitude—whether it be social and linguistic informality or a propulsive musical approach—helped break folk out of a cul-de-sac of stagnation and solipsism. Adding to an aura of newness was his often lengthy comedic and self-deprecating raps between songs. Ditto the fact that he played mouth harp, not that common an instrument at the time. On top of that was the additional novelty of the rack he employed to enable him to play harmonica and guitar at the same time. It was such a little-known tool at the time that one DJ who interviewed him expressed her admiration for his harmonica 'necklace'. (Dylan had got the idea from folk/blues singer Jesse Fuller, whom he had met in a stint playing Denver clubs.)

Although his set didn't yet feature what might in this context be termed 'originals' (old tunes with his own lyrics), by September 29, 1961, *New York Times* music critic Robert Shelton had spotted something new and superior about Dylan. Reviewing a performance at Gerde's, Shelton hailed a 'bright new face in folk music' and 'one of the most distinctive stylists to play a Manhattan cabaret in months'. While conceding that his 'clothes may need a bit of tailoring', his 'voice is anything but pretty', and his 'stylization threatens to topple over as a mannered excess', he also insisted that 'he is bursting at the seams with talent', that 'a searing intensity pervades his songs', and that he purveyed a 'highly personalised approach toward folk song'. Shelton also admired the way that Dylan as a performer oscillated easily between pathos and humour. He concluded, 'Mr. Dylan is vague about his antecedents and birthplace, but it matters less where he has been than where he is going, and that would seem to be straight up.' Shelton would be a significant figure in Dylan's life from hereon, writing the liner notes to his first album under the name Stacey Williams, mentioning his chilling song 'The Death Of Emmett Till' in a *NYT* article about the civil rights movement, serving as an eyewitness at several of the seismic events in his career, and ultimately writing a major Dylan biography, *No Direction Home*. His initial involvement in his career, however, may have been the most significant in that it put this ragamuffin, nascent talent into the public spotlight.

Not that Shelton's Gerde's review led to a chain of moguls beating a path to Dylan's door. It's almost certainly Dylan's very unconventionality that initially led to his talent failing to translate to that chief yardstick of success for a musician: a recording deal. Elektra, Folkways, and Vanguard were major folk labels, but all failed to make him an overture. He was a fine, expressive singer but, as with his harmonica playing, his technique was so unconventional that it caused music labels to overlook its qualities. Even the fact that he was only just out of his teens (accentuated by his chubby cheeks, doe eyes, and penchant for Huckleberry Finn caps) counted against him in an idiom so stepped in tales of long suffering and hard lives.

For a while, Dylan may even have assumed that he was destined to rise no higher than the likes of Dave Van Ronk, Eric Anderson, or any of the other scuffling one-man-and-a-guitar merchants to be found in and around the village at the time who, in lieu of a structured career, relied on crashing on people's sofas and divvying up the contents of passed-around hats while trying to put out of their minds the thought of whether they would be able to sustain this sort of life indefinitely. There were, though, glimmers of promise.

It was on the very day of the Shelton write-up that Dylan first entered a recording studio. He provided harmonica on a session for folk singer Carolyn Hester. The latter wasn't the only person to see past his unconventional approach to the instrument. Within a short time, he was performing the same services for Victoria Spivey and, most notably, Harry Belafonte. The latter was hugely prominent at the time, his 1956 effort *Calypso* being the first album to sell a million copies. A career as a sideman for successful artists might have been a highly respectable and even enviable proposition for a lot of other people. However, it was not

24

what this intensely ambitious young man was aiming for. It was one John Hammond who provided Dylan the path to something greater.

Hammond was fairy godmother to many artists both before and after Dylan, the archetypal Artists & Repertoire man who, if he believed in an artist, would champion him in the face of employer resistance and detractor ridicule. Born in 1910, his privileged hinterland can be guessed at from the fact that his father was a banker, and he was related to the Vanderbilts. Yet despite his wealth and access to elevated pathways, he became both a noted civil rights activist and a champion of things then deemed to be low culture. He dabbled with music, journalism, and DJing before finding his true calling nurturing talent. He served as an A&R man and producer at Columbia/CBS for, off and on, five decades. Like with all talent scouts, some of the horses he backed in his long career were duds, but at the end of the day, few could match his track record of discoveries. As well as Dylan, Hammond propelled into the spotlight incandescent talents like Count Basie, Aretha Franklin, Benny Goodman, Billie Holliday, Bruce Springsteen, and Stevie Ray Vaughan. He as much as any actual recording artist deserved to be inducted into the Rock And Roll Hall Of Fame. The latter institution has often been criticised for being mystifyingly tardy with formally recognizing some of popular music's treasures, but they called it exactly right with Hammond: his induction in 1986 came a year before his death, thus providing a gratifying capstone to his life.

Not that there wasn't a suspicion of dregs-of-the-casket about the fact that on October 26, 1961, Hammond signed Dylan to a Columbia recording contract. Dylan was the only artist of the vibrant Village folk scene Hammond managed to snag after all the acts considered to have more gravitas had been snapped up by rivals. There was also no advance for Dylan. However, a record deal was a record deal—something beyond the wildest dreams of the vast majority of musicians on any scene. On November 20, 1961, the newly signed Dylan entered Columbia's 7th Avenue recording studio to begin laying down his debut album.

•

Released on March 19, 1962, Bob Dylan's eponymous first LP has had a wide influence.

British R&B outfit The Animals found their first two singles on it. They turned the high-spirited 'Baby Let Me Follow You Down' into 'Baby Let Me Take You Home' and, of vastly more cultural significance, Dylan's rendition of the old traditional 'House Of The Risin' Sun' was transformed by them into a transatlantic 1964 no. 1—one whose imaginative electrified rearrangement not only helped create the genre of folk-rock but fed back into Dylan's own tectonic career turns. The Animals were by no means alone in their admiration.

Interpreters of Dylan's material were two a penny within a few years of *Bob Dylan*'s release, but during the 1970s Rod Stewart became known for particularly thoughtful and sensitive readings of his songs. Furthermore, the fact that he usually chose to cover songs that Dylan himself hadn't yet released, such as 'Only A Hobo', 'Tomorrow Is A Long Time', and 'Mama, You Been On My Mind', suggested he had specialist knowledge of and particular interest in Dylan. This in fact wasn't the case. The only album of Dylan's that Stewart was ever partial to was his first one, its release coinciding with the start of his own journey down the folkie path, which of course ultimately transmogrified into a career trajectory of a much more populist bent. The version of 'Man Of Constant Sorrow' on Stewart's debut album, *An Old Raincoat Won't Ever Let You Down*, aka *The Rod Stewart Album* (1969), was more to Stewart's tastes. It wasn't a song written by Dylan, but Stewart's recording was clearly inspired by the latter's performance of said traditional on his own first LP. A similar thing happened with 'In My Time Of Dyin''. At a point when they were the biggest recording act on the planet, Led Zeppelin placed on their 1975 double album *Physical Graffiti* a version of this traditional that owed a clear debt to the *Bob Dylan* iteration.

Nor were Dylan's musical peers the only people impressed by the record. The first edition of *The Rolling Stone Record Guide* (1979) graded *Bob Dylan* a maximum five stars, stating it to be the work of 'an amazingly original singer' of both his and others' songs, thereby placing it in their estimation two stars higher than the artist's far more famous work, *The Times They Are A-Changin'*.

This is all somewhat curious. Not because *Bob Dylan* was recorded in such a short space of time (it was wrapped up on the 22nd after three sessions, but such quick turnarounds were not uncommon in the era, especially for what was a one-man proposition). Rather, it's surprising because it's difficult to imagine a more atypical Dylan album. Dylan is known as an original songwriter. He's also known as profoundly more than that: he is widely considered to be the greatest lyricist of post-Presley popular music, the poet laureate of rock'n'roll, the man who turned pop/rock from a musically exciting but lyrically simplistic genre into a medium that could make one not only tap one's toes but think deep thoughts at the same time. What worth, then, a collection of thirteen songs that, with two exceptions, were not written by him and often not written by anyone that history records (i.e., songs so old as to precede the very legal concept of copyright)? The fact that there are so few originals on the album is of course a function of the fact that, in the foothills of his career, Dylan had a paucity of songs penned by his own hand fit to withstand public scrutiny. That beginner status is reflected in a cover photograph in which his chubby cheeks and baby-deer eyes scream 'greenhorn'. Covers of oldies, of course, can be an enjoyable listening experience, but that is usually dependent on adroit use of instrumentation: such scope for interesting arrangement is somewhat limited in the context of one voice, one guitar, and one harmonica. Moreover, all of those things are, in this particular artist's case, as mentioned, an acquired taste.

It's also hard to think of an official album by this artist held in lower esteem by the general public, at least in terms of commercial success. It has never registered on any American chart. Its paltry sales of five thousand in its first year supposedly caused people at Columbia to dub

Dylan 'Hammond's Folly'. It did manage to climb to no. 13 in Britain, but that was a consequence of an indiscriminate Dylanmania sweeping the nation on the occasion of him touring the country. More representative of its UK fortunes is the fact that, in the 1980s, it was one of Woolworth's 'Music For Pleasure' albums: a record that could be found on its stores' discount spinners priced at 99p, at a time when a new album cost a fiver.

So, where lies the truth between such contrasting perceptions of *Bob Dylan*'s quality?

For what it's worth, the album is representative in many ways of the 1960s Greenwich Village coffeehouse scene. Although emblematic, however, *Bob Dylan* was also slightly different to the scene's norm. While this is partly down to the title artist's more youthful, energetic, and humorous style, another part of the departure from the Village mould is Dylan's singularly odd, even inexplicable, obsessions. The overarching miserabilism is to be expected—it's difficult to inject levity into vistas of suffering, even for someone as unusually mischievous as Dylan—but what's not is the fascination of a man barely out of his teens with impending death, particularly impending death after a grinding life.

Dylan softens us up for the miserabilism to come by opening the album with 'You're No Good'. A love song of a nuanced stripe by Jesse Fuller (1896–1976), who straddled blues, folk, and jazz, it's a spirited if ambiguous composition, and Dylan's playful vocal, galvanizingly scrubbed guitar, and plucky harmonica all please. Nor is there much bleakness in 'Talkin' New York', a track that was a milestone insofar as being the first Dylan original heard by people who had not seen him live. However, it wouldn't have alerted anyone to the fact that this was a major new talent about to blossom. A talking blues is never going to be a classic: the reason so many folkies devised them is because the fact of them having no melody makes them easy to write. Any virtue a creation written in this idiom can possess is dependent on compelling performance and sparking content. 'Talkin' New York' has neither, being the reminiscence of a hick outsider arriving in the titular East

Coast metropolis that can offer observations no more searing than that in New York, while people go down to the ground (presumably the subway), the buildings are 'going up to the sky'. The one line that does approach cleverness—in which he refers to the robbery of people via the means of a fountain pen—was actually pinched from Woody Guthrie's 'Pretty Boy Floyd'. Again, though, the track at least has a humour that's shortly to be thin on the ground: the gloominess of the trilogy of songs that follows is emblematic.

'In My Time Of Dyin'' is one of the copyright-doesn't-apply album cuts that enable the publishing attribution 'Trad. Arr. Dylan', as potentially lucrative a proposition as an artist's name in the publishing parentheses *sans* those two preceding words. An embrace of the thought of death and the paradise offered by heaven, it was the kind of spiritual very popular with African Americans at a grim time in history when for many of them life had meaning only in the context of the everlasting paradise promised upon their death. The only thing preventing one from asserting that the song is absolutely absurd from the mouth of a middle-class white boy is that so already weathered sounding is Dylan's voice that it bizarrely confers an illusion of authenticity. Despite whatever qualities might be attributed to the weird verisimilitude, though, the cut is doomy and depressing. As is anthem of self-pity 'Man Of Constant Sorrow', although the spiritual heaviness is slightly leavened in this case by the remarkable sustain heard in both Dylan's voice and his harmonica. 'Fixin' To Die' (Bukka White) is yet another lament about what a crushing hand has been dealt the narrator by fate. It has retroactively been further diminished by the fact that three years later Dylan reused its riff in his own, far more worthy song, 'It's Alright, Ma (I'm Only Bleeding)'.

The sprightly and cheerful-seeming traditional 'Pretty Peggy-O' would be a merciful relief bar the fact that paying close attention to its lyric reveals it to be a story of a maid who falls in love with an army captain, only to shortly become bereaved. It's apropos of nothing to do with even vaguely contemporary life.

Side one of the original vinyl album closes with Curtis Jones's 'Highway 51 Blues' (listed on the first pressings of the sleeve as 'Highway 51'). As with so many blues, first lines of verses are repeated—a potentially tedious format, yet Dylan injects an energy that at least pulls it clear of boring.

Even this early in his career, on the first cut of side two Dylan is approaching formulaicness-cum-self-parody. Devotional song 'Gospel Plow' is actually quite enjoyable, but one is tempted to snort at the fact that even something so worshipful is subjected to the quintessentially/ cartoonishly Dylanesque treatment of puffed harmonica and furiously strummed acoustic guitar. 'Baby, Let Me Follow You Down' is a traditional recently given a new arrangement by one of his coffeehouse contemporaries, Eric Von Schmidt, whom Dylan namechecks in a spoken-word intro. A genuine love song—albeit one dealing in the nuance of real-life, rather than the banalities of then-contemporary pop—it's both the most endearing song present and a ray of sunshine in the predominant gloom.

Dylan takes care to credit the arrangement of his recording of traditional 'House Of The Risin' Sun' to another warbler on the coffeehouse scene. Yet while Dave Van Ronk gets a 'Trad. Arr.', neither this nor the type of royalties he could never have generated from his own releases were sufficient consolation to him. Van Ronk claimed he had elicited from Dylan a promise that he wouldn't pre-empt his own planned recording. That Dylan hereby broke that promise was one of the first glimmerings of a disconnect many would note between Dylan's macro humanitarian values and his micro mistreatment of fellow human beings. The song itself is the lament of a world-weary prostitute who has been 'ruined' by the titular bordello but at its end is resignedly making her way back to the financial security it offers. Most audiences would find it odd that either Dylan or Van Ronk would tackle a song surely only suitable for a distaff performer, but folk is a medium chockful of narratives sung from a dispassionate and hence depersonalised perspective. Almost contradicting that fact, Dylan emotes quite impressively.

The traditional 'Freight Train Blues' provides another indication of things to come. Whatever pejorative description can be applied to Dylan's vocal style—and many have been, ranging from whine to honk to bellow to monotone to irritating to rough as a bear's backside to a prairie dog caught on barbed wire—the fact is that he is one of the greatest singers in the history of recorded music. He achieves this by presence and soulfulness, investing such unselfconscious passion into his performances as to create an effect that may not be technically slick but has its desired effect of inspiring emotion. Even his insertion into his delivery of a phoney Southwestern accent creates an exotic frisson. In the mid-70s, during his married-bliss period, his voice became rather dull, apparently deliberately, while from around 1978 it has suffered a slow decline into a pebbles-and-gravel proposition. On *Bob Dylan*, he was just finding his feet, singing-wise. At every other point in his career, however, he has been a magnificent vocalist, as great as any artist whose singing prowess is widely acknowledged, whether it be Smokey Robinson, Dusty Springfield, Sam Cooke, Eric Burdon, or John Lennon. It is simply absurd to suggest that a man who has given us vocal performances like 'The Times They Are A-Changin'', 'Like A Rolling Stone', or 'You're A Big Girl Now' is a bad singer. 'It's a presence, it's a style,' says Harvey Goldstein. 'He presents his lyrics. He puts certain twists to the words to emphasize certain words. He's more concerned with getting his lyric across, he's not worried about the actual singing of it. He hears the melody. And the evidence of that is the way he also evolves the melodies over the years. Some of them are totally unrecognisable. It's phrasing. The vocal phrasing is incredible. If you listen to all those albums, you understand almost every word he's saying.'

'Freight Train Blues' points the way to Dylan's future greatness in the way he pays no attention to his limited range or lack of smoothness as he outrageously extends notes and puckishly throws in whoops while narrating the story of living the kind of hobo life made possible by the United States' unenclosed railway lines and slidable train doors. Dylan loved this sort of romantic, picaresque tableaux and—as indicated from the very first quotes he gave anyone—was apt to insert himself in them. While he did his fair share of hitchhiking, though, circumstances and money mailed by his parents meant that train-hopping was never part of his experience.

Someone who did live that life was Dylan's great idol, about whom the following track, 'Song To Woody', was written. The second of the album's brace of Dylan originals, it has a sweet melody and a touchingly devotional flavour ('There's not many men that done the things that you've done'), although the guitar riff seems possessed of marginal differentiation to ones we've heard already herein. We're also inescapably left pondering the fact that the track's quality doesn't come near the greatest of Guthrie's own creations.

We're left pondering another juxtaposition by the closing track, 'See That My Grave Is Kept Clean'. Whatever the false verisimilitude lent the album's material by Dylan's lived-in voice, it can't transcend the ridiculousness of him covering a composition by Blind Lemon Jefferson, an old Black bluesman whose lifetime of suffering gave him every right to purvey the morbid narrative of a man facing an impending death that might well be a blessing. There is no gainsaying that Dylan's hinterland was psychologically difficult—what else could generate the obsession this album reveals with vistas of persecution and intimations of unrelieved misery (as well as his public claims that his parents were dead and his often obnoxious and self-serving behaviour)? However, whatever familial difficulties he faced and whatever suffering he may have endured as a Jew, Dylan at base was male, had white skin, had never gone hungry except by choice, had no physical infirmities, and had a potentially bright future. His performance of the song is competent enough, but it's also a fittingly absurd capstone to a psychologically silly album.

While folk music has very often dealt in doom and gloom and the adoption of points of view of people who have suffered greatly, *Bob Dylan* takes those traits an embarrassing step too far. These are losers' anthems from somebody who it's difficult to accept has earned the right to sing them. It's the work of a kid with something to prove; some sense of injustice at the way he has been treated that he isn't yet able to articulate with his own songs (and may not even be able to define in his own head) and can only strain to convey with his choice of others' material. Perhaps better that he works out his grievances on this safe ground rather than employ the other—sometimes violent—ways some young men do. Perhaps it's even to his credit that his unhappiness and resentment are manifested in bringing to public attention writers who could very much do with the exposure and royalties. As a work of art, though, *Bob Dylan* is close to meaningless, even in the sense of indicating where the artist might be able to take his abilities once he is able to proffer his own visions. Sometimes those visions would be just as depressing—*The Times They Are A-Changin'* was even more of a downer than this LP— but at least he was finding with them a way to analyse the world and himself without resorting to trying on outfits that just didn't suit him.

Of course, if Dylan hadn't become a world-famous genius, all of this might not matter: the public might never have become apprised of the relatively privileged background he'd enjoyed over and above that part of it that was visible from his male sex and white skin, nor would it have been able to unfavourably compare it to his profoundly more impressive later efforts. Had it been the only effort of an artist of whom we never heard of again—and that possibility existed for a while after its release—the few people exposed to *Bob Dylan* would have viewed it somewhat differently: its main demerits would have been its spartan sound and depressive timbre, while its attributes of enthusiasm and deep love of blues and folk might have seemed more noteworthy and admirable. We'll never know.

A postscript to any debate about the album's qualities is the fact that it would have been improved by the inclusion of material Dylan decided to leave off. People who'd caught his coffeehouse act must have been mystified that he didn't tackle any of the Woody Guthrie songbook, much of which he knew backwards. The LP's sessions did in fact see him render Guthrie's 'Ramblin' Blues', but it didn't make the final track listing. Dylan actually expressed to friends his regret that he'd also left on the cutting room floor 'Hard Times In New York Town', which is not surprising as it easily trumps 'Talkin' New York' in the stakes of a Midwesterner's bewilderment at Big Apple culture, being both insightful and funny. Such questionable decision-making would be a motif throughout Dylan's life. The vaults would ultimately bulge with great songs of whose qualities he was apparently oblivious—something that caused immense frustration to fans who became cognisant of them by press reports or bootlegs, not least because they would at some junctures in that long, mixed career have enhanced mediocre albums and rescued a reputation in decline.

•

That *Bob Dylan* sold so few copies in its first year may well have been a relief to the artist whose name constituted the title. He had outgrown it before it was even on the market.

Partly this was down to bureaucracy causing an inordinately long five-month delay before its release. Partly it was down to the fact that the Bob Dylan of the 1960s developed at a lightning pace, and perhaps never more so than in 1962–63. John Hammond had not signed a songwriter but a performer in the classic folk tradition of an oldies purveyor, even if he felt him a punkier, zestier variant of such and knew that he could compose at least to a degree. Yet, no doubt to Hammond's great surprise, not to mention pleasure, in that aforesaid time period Dylan proceeded to become a great original songwriter and at the very same juncture the voice of his generation.

That the callow artist singing songs as old as the hills blossomed within a few months—weeks, even—of the debut album's recording into a prolific composer would have been remarkable enough even had his original songs been mediocre, but the creations he began to

34

churn out were of a high quality indeed. By April 1962, he had come up with 'Blowin' In The Wind'. A contemporary protest anthem that also sounded like a hymn, it was instantly acclaimed as a classic and quickly taken to the heart of his cohort. Virtually overnight, the puppy-faced kid had turned himself into a spokesman-cum-seer.

Curiously, that reputation was not begun with any release by Dylan himself, for 'Blowin' In The Wind' actually became famous before he did.

Broadside was a mimeographed Greenwich Village underground magazine that debuted in February 1962 and printed a Dylan lyric—'Talkin' John Birch Paranoid Blues'—in its first issue. It soon assumed the status of a must-read for those on the scene, and in its sixth issue (May 1962), it printed on its front cover—a full year before the song's release by Dylan—the lyric of 'Blowin' In The Wind' in its entirety. It was immediately clear that it was a creation that superbly articulated the sentiments of the era's increasingly questioning young. Several things had in recent years served to impose a crushing conformism on American culture: the patriotism dictated by the atmosphere of the Second World War and its aftermath, the supine attitudes created by the fear of being labelled a Communist in the McCarthy era and a feeling that people should be grateful for the unprecedented median wealth that had occurred in the last couple of decades. Such restraints increasingly no longer applied. Dylan himself perfectly summarised the mood of the era when he said in the *National Guardian* in August 1963, 'There's a feeling in the air. More people are willing to say: To hell with my security. I want my rights.'

'Blowin' In The Wind' was an anthem that summed up his peers' grievances at the failings of what they had always been led to believe were their 'elders and betters'. Whether by cunning design or freakish accident, the phrase 'blowin' in the wind' sounded like an expression of world-weary resignation from a wise old man, only strengthening the song's air of authority.

It was, however, an odd kind of authority. The line 'How many times must the cannonballs fly before they're forever banned?' was exactly the type of sentiment proliferating in a culture where children had to undergo drills in school to train them what to do in the event of a nuclear strike. Yet the line, like almost all the others, is written in the form of a question, not a statement. Similar queries are posed about how many roads a man must walk down before he's fit to be called a man, how many seas a bird of peace must sail before its mission is completed, how many years some people must exist before they're allowed freedom, how many times a man can turn his head pretending he doesn't see, and how many deaths it will take before its apprehended that too many people have died. The only line that doesn't have a question mark at the end of it is the one that appears at the close of each verse, which states that the answer to the preceding litany of enquiries is blowing in the wind. In other words, the narrator is saying merely 'Beats me, pal,' or as the British would put it, 'Don't ask me, mate.' It is a quite extraordinarily sustained study in non-commitment, an exercise in ambiguity. The suspicious mind—and many who met Dylan were inclined to be suspicious—might assume that it represented the composer pulling a fast one on his listeners, even mocking them. We can perhaps disregard the fact that in later years Dylan began expressing opinions that could be termed right-wing on the grounds that it proves nothing other than that people often shrug off their youthful idealism in middle age. Nor can we read too much into the fact that he has always been disinclined to didacticism—he always had what might be termed the wisdom to understand that there are no tidy answers. However, pandering to the left-wing opinions of the folk audience would fit in perfectly with Dylan's comment to Echo Helstrom that folk was the coming thing and the way he was going to make it. It also ties in with the fact that Dylan didn't join his fellow guitar-wielding folkies and chroniclers of contemporary injustice like Joan Baez, Phil Ochs, and Pete Seeger in attending protest marches or even really espousing causes, his participation in a voter-registration rally in Greenwood, Mississippi, and the March On Washington (both 1963) being rare exceptions. The ambiguity also ties in with Dylan's mischievous bent, manifested in so many veiled song lyrics and red-herring interview quotes and testified to by so many who have known him.

Not that it can be credibly asserted that Dylan's protest days were fraudulent. Underlying it there may well have been some hard-nosed ambition and an understanding of which way the—as it were—wind was blowing. However, his hatred of racism is palpably sincere, proven by his heartfelt anti-racism songs, his working with Black musicians, his marrying Black singer Carolyn Dennis (with whom he had a child), and even his taking up of rather dubious causes like those of George Jackson and Reuben Carter, incarcerated Black men who were not as saintly as some of their champions maintained. Nor can it be gainsaid that he has always been discomforted by inequity and underprivileged, going right back to those grisly days wherein he had the mortifying duty of entering poor people's houses to repossess their furniture.

For some—although in this instance not so much within folk circles—there was another issue with Dylan's songwriting. He had blossomed as a writer only in the lyrical sense. As quickly became apparent with other new songs, he proffered uncommonly imaginative phraseology, acute insight, memorable imagery, and audacious rhyming schemes, but little originality with melody. Those who heard—as opposed to read—the lyric of—'Blowin' In The Wind' and who had a passing knowledge of folk music instantly discerned that the song utilised the tune of an old anti-slavery spiritual called 'No More Auction Block'. As Dylan himself noted in his book *Writings & Drawings* (1973), the lyrics of this new slew of songs were 'rolled up' in pre-existing melodies. Folk is a musical form predicated not on original melody or even ideas but on utilising tunes and lyrical motifs generations old. That being the very definition of folk music, it poses no problem to aficionados, but for lovers of rock and pop it bespoke a lack of inventiveness. It also bespoke an adherence to tradition and therefore implicitly hidebound rules—or to use one of the worst putdowns of the era, it was square.

Whether 'Blowin' In The Wind''s hedge-betting was motivated by insincerity or sagacity or both, it proved to be the mechanism by which Dylan became the king of a new form of music, one that would be all the rage for a year or two and help shape the way that popular music went during the entire decade; one in which pop became not just a means of entertainment but an expression of the public's social concerns and even a sociopolitical force in and of itself. The new genre would acquire the sobriquet *protest*. The genre was intertwined with the civil rights movement, a crucial component part of which was marches, rallies and demonstrations. 'Blowin' In The Wind' quickly became a staple of such mass events, immediately being granted a place alongside far older activist anthems like 'We Shall Overcome'. So much was it a temperature of the times that within a year of its first cover version, there had been nearly sixty others, including ones by artists as varied as Glen Campbell, Marlene Dietrich, Duke Ellington, Percy Faith, and Lena Horne. The most important one, though, was the first. It was by a folk trio who happened to be clients of Dylan's new manager.

After the release of his first album, Dylan was approached by Albert Grossman, an entrepreneur in the folk field who had produced the first Newport Folk Festival (1959) and was manager of the singer Odetta and Peter, Paul & Mary. He had also effectively discovered and to an extent promoted the new folk sensation, Joan Baez. Born in 1926, Grossman was a figure whom some viewed as a simple vulgarian, something assisted by his bulk and apparent lack of social skills (he remained silent for stretches of time that would make just about any other human being intensely awkward). However, while it could be said that he always had his eye on the main chance, Grossman was also steadfast in his protection of the artistic rights of his clients (which would later also include The Band, Paul Butterfield, John Lee Hooker, and Janis Joplin). He was also educated, possessing a master of science degree in economic theory. Hitherto, Terri Thal and then Roy Silver had been Dylan's managers in the sense that they booked him gigs. When Grossman expressed interest in adding Dylan to his roster, Dylan—after taking advice from Shelton—signed on the dotted line in May '62. (Grossman bought out Silver for a then-princely $10,000.) One of the first things Grossman did was to try to get him out of his Columbia contract. Some have suggested that the terms of the contract were bad and that, had Dylan had a manager at the time he signed it, its terms would have been amended to his benefit. However, Grossman was a man whose surname many of those who dealt with him found utterly fitting, and it may well have been his belligerent style that resulted in Columbia not only insisting on retaining Dylan but refusing to renegotiate. Although he was unsuccessful in getting the contract cancelled, Grossman's stewardship of Dylan's affairs quickly had a very beneficial effect in that he apprised Peter, Paul & Mary of the quality and commercial potential of 'Blowin' In The Wind', and that mixed-sex vocal trio helped turn Dylan from an artist with sales in four figures into a composer of Top 10 smashes.

Peter Yarrow, Paul Stookey, and Mary Travers were folkies of a more polished stripe than the coffeehouse performers. Some suspected that their previous hit, 'Puff, The Magic Dragon' (1963), surreptitiously proselytised marijuana usage, but the trio were far too sweet and nice (and, frankly, unimaginative) to be so subversive, as demonstrated by their other chart entries, 'Lemon Tree' and 'If I Had A Hammer (The Hammer Song)'. However, in the summer of 1963, their more 'accessible' version of Dylan's song soared to no. 2 on both the *Billboard* and *Cash Box* charts, eventually selling over a million copies. The world was suddenly intrigued to find out who had written this instantly memorable and thought-provoking number nestling among the banalities and platitudes otherwise found on the hit parade. The fact that the composer turned out to be an adorably unkempt, winningly impish, and highly photogenic young man was a bonus for journalists looking for a hook. Straplines like 'Voice Of A Generation' or 'Conscience Of Youth' were manna from heaven for hacks—and, as an added bonus, were not even necessarily inaccurate.

Publishing and airplay royalties were soon pouring into the Dylan camp's coffers. It set the pattern that would prevail, certainly during the course of the 60s. Come September, Peter, Paul & Mary were on their way to providing Dylan a second US Top 10 with their version of another of his songs, 'Don't Think Twice, It's All Right'. Dylan's own releases would soon be good—although never spectacular—sellers, but his big money would derive from the fact that every Tom, Dick, and Harriet was eager to record the efforts of a man perceived to have his finger on the pulse, both sociologically and commercially. This eagerness was handily assisted by the fact that cover artists were happy to record even his discards. Courtesy of their client's prolificness and penchant for discarding material, Dylan's publishers, M. Witmark & Sons, were often able to furnish them with songs Dylan had no intention of releasing himself but which were rarely second-rate.

The success of Peter, Paul & Mary's 'Blowin' In The Wind' was partly down to the fact that their smooth harmonies and clean-cut image enabled access to an American media then often dubious about anything that smacked of 'alternative' or 'leftist'. Early Dylan covers were usually alternatives in the true sense of the word in this context: full-band extrapolations of his bare originals. They were more conventionally delivered as well, something that was important to the considerable number of people who averred that they 'can't stand' Dylan's voice.

•

In December 1962, Dylan flew to the UK to appear in a television play entitled *The Madhouse On Castle Street*. As with so many British TV recordings of the time, no copy of the show survives, but the fact that he played a cap-wearing folk singer and sang 'Blowin' In The Wind' over the opening titles and end credits hardly suggests he was stretched, acting-wise. The visit saw him taking in the local folk scene, where he absorbed English folk melodies that had not permeated Greenwich Village and—ever the magpie—incorporated them into the songs he was churning out.

Despite his prolificness, Dylan's second album would take a cumulative year to finish, and he would jettison more than one complete or quasi-complete track listing before the final version was decided on. The process was punctuated in December 1962 by an odd false start. 'Mixed-Up Confusion' b/w 'Corrina, Corrina' was Dylan's first single. It was treated almost as a burp by the principals, its withdrawal shortly after release serving as a 'pardon me' from Dylan and Columbia. This seems unrelated to any issues of quality: both sides are quite enjoyable, especially the sweet, gentle flip. Rather, it seems to have been viewed by label and/or artist as a mistake. It certainly has no connection to the way Dylan was perceived at the time or what (at least in the immediate future) he would become. 'Mixed-Up Confusion', a Dylan original, is a raucous rocker that bears a resemblance to Elvis Presley's records in his pre-fame recording days on the Sun label. 'Corrina, Corrina' is a folk standard given a new arrangement by the artist. Both feature a band. (There would also be a clutch of tracks recorded for the album with the accompaniment of a band and/or a bassist. These—all covers—were discarded, according to Dylan because Columbia didn't want non-originals on the LP.) Memories of the single were soon expunged by the wild success of the acoustic album that did emerge, but in retrospect, it's almost as if Dylan was blowing his cover as a rocker sailing under a flag of convenience and a dry run for what was to come.

In terms of his social life, Dylan was in love with Suze Rotolo, a teenage Italian American New Yorker who shared his passion for equality and social justice and, as all partners of songwriters do, often acted as his unwitting muse. Despite her youth, Rotolo was highly intelligent and highly active, working in the offices of equality and anti-nuclear campaign groups and as a staff member of *Streets* magazine. Come May 27, 1963, she was immortalised when she appeared on the front cover of Dylan's second album. Nor was that record any less fame-making for Dylan. 'Epoch-marking' is a frequently overused phrase, but if one can pinpoint events that signified the proper start of the 1960s—

moments that encapsulated the insurrectionary tone in Western society that hitherto had been *sotto voce* but would for the rest of the decade be up front and centre—the appearance of *The Freewheelin' Bob Dylan* is certainly one of them.

It might be said that this leitmotif of the age had a perfect preamble. The public perception of Dylan as an Angry Young Man—to use a phrase common on the other side of the Atlantic about artistic types of the same mindset—was cemented in the second week of May, a fortnight before *Freewheelin'*'s release, when he made the national news after being denied the right to sing on television what he had now retitled 'John Birch Society Paranoid Blues'. The song was a satire of one of the hysterical anti-communist organisations proliferating in the States at the time, the sort to whom any questioning of authority or slightest suggestion of wealth distribution marked someone out as a 'fellow traveller' (i.e., sympathetic to the brutal communist regimes of the Union of Soviet Socialist Republics). Grossman pulled off the coup of securing his client a slot on *The Ed Sullivan Show*, a greater piece of mass-market exposure it's difficult to imagine. The slot was for May 12, and Dylan's plan to perform 'John Birch' was approved by, among others, Sullivan and his producer, Bob Precht. Some might be surprised that Sullivan would even be interested in Dylan, let alone willing to broadcast such a number, but his reputation as a dry old stick and showbiz-establishment lackey is clearly exaggerated. Unfortunately, Stowe Phelps—responsible for programme practices for the CBS TV network—expressed concern about the admittedly over-the-top comparison of the Society's members to Hitler. Fearful of a libel writ, he banned its performance.

Although unhappy with the decision, Sullivan suggested to Dylan that he might replace it with another song. 'If I can't sing that song, I won't sing *any* song,' came the reply as Dylan stormed out. Although there's no denying Dylan's genuine fury, perhaps the resulting furore benefitted him more than performing the song would have—it was a talking blues, after all, whatever the lyric's biting wit. With parts of the media now anxious to make amends for the terror and supineness of the all-too-recent McCarthyite days, CBS was excoriated in the press ('Higher-echelon thinking at CBS continues rigid, narrow and indifferent to the grave moral issues of our time,' thundered national columnist Harriet Van Horne of the incident). More important than the public support was the iconoclastic cachet of the controversy: the tide may have been turning as regards anti-red hysteria, but at this point in history, young entertainers did not storm off entertainment national institutions and spurn great media showcases.

'John Birch' didn't make the *Freewheelin'* album—Columbia's lawyers also quibbled over the implication that the Society's members had no problem with Hitler killing six million Jews—but the LP was also iconoclastic. It starts with the front cover. It is now overfamiliar and unremarkable in the way that so many images that have become iconic are, but at the time it was startlingly different. Although the jacket adheres to the then-common corny and consumerist practice of plastering the album's entire track listing on the front, in all other respects it's almost avant-garde. On the front of the first album, Dylan looks like a virgin. (He wasn't—he'd always had a way with the female sex from back in the Hibbing days.) This one pretty much shouts the fact that he isn't from the rooftops. Don Hunstein's full-colour, borderless photo shows him walking down the middle of a snowy Big Apple street with Suze Rotolo. Furthermore, that this is not the conventional clichéd, stiltedly posed studio shot is emphasised by the fact that neither participant is looking at the camera: Dylan is moodily hunched over with his hands dug in his jeans pockets while a laughing Rotolo clings to his arm.

The album title has more than one suggestion of new values. The ostentatiously dropped *g* of the second word could have been a reference to the way Dylan trended to dispense with that letter in his singing and his song titles, but it also clearly embraced an informality and grammatical heresy that in the crushingly obedient atmosphere of the crew-cut, God-and-country Eisenhower years was a subtle act of insurrection. 'Freewheeling', meanwhile, is a word that means groundbreaking and risk-taking, but in the context of the era those things were considered by some a synonym for 'commie/'red'/'pinko'. Others still may have assumed it to be some sort of sexual innuendo.

The cover was as nothing compared to the contents. Rarely has an artist made such a quantum leap between albums as Bob Dylan did between his first and second long-playing works. In contrast to the two unimpressive new songs on his debut, all but one of the thirteen selections here is a Dylan original, and most of them very good, with more than one subsequently acclaimed as a classic. The issue of self-reliance aside, the songs absolutely capture the *gestalt* in their concerns, and they do so in an age where stakes in such matters were genuinely high. In the early 60s, protest music/topical songs were not the stuff of self-aggrandisement and posturing that they have become in a now far less authoritarian society. This was an era where Southern Blacks insisting on their right to be served at lunch counters had food humiliatingly poured over their heads by outraged white patrons while the police looked impassively on. It was an era where the general public had a background terror that they and their loved ones could be blasted off the face of the earth at any moment by a nuclear bomb—a background that became terrifying foreground in October 1962, when the USA and the USSR squared up to each other over the issue of the Soviet Union supplying nuclear missiles to Cuba, less than a hundred miles of America's coast. It was an era where welfare on both sides of the Atlantic was still in its infancy, and where there existed large gaps in provision, creating areas of genuine—as opposed to relative—poverty in the form of hunger, homelessness, and lack of access to medical treatment. It was an era where young Americans who led a lifestyle that authorities deemed to be too alternative could have profound difficulty finding jobs and, at the far extreme, literally be committed to mental asylums. Much of this reality failed to filter through to the media, which was controlled by conservative forces uninterested—especially in the States—in advertising society's faults, creating a feeling of infuriated impotence among the public in the face of unfairness and cruelty. With the lack of scrutiny that goes with the media being in the hands of the well-off and reactionary, public officials were far less likely to face exposure or be punished, as a consequence of which officiousness and iniquitousness were woven into the fabric of society. All of this meant that *The Freewheelin' Bob Dylan* was not merely enjoyable music but a merciful blast of truth. It was a work that was a vital safety valve for angry youth (and not necessarily only the youth), and a rallying cry for the activist elements of it.

Remarkably—but, for Dylan's career, predictably—the album could have been even better. Whether the formulaic and sensationalist 'John Birch Society Paranoid Blues' was a loss is debatable, but Dylan's unforced omission of 'The Death Of Emmett Till' is inexplicable. The latter may well be the first proper protest song he ever wrote. It's also one of his best, a song detailing the horrific true story from 1955 of a fourteen-year-old Black boy beaten to death for whistling at a white woman and whose murderers went unpunished, containing harrowing lines like, 'They tortured him and did some things too evil to repeat.' As with other great protest songs he wrote, it doesn't destroy his point too much that he gets some facts wrong. Then there is 'Tomorrow Is A Long Time', a beautiful expression of loneliness. To us the listener, of course, the 'waste' of the latter is bewildering, but the composer seems to have decided not to include it for complicated emotional reasons. It's Dylan's song about his heartache over Suze's absence in Italy, where she had gone in May '62 to study art. As with so many Dylan compositions that he registered for copyright and/or made an acetate of but didn't release commercially, it was left to other recording artists to realise its potential, starting with Ian & Sylvia (1963) and including none other than Rod Stewart (1971) and—to Dylan's delight—Elvis Presley (1966).

'John Birch' was included on a very early Los Angeles *Freewheelin'* pressing that also encompassed 'Let Me Die In My Footsteps', 'Rambling Gambling Willie', and 'Rocks And Gravel' (aka 'Solid Road'). It was recalled in April. Numbering an estimated three hundred copies, this pressing is one of the most sought-after collector's items in music history. Whether it's artistically superior is, of course, a matter of taste.

'Let Me Die In My Footsteps' amusingly mocks the many people at the time building fallout shelters, but the tracks that replaced the jettisoned quartet were 'Masters Of War', 'A Hard Rain's A-Gonna Fall', 'Bob Dylan's Dream', and 'Talkin' World War III Blues', major compositions all.

John Hammond's album production credit is only partially correct. A consequence of the unpleasant and ultimately failed attempt by Grossman to get Dylan's Columbia contract nullified was the displacement of the man who had given Dylan his break and produced his first album. Although the label's sidelining of Hammond as a political manoeuvre may have been graceless and Dylan's acquiescence to it ungrateful, it can't be denied that his replacement was ultimately beneficial.

Tom Wilson was born in 1931 and raised in Texas. 'He was a very sweet man,' says Al Kooper. 'He was a Harvard graduate. He was very intellectual and just a wonderful person.' Frank Owens, a keyboardist who worked with Wilson on at least one Dylan session, describes Wilson as 'a tall gentleman of African American descent. A clean-cut gentleman. Very friendly, easy-going, very affable, very nice.' He also observes that he was unusual: 'You didn't see many producers of that colour doing things like a Bob Dylan album.'

Wilson launched jazz label Transition Records and subsequently worked for United Artists and Savoy before he became a Columbia staff producer. A studio hand who had previously worked on sessions for jazz artists such as Sun Ra, Cecil Taylor, and Donald Byrd, he had not been much interested in folk previously, but—as with so many who hadn't— was enervated by Dylan's vibrant, cutting-edge variant. He would guide Dylan's studio work for the next two years, overseeing one of the most profound and culturally far-reaching changes in style and demographic any artist has ever made.

On *Freewheelin'*, Dylan was already making a pretty big change. The first album contained little in the way of what at the time would have been termed radicalism. It possessed a bohemian ambience, material favouring a pessimistic worldview, and, in 'Talkin' New York', a verse containing a reference to people robbing other people with fountain pens and a slightly confusing metaphor about hungry people still needing to cut something with their knives and forks. That, though, was the extent of its sociopolitical commentary. In the fourteen months between the two LPs, Dylan seemed to have become politically educated and engaged.

For those who found the transition a little too convenient and Damascene, especially in the context of Dylan restricting his activism to his songs and his subsequent supposedly even more cynical embracement of rock music, the case was closed by comments Dylan made to *Long Island Press* in October 1965. There, he said, 'I never wanted to write topical songs. That was my chance. In the Village there was a little publication called *Broadside* and with topical songs you could get in there. I wasn't getting far with the things I was doing…*Broadside* gave me a start.' It's a pretty stark admission of opportunism, but it's not quite the same thing as stating that his diatribes about nuclear arms proliferation, poverty, and racism were insincere. Moreover, context is important here: Dylan had not long before that particular interview renounced protest and even more recently removed himself from the folk idiom. His comments may have been an attempt to get off his back the legions of disgruntled fans who were badgering him to go back to protest, and/or a justification for his change of style.

The rather unfortunate fact for Dylan's detractors is that, whether wholehearted or otherwise, it is his protest songs that are the greatest of the era, not those of Pete Seeger, Phil Ochs, Tom Paxton, or anyone else. The compositions of the aforementioned have largely passed from the public consciousness, even though they—having stuck with the genre for longer—wrote far more of them than did Dylan. That Dylan's have not is a consequence of his mind and creativity working on a far higher level. His protest was rarely simplistic sloganeering or agitprop. Instead, he specialised in nuance and cleverness, and furthermore, he had a facility with language that encompassed both the poetic and the colloquial. This poetic element was something Dylan was quite serious about and conscious of. He told Paul Robbins of *In-Beat* magazine in 1965, 'They're written so you can read it, you dig? If you take away whatever there is to the song—the beat, the melody—I could still recite it.'

The poetic and the colloquial are cheek by jowl in album opener 'Blowin' In The Wind', where Dylan's phraseology feels slightly olde-worlde and hence possessed of ancient wisdom but yet is delivered like a barroom conversation, with lines almost comically beginning with a 'Yes, and...'

If 'Blowin' In The Wind' is an exercise in ambiguity, 'Masters Of War' is the very opposite. In fact, it could be said to be the track where Dylan embraces the very one-dimensionality he is usually careful to avoid. This denunciation of warmongers is intense, pitiless, and unlayered. In a seething litany, Dylan tears into those who build guns and bombs, his fury incrementally mounting to such a pitch that by the final verse he is declaring to arms manufacturers that he hopes that they die 'and your death'll come soon'.

It's simplistic, of course, but the climate of the times militated against the type of clear-headedness that would make one reason that, without wars, the world would never have been able to, say, overcome the Nazis. Such was the global terror engendered by the Cuban Missile Crisis that many simply hated the very idea of weapons, and in this sense, the song captures the mood of the young and/or engaged of the time. It could be argued that it didn't capture *Dylan's* mood—that he was far too clever to think in such naïve and emotional terms—but expressing the opinions of others rather than oneself is a not-illegitimate pursuit and certainly not uncommon in folk music. It also became an irrelevant point by virtue of the performance. The melody—based on standard 'Nottamun Town'—is superbly appropriate for such an anthem of cold fury, relentless without being monotonous and as tight as a coiled spring. If we can't agree with the song's message, we can at all times understand the impetus for it.

The magpie and revivalist traditions of folk in no way ruled out some of the genre's artists having proprietorial attitudes. Singer Jean Ritchie claimed Dylan had stolen 'Masters Of War' from her because 'Nottamun Town' was in her repertoire after being rediscovered by her great aunt. Ritchie took legal action. Considering that 'Nottamun Town' goes back to the Middle Ages, some might consider her suit laughable, but she later said that a settlement was agreed to (although no writing credit). Such quasi-scandals pocked Dylan's career at this point, although they never gained too much traction because there was never any suggestion of outright plagiarism.

In a similar vein, in 1982 Pete Townshend released an album named *All The Best Cowboys Have Chinese Eyes*, which featured a song titled 'North Country Girl'. Some will have been surprised at its publishing attribution of 'Traditional; arranged by Pete Townshend', as they had always thought it was a Bob Dylan song. It certainly owed more to *Freewheelin'*'s 'Girl From The North Country' than did the 1966 Simon & Garfunkel song 'Scarborough Fair/Canticle', which the latter pair took intact from English folkie Martin Carthy's arrangement of the public domain song 'Scarborough Fair', whereas Dylan merely took the tune (with Carthy's approval) and devised a lyric that truly personalised it. The North Country girl in question could be Echo Helstrom or Bonnie Beecher (a university girlfriend), or both. Either way, it's a sweet track, and the guitar picking suggests Dylan has come on in leaps and bounds on the instrument since the debut album.

'Down The Highway' is about a newer Dylan squeeze, one of a pair on the album that appears to address his somewhat tumultuous and bitty relationship with Rotolo. This one is of a more generous nature, although he does cavil a little at her for abandoning him for foreign shores (she was in Italy for much of the time they were 'together'). However, it's less interesting than the other, less generous-hearted song because it has a repetitive blues structure that even his intriguing, wiggly guitar lick can't compensate for.

'Bob Dylan's Blues' is a slight song but a development in that it sees Dylan addressing in his own words rather than someone else's the glum and world-weary subject matter that predominated on his debut. Lamenting that the Lone Ranger and Tonto are fixing everybody's problems except his, the narrator for two and a half minutes comes across like a drunkard muttering into his whiskey glass, although his scuffed vulnerability makes him more agreeable company than the average disillusioned barfly.

'A Hard Rain's A-Gonna Fall' is Dylan's first epic. With such extravaganzas, he would transform the notion of the acceptable length of an individual recording. Seven minutes long, it closed the album's first half in its original vinyl configuration. It's a song that has been misinterpreted and misrepresented, starting right at the beginning with Nat Hentoff's album sleeve notes, which state that Dylan wrote it during the Cuban Missile Crisis, something Dylan scholars assert the chronology doesn't support. It's partly Hentoff's claim and partly Dylan's quote on the back of the album—'Every line in it is actually the start of a whole song. But when I wrote it, I thought I wouldn't have enough time alive to write all those songs so I put all I could into this one'—that led many to assume that the rain in the title is a reference to nuclear fallout, something Dylan was subsequently anxious to dispute. Frankly, Dylan would have been better advised to go with the misapprehension, as whatever chilling quality the song has ever possessed derives from it. Without it, we are left with an overlong creation written in courtly vernacular—deriving from its source material, 'Lord Randal'—in which a returning wandering son tells the father who has missed him about experiences that are, to modern ears, antediluvian and therefore not of much relevance ('I saw a newborn baby with wild wolves all around it').

Although Dylan had improved as a guitarist since his first release, no one in the know was going to mistake the fingerpicking on 'Don't Think Twice, It's All Right' as his handiwork. It was almost certainly played by session man Bruce Langhorne. Fellow session musician Al Gorgoni recalls, 'He was a folkie. He played with stumps. He was pretty amazing.' He is referring to the fact that, like Django Reinhardt and Black Sabbath's Tony Iommi, Langhorne became an excellent guitarist despite being deformed by an accident, in his case a childhood fireworks mishap that caused the loss of three fingers on his right hand. His mellifluous contribution to 'Don't Think Twice, It's All Right' helps make the track the album's highlight. Clearly written after another row with the young woman on the album's front cover, it sees the narrator inform his partner that, when her rooster crows at the break of dawn, he'll be long gone. However, he injects ambiguity by admitting that he wishes there was something she could say to make him change his mind. The wistful tone, furthermore, belies the insults he strews in his wake about her being a child rather than a woman and having wasted his precious time. Underlining the rather sweet fact that it's all a big bluff is the fact that the pair's romance would endure for a while yet.

Less sweetly, Dylan was accused of ripping off Paul Clayton, having based his melody on that of 'Who'll Buy Your Chickens When I'm Gone', a composition his fellow folkie had found on one of the song-excavating expeditions popular in those days and in those circles, the kings of which activity were the Lomax family. Clayton had refashioned the lyric as 'Who's Gonna Buy Your Ribbon Saw', but the melody was public domain, so Dylan had the perfect legal right, although it was considered at best a discourtesy not to offer Clayton a co-composing credit and royalties. Dylan didn't put a 'Trad. Arr.' before the word 'Dylan' in the publishing credit.[*]

Dylan might have detested the parochialism of his hometown but,

---

[*] Dylan claimed that Clayton was later given substantial financial recompense from an unspecified music publisher.

as with any human being, he had a sentimental attachment to his old stamping grounds. In 'Bob Dylan's Dream', he laments the fact that his old Hibbing friends are now a distant memory.

'Oxford Town' is a protest song of a far cleverer stripe than 'Masters Of War'. Its subject matter is grim, being the recounting of the harassment and humiliation faced by James Meredith when, in 1962, he became the first Black student to enrol at the University Of Mississippi—something achieved at the cost of the deployment of troops. The terrible things that went down in and around that event are communicated by the line 'Two men died 'neath the Mississippi moon', but otherwise the sprightly melody and Dylan's laconic lyric keep things as light as possible in the circumstances without undermining the grave point being made.

'Talkin' World War III Blues' makes its point with a similarly velvet glove. It's pretty much the song that many mistook 'Hard Rain' for, being concerned with nuclear war and its aftermath and being almost as long. The depiction of the upshot of the dropping of the Big One is humorous, warm, and funny, featuring a man wondering who turned the lights out as he traverses streets deserted but for a madman who runs away from him and a woman who declines to play Adam and Eve on the grounds that 'You see what happened last time they started'. The banal pop songs he spins on his record player and the voice on a speaking clock stuck permanently at 3pm aren't exactly satisfying substitutes for human company. The song is even sufficiently inventive to transcend the limitations of the talking blues format.

'Corrina, Corrina' is not the full-band version from Dylan's first single, but it is the only track on the album augmented with drums. A sweet and gentle folk-blues, it's the most sentimental thing on the record—certainly far more so than the succeeding 'Honey, Just Allow Me One More Chance', a raucously importunate composition with a breakneck pace. Even more raucous is the closing track, 'I Shall Be Free', an impressionistic sequence of images from Dylan's sex life (or idealised sex life—it's doubtful he caught hell from Richard Burton for making love to Elizabeth Taylor). Such songs may seem chauvinistic from today's perspective—in 'Honey, Just Allow Me One More Chance', the narrator tells the woman he is addressing that he has been seeking a girl like her but 'I can't find nobody, so you'll have to do'; in 'I Shall Be Free', he jumps out of a bedroom window stark naked when his partner asks him how she looks without her make-up. They aren't without self-criticism, though: Dylan admits in 'I Shall Be Free' that he sometimes smells like a skunk. Moreover, both numbers exemplify how even the songs here that aren't overtly political seemed implicitly so at the time: such frankness about sex and relationships was itself throwing down a gauntlet to the chaste, squeaky-clean version of America seen in the media.

'Blowin' In The Wind' b/w 'Don't Think Twice, It's All Right' appeared as a US Bob Dylan single in August 1963. It was a stunning combination of songs, but it did little business, partly because, by then, Peter, Paul & Mary had hit with their interpretation of 'Blowin' In The Wind'. However, Dylan did quickly become a star in his own right. In the last week of July, he appeared at the Newport Folk Festival and turned out to be the highlight of a weekend at which 47,000 attended— the largest crowd the event had attracted, and clearly so big primarily because of him. Among the numbers he performed were 'Playboys And Playgirls', an anti-privilege/hedonism anthem, another of his early songs that was well known to and loved by his fans from live performance but transpired to not become part of his familiar canon because he didn't release a recorded version of it. He also, of course, sang 'Blowin' In The Wind', whose status as a national anthem for the Movement was confirmed when all the fellow artists arrayed on chairs on stage with him stood up and joined in. As well as his own set, Dylan was omnipresent in the fact that Peter, Paul & Mary sang his songs and verbally exalted him in their set, as did Joan Baez, who by the way couldn't resist introducing 'Don't Think Twice, It's Alright' as being about 'a love affair that has lasted too long'. (Suze Rotolo was in the audience and was rendered distraught.) This event marked the occasion

53

when Dylan and Baez publicly sang together for the first time, the start of a brief period when their names became synonyms.

In some ways, Newport '63 was as significant as 1967's Monterey International Pop Festival or the Woodstock Festival of 1969, but that fact has been rather washed from history because it marked both the apotheosis and the end of the folk revival, that brief moment in time when folk was the new rock'n'roll, before The Beatles came to America and asserted that actually rock'n'roll—or the way they and their compatriots had reconfigured it—was. That deal was sealed when Dylan himself proceeded to infuse rock with the attributes of folk, thus making the whole debate and divide redundant, but that's a story for a later point in this narrative.

By September, *Freewheelin'* was nosing into the *Billboard* album chart, eventually climbing to no. 22. (In 1964, Dylan's British fans sent it all the way to the top of that nation's chart.*) By October, he was headlining and selling out New York's famous Carnegie Hall. Reviewing the concert, his old champion Shelton put the status he was acquiring in a nutshell: 'To regard Mr. Dylan as merely an entertainer is to slight his importance. Rather, he is a moralist, a pamphleteer, an angry young man with a guitar, a social protest poet, a latter-day James Dean who knows what he is rebelling against.'

Bob Dylan was a kid speaking truth to power, a ragged troubadour articulating the grievances of contemporaries who had no platform or skills to express them. His stature would become in some ways no less important than that of John F. Kennedy or Martin Luther King. He purveyed through his songs the same sort of progressive values of a reformist president or a civil rights lynchpin, and while he didn't have either the formal power of a head of state or even the sort of informal power that comes from being the figurehead of a political movement, he

---

* The US chart stats used in this text are unless stated otherwise for *Billboard* and the UK chart stats are from *The Guinness Book Of British Hit Singles*, which for the period in question has usually employed the chart published in *Record Retailer / Music Week*.

reached people that luminaries like those men couldn't, whether because of his appeal to those not attuned to or hostile to politics and/or the opinions of the middle-aged, or because of the communal and joyous nature of the consumption of music.

The Freewheelin' Bob Dylan and its effect and influence made Dylan a man of the moment. He may not have intended it, he may not have wanted it (as opposed to fame or success), but it couldn't be much doubted that he deserved it.

.

In the last couple of months of 1963, it might have looked to some as though Bob Dylan's star was about to wane.

The first instance of his halo slipping a little came with the issue cover-dated November 4 of the mass-circulation magazine *Newsweek*, which ran a profile of him that exposed him as a fraud. Journalist Dick Schaap wasn't the first journalist with a national audience to find amusing Dylan's accent, appearance, syntax, and singing voice, but he—or more accurately his researcher, Andrea Svedberg—was the first to stumble upon the fact that his name was Zimmerman and—more importantly—he had never been poverty-stricken, a runaway, or a quasi-orphan. Schaap juxtaposed his subject's barefaced lies to him about his true name ('Dig my draft card, man. Bob Dylan') and his airy, myth-making pronouncements about his hinterland ('I don't know my parents . . . I've lost contact with them for years') with assiduous reportage that couldn't help but make him look ridiculous ('A few blocks away, in one of New York's motor inns, Mr. and Mrs. Abe Zimmerman of Hibbing, Minnesota, were looking forward to seeing their son sing at Carnegie Hall. Bobby had paid their way east and had sent them tickets').

Then there was Dylan's boorish, even shocking, behaviour on December 13, when he turned up at the Grand Ballroom of New York's Americana Hotel to accept campaigning group the Emergency Civil Liberties Committee's annual Tom Paine Award for work for freedom

55

and equality. Dylan was possibly inebriated, possibly nervous, and (in light of the *Newsweek* exposé) possibly undeserving feeling. He was also taken aback at the sea of grey and balding heads he saw before him, and—blithely assuming that lack of youth implied lack of progressivism—made a rambling, ungracious speech in which he said things like, 'My friends don't wear *suits*.' That in itself might have been harmless, but he then made a bizarre remark about Lee Harvey Oswald, the presumed assassin of John F. Kennedy, the president slain only three weeks before and the great hope for the (in fact very progressive) audience members: 'I saw some of myself in him.' He was rewarded with boos.

Yet neither matter seemed to do Dylan any particular long-term harm. In the case of *Newsweek*, it was possibly because the climate of the times made it seem to many that an 'establishment' magazine was trying to delegitimise a voice of dissent, and possibly because Schaap/ Svedberg undermined their exposé by giving credence to what soon turned out to be a totally false story that 'Blowin' In The Wind' was written by a New Jersey student named Lorre Wyatt who then sold it to Dylan. In the case of the Tom Paine Award, the audience members and those linked to them weren't exactly Dylan's demographic and therefore had no know-how or ability to harm his career with their reaction to him, even in the unlikely event that such liberals might want to. Moreover, Dylan's subsequent contrition—even if partial and mealy-mouthed—seemed to appease them enough to make things die down.

.

If in fact Dylan had never truly wanted to be a protest singer, he did a pretty good job of hiding it. For a brief period, he seems to have fallen in love with his role as voice of a generation and moral arbiter.

Who really can blame him? The blandishments of fame are seductive in any circumstances, but in this individual's case recording artists were queuing at the door of his publisher in the hope of getting an unheard song, convinced that his name in the parentheses beneath a song title on a record label was a virtual guarantee of chart success or at least credibility; the likes of Joan Baez, The New World Singers, and Peter, Paul & Mary were asking him to write album sleeve notes for similar cachet-by-association reasons; and journalists were seeking him out so they could nod solemnly at whatever witticisms or social critiques or even piss-taking he proffered them. Such things could turn the head of even the most humble of individuals—and it's fair to say that Dylan was never in the latter category. The fact that the voice of a generation role was also a lucrative one was brought home to Dylan early on when he was told that the success of Peter, Paul & Mary's version of 'Blowin' In The Wind' guaranteed its composer a minimum of $5,000 in royalties ($50,000 in today's money). Dylan was reportedly speechless. The revenue stream grew exponentially from there: by approximately August 1964, Dylan was reporting to Robert Shelton that he was about to gross his first million (ten million dollars today, over two million dollars even as an approximate net figure).

There was perhaps another incentive to further embrace the role. Joan Baez had been successful longer than Dylan and was to a remarkable extent his distaff bookend: a young, acoustic-oriented folk singer, albeit one with a far more conventional singing voice. She also had a widely known concern for social issues, although she hadn't yet incorporated such into her music. When the two became romantically involved and began to share concert stages, it seemed to many to make perfect sense. People were enchanted by the modern-day fairytale of the King & Queen Of Protest. (That is, with at least one exception in the shape of Suze Rotolo, with whom Dylan was still involved when he took up with Baez.) Dylan and Baez's reign—and relationship—was actually brief, but such was the perception of them as two peas in a pod that their names are intertwined in the public mind to this day.

The same could be said about Dylan's protest and folk eras: both were already coming to a close, but even in the 70s, an enquiry at a record shop about where Dylan's catalogue could be found would sometimes result in the customer being directed to the folk section. The reason that phase cast such a long shadow is exemplified by Dylan's third album. Recorded in six sessions in August and October 1963, *The Times They Are A-Changin'* is the LP on which he embraces for the final time, but in the most unequivocal and self-conscious way ever, his status as conscience of a cohort.

Almost everything about the album is stark and serious, from its unsmiling, monochrome cover photo to its grim contents. The humour that leavened his broadsides on *Freewheelin'* and was a big part of his stage act is completely absent, with his vignettes of poverty and oppression relieved only by the hardly mirthful subject matter of failed romance. Furthermore, his social critiques this time tend to offer not rousing solidarity or hope but instead little more than the message that the world is a cruel place, about which fact one can do nothing.

One of the only exceptions to the album's overarching glumness is the opening title track, and it's a glorious exception. Some aver that 'The Times They Are A-Changin'' is no less shallow and one-dimensional than 'Masters Of War', and that additionally it has been devalued by the passage of time: the insurgent 60s new-values young that the song celebrates have by this current point in history long had their chance in power, and while they notched up many entries in the plus column regarding nuclear brinksmanship, wealth inequity, racial injustice, and social authoritarianism (none of which are ever specifically mentioned in this song but all of which obliquely underpin its sentiments), the society we inhabit is hardly the utopia the protest generation were demanding. None of that makes it untrue, however, that it is a perfectly constructed creation that sweeps the listener up in its exhilarating rhetoric.

'The Times They Are A-Changin'' is almost a form of shorthand for the values of the Baby Boomers, the cohort that resulted from the vast uptick in the Western birthrate after the end of the Second World War. That generation had very different values to their parents. Never before in modern history had such a canyon yawned between the values of age groups. This might have been irrelevant were it not for the fact that Boomers had power not just numerically but economically. Rising living standards gave them much in the way of financial independence and thus enabled them to challenge without ruinous resistance the edicts and assumptions of their families, cultures, and governments. Or, as Dylan pithily and intoxicatingly put it in this song, 'Your sons and your daughters are beyond your command.'

Despite its heady qualities, that line is far from the best herein. The song has none of the gritty specificity of some of his other protest numbers, and in many ways it doesn't even feel contemporary, starting with the olde-worlde smack of that title phrase and continuing with an opening line wherein Dylan—as though he's a biblical prophet about to deliver a sermon—instructs people to gather around him. There are also vaguely timeworn-seeming references to lines being drawn and curses being cast. However, his talk of senators is not an Ancient Roman or Greek reference but unmistakably modern—something that makes all the more piercing his advice to Capitol Hill lawmakers that there is a battle raging outside that will soon shake their windows and rattle their walls. The melody and tempo are propulsive and perfectly matched by Dylan's torrential, defiant language, which itself is rendered glittering and persuasive by his dazzling rhyming schemes. Millions of teenagers and twentysomethings exulted in the vision the song proffered of politicians, parents, bosses, civil servants, and other authority figures who had failed to heed the call, spoken too soon, or blocked up the hall being consequently stalled, stymied, or drenched to the bone.

The album's joyous sense of solidarity ends there (unless one is prepared to give the benefit of the doubt to 'When The Ship Comes In', a poor man's 'The Times They Are A-Changin'' that sits in the middle of side two). Immediately following the opener comes 'Ballad Of Hollis Brown'. A mainly second-person narrative, it tells the story of the titular fictitious South Dakota man who lives in a decrepit, rat-infested cabin with his wife and five children. Unable to find work, he has to endure his spouse's screams and the despair in his hungry kids' eyes. Receiving no answer from the God he beseeches for help, he spends his last dollar on shotgun shells and kills his entire family and then himself. Dylan switches back to the third person with which he started the song for its two concluding verses, the second of which notes that, while seven people lie dead in Hollis Brown's cabin, somewhere else, 'There's seven new people born.' This would be wrist-slitting stuff in any circumstances, but Dylan rachets up the nagging quality of the song by using the format of the blues, repeating lines in almost a taunting chant about the man's babies tugging at his sleeve and him praying to the Lord above. It may be tedious, but it's a quite stunning contrast to *The Beverley Hillbillies* and other all-American, dimple-cheeked fare then being pumped into US dens.

That the following track, 'With God On Our Side', is also powerfully argued and also boring encapsulates the problem with *The Times They Are A-Changin'*. It's as though Dylan doesn't care about listenability as long as his point is made—an attitude that would have had some support at the time because social commentary was far more gratefully received than today, simply because it was so rare. This cut is more daring than the previous one in the sense that the United States was nowhere near Britain at the time in being a post-Christian country, and the church still had great sway in vast tracts of it. It denounces the way that the Almighty has traditionally been invoked to justify the latest conflict and concludes with a line that would have been received as sheer heresy in the Bible Belt: 'If God's on our side, he'll stop the next war.' Unfortunately, the straining melody is perfectly unsuited to the shortcomings of Dylan's voice, and here he is at his caterwauling worst, something a well-argued lyric can't assist.

In complete contrast, his singing on 'One Too Many Mornings', the album's other classic, is lovely, as is the entire song. A malice-free fare-thee-well to an ex-lover ('You're right from your side, I'm right from mine'), it's the perfect demonstration of the effectiveness of the one-man format, Dylan intoning sensitively as he picks delicate guitar shapes and injects melancholic harmonica patterns.

'North Country Blues' is one depressive poverty tableau that does work, possibly because Dylan has direct experience of dying mining towns, if not of being an old woman, from whose perspective the composition is sung. In tracing the course of a difficult life, he doesn't resort to stereotype, acknowledging the joys along with the hardships, although he winds up pointing out that the woman—now alone through either abandonment or widowhood—knows that her three children will sooner or later be departing ('For there ain't nothin' here now to hold them'). Nor does Dylan go over the top in delivery, his singing impressively understated. Although he is probably using a lot of stock phrases and scenarios from old folk numbers, this is a superb example of journalistic reportage in song, bringing to people's cognisance lifestyles and experiences of which they may have been barely aware.

Similar subtlety is on display in 'Only A Pawn In Their Game', which opened side two of the original vinyl album. It was songs like this that marked Dylan out as a cut above his contemporaries. A sort of sequel to the previous album's 'Oxford Town', its considerable nuance means it can really only be described as social commentary rather than protest. It's concerned with the recent murder of Medgar Evers, a Black civil rights activist who had been part of the beleaguered campaign to enrol James Meredith in Mississippi. Dylan declines to paint those behind or supportive of the slaying as pantomime villains. The logic is circular but not nonsensical: the poor white bigot, he asserts, is kept distracted from the fact of his poverty by the race-baiting Southern politician, leaving the latter and his shady allies free to continue to fail to address the poor white's economic grievances. Although overall the song is simpatico with the beliefs of the demo generation, its refrain of 'It ain't him to blame' is almost the antithesis of the fist-pumping, culpability-apportioning anthem favoured by that group.

As with several of his reportage songs, Dylan let his emotions take precedence over his fact-checking. The killer, Byron de la Beckwith, was indeed a bigot and white, but hardly poor: he paid his $10,000 bail in cash.

'Boots Of Spanish Leather' is yet another kiss-off to Suze, who does seem to have endured an inordinate number of complaints in song about her absences and faults when the reality is more likely that she was a saint to put up with Dylan. A dialogue between a man and the lover who is asking him whether he wants anything brought back from the travels on which she's about to embark, the song has a surprisingly elevated position in the esteem of Dylan's fanbase. However, its debt to folk standard 'Blackjack Davey' is made obvious by its dully old-fashioned phraseology, which denies it the contemporary, slangy verisimilitude of a song like 'Don't Think Twice, It's All Right'.

'When The Ship Comes In' would be merely a frustratingly vague you'll-get-yours sentiment if it weren't for the wide public knowledge of its genesis, which reduces it to the status of the simply silly. In August 1963, Dylan and Joan Baez were travelling together. When Dylan approached the desk of the hotel in which Baez had booked a room, he was turned away, and only the intervention of Baez confirmed the booking and secured Dylan himself a berth. Dylan's fury at the obvious disdain and suspicion his unkempt appearance had aroused in the desk clerk led to him sitting down that very night and hammering out a denunciation in which he talks of chastened foes agreeing to meet demands, only to be told, 'We'll shout from the bow your days are numbered.' Not only is the Armageddon rhetoric disproportionate, to say the least, but its phraseology is preposterously ornate, and the nautical metaphor is sustained beyond breaking point. It's all a rather unfortunate contrast to the on-the-button relatability of the anger expressed in the similarly themed 'The Times They Are A-Changin'', the song he wrote immediately after 'Ship', which therefore makes the latter a dry run.

'Ship' is also, it has to be said, slightly unsettling in the insight it gives us into Dylan's tortured mindset, and by extension his difficult childhood:

from which psychological cranny of resentment does this lopsided and overblown but clearly genuine sense of persecution spring? All in all, it's a song that almost undermines the superior artistry and thought processes he displays in the likes of 'Only A Pawn In Their Game'. That latter multi-dimensional creation is beyond the ken and craft of Seeger, Paxton, Ochs, et al, but the type of confused, hysterical resentment in 'When The Ship Comes In' is something to which they would never stoop. It serves to confirm what many people close to Dylan have always asserted: that he is an almost disturbingly complicated individual.

Still, that his heart is in the right place is illustrated by 'The Lonesome Death Of Hattie Carroll'. Using the tune of 'Mary Hamilton', he gets several details wrong in this supposedly true, contemporaneous story of white rich boy William Zantzinger, who escaped punishment for causing the death of a Black maid. Additionally, he makes his point over too extended a time, but within those six minutes, Dylan proves why he is head and shoulders above his peers. He proffers a protest song, but one in which he does almost the reverse of invoking a sense of solidarity, as at the end of each verse he admonishes the listeners to refrain from weeping, finally telling them at song's end, after Zantzinger's paltry sentence is revealed, 'Bury the rag deep in your face for now's the time for your tears.'

The album closes on what was then a curious note, but one that subsequent events caused to drip with meaning. In 'Restless Farewell', a narrator is looking back on his life and contemplating the fact that he will soon be cutting current ties. Some of the verses concern good times and lovers, one addresses foes and causes. Of every one of the latter, Dylan says, 'I fought it full without regret or shame.'

•

The Times They Are A-Changin' was released on January 13, 1964. It made it only to no. 20 on the *Billboard* chart, a position that would have been perfectly respectable were it not for the breakthrough *Freewheelin'* had effected. In the UK, it initially made no. 20 but climbed to no. 4 in May 1965 in the wake of mounting Anglo Dylanmania.

The first album Dylan made as a famous person, it's difficult to escape the impression that *Times* constitutes him deliberately conforming to public perception. To some extent, it's almost a parody of both his public persona and the protest genre. It will have been many people's first Dylan album, and as such it's a pity that it's not that good, but, as touched on previously, for some people protest music was less a matter of experiencing enjoyment than of being caused to feel solidarity. Some, in fact, might even have found distasteful the notion that the soundtrack to dissent and/or insurrection could be a matter of pleasure.

To such people it may have been irrelevant that, as was now already traditional in Dylan's short career, his latest album could have been enhanced by the inclusion of discards, in this case the imperial 'Lay Down Your Weary Tune', the coiling 'Percy's Song', and—especially— the beautiful compassionate eulogy to an anonymous, dead homeless man 'Only A Hobo'.

Whereas the two previous albums had back-cover sleeve notes written by supportive journalists, Dylan provided his own text for this release in the form of verse titled '11 Outlined Epitaphs', something that happened to feed into the reputation he was acquiring as a people's poet. They're very much in the vein of the Beat writers, whose most prominent example, Allen ('Howl') Ginsberg, was a friend of his. If one takes the position that blank verse and unconventional spelling make one a rebel, they're no doubt impressive. Others will be more intrigued by the fact that they seemed to offer Dylan a means to be self-critical and confessional in a way that he clearly felt unable to be in his song lyrics—and in fact would never really be able to be, except by using distancing mechanisms like metaphor and second-person perspective.

Soon, he would be using such techniques in song to explain why he no longer wished to cater to a demographic he had largely created. Unthinkably, the King Of Protest was about to abdicate.

Chapter two

Things Have Changed

Dylan's appearance at the Newport Folk Festival on July 26, 1964, was not quite as triumphant as his Christ-like arrival the previous year. The audience was puzzled by a set of new songs that seemed to have no political content. The title of Dylan's fourth album, released a fortnight later, only confirmed this supposedly disturbing new trend.

Dylan later claimed that it was Tom Wilson who came up with *Another Side Of Bob Dylan* and that he 'begged and pleaded' that it not be used because it suggested the contents were 'a negation of the past'. Leaving aside the utter unlikelihood of his producer having more power over the matter than Dylan, the title was actually pretty much perfect for an LP that was a marked departure. Rather than another collection of protest songs, he delivered an array of romantic compositions, picaresque stories, and comedy numbers. This wasn't completely unprecedented in his career, of course. However, his protest-free first album predated him acquiring the ability to consistently write his own material. Since finding his feet and voice as a composer, he had set out his stall as a man who proffered sociopolitical broadsides. That his latest offering contained nothing that could be posited as in that vein seemed for many like a cop-out.

Left-wingers of the time—especially in the States, where the McCarthyite terror had seen many progressives, fearful for their livelihoods, recant their previous idealism—were highly attuned to the prospect of their brethren capitulating to pressure. While McCarthyism itself was gone, there was still much in the way of social pressure militating against progressivism. *Another Side Of Bob Dylan* seemed to fit a depressingly familiar pattern of a losing of nerve. Theoretically, it could signify something even worse—a loss of ideals. On top of that was the aesthetic consideration of a blanding out. Certainly, the album's front cover—featuring a picture of the artist with his arm resting on an upraised knee as he gazes thoughtfully into the distance—is not too far off the type of anodyne, corny publicity photos favoured by the likes of Bobby Vee.

One possible cause for Dylan's abandonment of protest is the seismic event that occurred less than a month after he finished recording *The Times They Are A-Changin'*. Today, the possibility of the assassination of an American political figure is part of the background of life. Before November 22, 1963, when President John F. Kennedy was mown down, it was unthinkable. Singer Eric Andersen was just one of several people in Dylan's circle who suspected that Dylan was shaken to his core by the slaying, and not just because of compassion for a man whose value-set broadly reflected his own. Dylan was perceived by the public as part of the same movement as Kennedy. If someone could kill a president for, it was presumed, his values, it didn't take a leap in logic to assume that someone like Dylan might also be in danger. For the record, Dylan has denied the linkage.

For some, there was an even worse possibility: that Dylan had never really meant any of it. In the context of his new direction, the previous LP's 'Restless Farewell' could make perfect sense: his kiss-off to protest music.* Both the song's contents and its suspiciously tidy placement at the close of *The Times They Are A-Changin'* bolstered an interpretation that Dylan's protest phase was calculatingly designed to be limited. The melancholy undertow to its lyric, which seems to acknowledge that he was destined to shortly lose friends, wouldn't have been of much interest to his disenchanted detractors. Nor would the fact that *Another Side Of Bob Dylan* is a more pleasurable listen than its admirable rather than enjoyable predecessor.

When an artist has been making records as long as Dylan has, his work tends to get divided by critics and fans into phases. *Another Side Of Bob Dylan* has suffered by being perceived as a bridge between two hugely notable and distinct parts of Dylan's recording career: his protest era and his triumvirate of electric rock masterpieces. Yet the album is nothing like the collection of underwhelming hedged bets that usually characterise transitional albums. It is an aesthetically superior work to

---

* Others have suggested his being shaken by the *Newsweek* exposé as a possible impetus for the song.

The Times They Are A-Changin', displays a more mature, rounded view on life than *The Freewheelin' Bob Dylan*, and—though its stark acoustic accompaniment cannot hope to compete with the shimmering sound paintings supplied by the sessioners on *Highway 61*, etc.—is lyrically a warmer, more emotionally direct disc than any of his 60s rock albums.

Not that it's without flaws. *Another Side Of Bob Dylan* epitomises a phase in Dylan's career that hasn't been discussed much—one that encompasses his first four LPs and constitutes an awkward period in his linguistic development. In this album's 'I Shall Be Free', he turns on its head the phrase uttered by people when somebody has said something that accidentally rhymes—'You're a poet / And you didn't know it'—as he jokily observes that he's a poet and he knows it, adding, 'Hope I don't blow it.' In fact, while he would very shortly assume the mantle and justify the description 'Poet Laureate Of Popular Music', at this juncture he constituted an unfinished and much more rough-hewn proposition. Although speckled with incandescent imagery and pocked with wonderful phraseology, the album is also replete with half-baked concepts and silly similes. Its two epics, 'Ballad In Plain D' and 'Chimes Of Freedom', whatever their considerable merits, are particularly guilty of this. Moreover, the album is a little slapdash, and not exactly heavyweight. This was perhaps inevitable: the bulk of it was written within the space of a week—at the end of May and beginning of June '64, while on a Greek holiday with German model (and later singer) Nico—while the actual recording was all done on one evening (June 9) and in less than optimum circumstances. The reason you feel you can hear Dylan showing off at times is that the control booth was packed with a bunch of his friends. As well as being sycophantic toward Dylan, they were disrespectful of Wilson (one of them drew a square in the air behind the producer's head). There was also much alcohol flowing. Nonetheless, the levity is actually merciful after the misery-fest of *The Times They Are A-Changin'*. Moreover, despite its lack of heft, the LP is alternately invigorating and absorbing, and in 'I Don't Believe You', 'My

Back Pages', and 'To Ramona', it contains a clutch of classics—a higher quotient of timeless works than the previous album.

There was, as usual, a classic that Dylan left off. By which is meant not 'Mr. Tambourine Man', which he wisely decided his attempt at was too primitive to bear public scrutiny, but the beautifully lovelorn 'Mama, You Been On My Mind'. That's lovelorn as regards a sexual partner rather than a mother, it should be pointed out. In American popular song, 'mama' has long been a term of endearment addressed to a romantic partner, in much the same way as the more common and enduring 'baby'. By the early 1960s, Dylan was one of the few still prepared to shrug off the self-consciousness Sigmund Freud's influence had injected into the sex/family terminology overlap.

Inevitably on an acoustic album, the focus is going to be on the lyrics, but *Another Side Of* proves as much as any Dylan album just what a good tunesmith and singer he is. The melodies are usually lovely, flowing things. His voice is passionate and versatile, well on its way to a quality that the following year would see it effecting arguably the greatest vocal performance in music history. Meanwhile, his sweet, tender playing on 'To Ramona' and 'I Don't Believe You' brings his harmonica work to new heights.

He begins proceedings with 'All I Really Want To Do', a merry and (entirely unconvincing, it must be said) declaration of un-sinister intent to a female friend. As well as a he-protesteth-too-much property, the song has a he-belabours-the-point strain: he's stated his case after a couple of verses. Again, though, the song's shortcomings would have been lessened by the climate of the times and the fact that it went against their grain, although for different reasons than the indulgence of the faults in his protest material. It's a song that demonstrates that while Dylan may no longer be a protest singer, that certainly doesn't mean he has embraced the banalities of rock and pop lyrics. This is a quite remarkably risqué composition: it was far from usual in 1964 to hear the phrase 'knock you up' in popular song, or a declaration from a singer that he would never beat someone. Bob Dylan may not have been interested anymore in writing manifestos, but he was clearly still simpatico with those who wanted to shrug off the clean-cut jib demanded by Western culture. Whatever he now was or wasn't, he was very much still an artist of the Movement. Whether he was self-aware is another matter. His stated ambitions for the treatment of his lover in this song are the diametric opposite of the manipulative and suffocating way witnesses say he treated Rotolo.

With 'Black Crow Blues', the world is introduced to Dylan the pianist, for what that's worth. His boxing-gloved style is employed on a meandering, lazily written, slight, but at the same time quite likeable creation. Atop a winding melody decorated with pleasing harmonica work, Dylan invests in his lyric a commitment that it doesn't really deserve as he explores an inner turmoil. A verse in which he says he sometimes thinks he's too high to fall and other times fears he's so low down he doubts if he can ever resurface is about as profound as it gets in a vague and unresolved song, an insubstantiality made all the more curious by the fact that he keeps cheating with the format of traditional blues to cram extra words into its stanzas, as though he has a lot to say.

If 'Black Crow Blues' finds Dylan in a lackadaisical mood, 'Spanish Harlem Incident' represents him at his poetic best. Although giddy and less than two and a half minutes in length, it constitutes a substantial-feeling ride, one in which he conveys evocatively his infatuation with a hot-blooded, palm-reading Gypsy lover. As well as it being chockfull of memorable imagery and sparkling lines ('I got to laugh halfways off my heels'), he repeatedly throws in a cute, tricksy guitar run.

The album's shortest cut is followed by a very long one. 'Chimes Of Freedom' sprawls across seven minutes. If it weren't for the seismic declaration constituted by 'My Back Pages' and the fact that one of the love songs is even longer, we could adjudge it the work's grand statement. Even so, it's a philosophical musing in the same profound realms as his later works 'It's All Right, Ma (I'm Only Bleeding)' and 'Desolation Row', if not so pessimistic. It would also have been seized on by his fans as proof that while he may at the moment no longer be purveying formal protest, he might still come back to the fold. In actual fact, it feels like more of a farewell to that form. However, it shares with his protest fare only the fact of its humanitarianism and anthemic qualities. He's not advocating a specific cause or inveighing against a particular injustice but engaging in pondering on a higher philosophical strata.

Dylan and unnamed, unnumbered companions take refuge in a doorway from a rainstorm. The lightning they see seems to them to represent chimes of freedom flashing for a host of unfortunates, ranging from reluctant warriors and homeless refugees to rebels, outcasts, the gentle, the kind, poets and painters ahead of their time, the broken-hearted, the unjustly imprisoned, the unfairly maligned and—in a final flurry of expansiveness verging on meaninglessness—the hung-up the whole universe over. Yet the pity, however hazy, is moving, and the goodwill in the listener is strengthened by the evocative lines with which it's peppered, such as 'Through the mad mystic hammering of the wild ripping hail'. However, the poetry is forever teetering between majestic and ludicrous. The song's central conceit and metaphor doesn't make sense: chiming is a sound, flashing is a sight. He may be referring to the reflection of light off bells, but a poet should not be this imprecise. Then there is the preponderance of phrases that sound superficially impressive but which are at base illogical, whether it be the sky purveying poems in naked wonder or indeed that mad mystic hammering .

In the 1960s, some liberals were known to mutter, *sotto voce*, that while they were all in favour of desegregation in schools and Black voter registration drives, that didn't mean they wanted a Negro family moving into their neighbourhood, or their daughter getting wed to a 'coloured'. Dylan mischievously turns that mantra on its head in 'I Shall Be Free No.10'.* In what is a rambling humour piece like its antecedent, Dylan is no less scornful of liberals than he has been of reds-under-the-beds

---

* If he had written nos. 2–9 since the original 'I Shall Be Free' on *Freewheelin'*, they have yet to be exhumed from the archives.

types as he states, through the voice of a conflicted narrator, that he's a liberal, but to a degree: he would in no way permit anti-desegregation politician Barry Goldwater to move in next door and marry his daughter. It's mildly amusing, as is the song as a whole—even despite its lazy rhymes and air of aimlessness.

Those who had come to this album knowing little about Dylan other than the fact that he was increasingly being spoken of as a bard for his generation no doubt might have been rendered sceptical by most of what they'd heard so far. They would have had their scepticism blown to smithereens by the track that closes side one. 'To Ramona' is a song that offers words of comfort to an individual anxious about scrutiny and criticism. Its first verse is possibly the finest thing to ever emanate from Dylan's pen or typewriter. After consoling his tearful lover with the assurance that her sadness will pass and that the virtues of the city are not unequivocal and therefore not worth her emotional energy, he wraps up with the admission, 'Though I cannot explain that in lines.' It is writing of a quality that defies belief: the sheer affecting tenderness of the sentiments, the incredible economy and precision of the words (a whole romantic situation and an entire philosophical viewpoint explained in two immaculate stanzas), and, to top it all, that final line, where our poet admits that there's a more complicated thought he's trying to articulate but that the form of a song is too restrictive to enable him to do it— something he still manages to adroitly phrase so that it rhymes and scans.

It doesn't end there, either. In the Dylan canon from around this point onward, what appears to be a straightforward second-person narrative is often actually Dylan addressing himself. With that possibility, the track explodes into a whole other dimension. On one level, Dylan may perfectly sustain the conceit/pretence of the scenario of a narrator comforting a distressed lover, but once decoded it seems clear that this song's talk of sorrow stemming from fixtures, forces, and friends is an articulation of Dylan's internal agony about leaving behind the protest scene and the intimates and allies associated with it.

Although by no means one of his more famous numbers, 'To Ramona''s delicate strengths have been recognised by both Dylan (who has featured it in his sets ever since) and many other artists: it has been the recipient of multiple cover versions, including most unlikely ones by the likes of Alan Price and Humble Pie. Meanwhile, the song's final line, in which Dylan admits to the person addressed (whomever it may be) that one day s/he might be the one needing comfort, was nicked by his good friend George Harrison for the Beatles track 'Old Brown Shoe'.

Illustrating how this album lurches back and forth between sublime and ridiculous is 'Motorpsycho Nitemare', a throwaway featuring slapdash rhyming and an inconsistent melody with the additional demerit of uncertain purpose. It tells the tale of a man stranded overnight in a rural locale where a farmer wants to kill him and the farmer's daughter wants to sleep with him. The listener would be forgiven for gravitating more toward the farmer's point of view on the grounds that they wonder why they're wasting their time listening to something Dylan seems to have written in his sleep.

Naturally, this piece of garbage is followed by something quite majestic. 'My Back Pages' is the album's keynote song. Another artist would have placed it at the start of the album, but Dylan wouldn't be so crass as to indulge in such signposting. In a composition of disillusion, he sneers at his old self (from all of one year ago) for believing the lie that life is black and white, a sin that he suggests made him as bad as the people his protest songs fulminated against. It's in the nature of Dylan's genius, however, that through the superbly phrased refrain, 'I was so much older then, I'm younger than that now', he paradoxically manages to inject what is a denunciation of solidarity-engendering rhetoric with the galvanising, euphoric flavour of an anthem.

'I Don't Believe You' is broken-hearted yet somehow cheery, the latter partly due to the fact that—not for the first time on the record—Dylan is audibly showing off to his mates in the control booth. The narrator is bewildered by the sudden coldness of a woman with whom he has just 'kissed through the wild blazing night time'. Such evocative turns of phrase align with a sprightly melody, jaunty harmonica, and attractively mewling singing to uplifting effect.

Because Dylan is the original singer/songwriter, it's easy to unthinkingly assume that his material deals in the type of confessional song with which that genre is associated. In fact, as well as non-first-person pronouns, Dylan consistently hides behind metaphor, self-mockery, and fiction. Where the word 'I' does appear in his songs, it's not with the intent of candour. 'My Back Pages' and 'Ballad In Plain D' from this album, and the much later 'Sara', are uncommon exceptions in dispensing with disguising devices. 'Ballad In Plain D' documents his final breakup with Rotolo. Written in the style of a traditional ballad, it's all flowery simile and old-fashioned language ('I courted her proudly, but now she is gone'), but beyond the stylised dressing lies stark frankness. Dylan and Rotolo split up in March 1964. The singer tells us the relationship was doomed by Rotolo's interfering mother and sister but also says there are no excuses for his own behaviour, not even the profound changes through which he was going. He sets well a climactic scene in which he and the sister are screaming recriminations at each other while Suze cowers between them. The song has its flaws: for some reason he compares his lover to a magnificent mantelpiece and uses the word 'scrapegoat' (embarrassedly corrected to 'scapegoat' in collections of his lyrics). However, the song is absorbing and harrowing, and it ends on a sweetly poetic note when friends ask the narrator how it feels to be free and he responds with the question of whether birds are free from the chains of the skyway.

For some, the closing track, 'It Ain't Me Babe', could have been Dylan's anthem. In his folk period, his scornful attitude toward romantic conventions and his use of the word 'babe' were virtually his trademarks. It wasn't so much that he was anti-love or anti-woman, but the saccharine way the Western media, especially that of his home country, portrayed romance and pussyfooted around the issue of what was then revealingly termed 'premarital sex' was, for Dylan and his peers, bland, dishonest, and suffocating. While the resentment of the female half of that generation of the idea that in these romantic scenarios they were restricted to hearth-bound adjuncts to a partner who at least had the freedom of a career has been well documented, not so widely addressed is the grievance of the male half that they were expected to be—including by many women their age—guardians and protectors. It's this matter that 'It Ain't Me Babe' addresses, and it does so in informal, slangy vernacular fit for a cohort chafing against the era's uptight notions of correctness. To a female who is looking for someone to never be weak and to protect her and take her side regardless of whether she's in the right, he retorts, 'It ain't me you're looking for, babe.'

The word 'babe' in fact was so inextricably associated with Dylan that when Sonny & Cher released 'I Got You Babe' in 1965, it was immediately understood to be a Dylan pastiche or even rip-off, even if its Dylanesque groaning, elongated melody line, and Sonny Bono's nasal delivery assisted the apprehension. The scepticism of the early 60s Dylan toward romantic convention was lost in the tumult that would engulf his image and career over the next few years. Subsequent generations unaware of his influence on peers like Sonny Bono associate 'babe' more with Sonny & Cher, and some don't even associate it with popular song (the word now occupies a place in common language). To such people, a song like 'I Got You Babe' can feel merely like a sexist putdown. Thus are context and common understanding eroded by the impassive passage of time.

To add a twist to that tale, 'It Ain't Me Babe' may not even be about a woman at all. If we substitute the assumption that it concerns a lover with the theory that it's in fact addressed to the protest crowd, then—like 'To Ramona'—it becomes a whole different ballgame, and once again a more powerful one.

'Some other kinds of songs,' declared the back cover of the album, atop five poems of predominantly slangy and staccato style. Although they were rendered in tiny print to fit onto twelve square inches, there

75

still wasn't enough space for seven others from the same cache that finally saw the light of day in Dylan's 1973 book *Writings & Drawings*, maybe the only good thing about a collection that saw him retrospectively tamper with his songs' lyrics, often to their detriment.

Another Side Of Bob Dylan was released on August 8, 1964. In the States, the album's chart peak (no. 43) suggested Dylan's new direction underwhelmed the public. It did respectable business in the UK (no. 8), where for many years Dylan had a fanbase more loyal than in his home country. However, even there it became, in the 80s, one of the few Dylan albums that CBS (the British wing of Columbia) reduced to 'Nice Price' status—a bargain £2.99 that implicitly stated it was of inferior artistic status. The scant attention and faint praise directed its way has never enabled it to become embedded in critical esteem. Yet of his four folk albums, it lies behind only *Freewheelin'* in quality.

Moreover, the album was a good source of material for the snowballing number of recording artists keen to get in on the Dylan goldrush. As well as the multifarious people who covered 'To Ramona' across the decades, the album quickly attracted covers of 'It Ain't Me Babe' from Johnny Cash and The Turtles (the latter securing a US Top 10 with it), while The Byrds would soon veritably plunder it, including on their debut album alone the songs 'Spanish Harlem Incident', 'All I Really Want To Do', and 'Chimes Of Freedom', as well as, of course, *Bringing It All Back Home* outtake 'Mr. Tambourine Man.' (They would later also tackle 'My Back Pages'.)

Despite its quasi-mediocre sales, the album paradoxically had a high profile at the time, if not for good reasons. The controversy it created was summed up by Irwin Silber, editor of folk bible *Sing Out!*, who mournfully wrote of Dylan's new direction, 'You seem to be in a different kind of bag now, Bob—and I'm worried about it. ...Your new songs seem to be all inner-directed now, inner-probing, self-conscious—maybe even a little maudlin or a little cruel on occasion. And it's happening on stage, too. You seem to be relating to a handful of cronies behind the scenes now—rather than to the rest of us out front.'

Silber's 'now'-peppered lament echoed the opinions of many. However, if these people suspected Dylan had sold out, it was as nothing compared to what they were to begin feeling over the following months. Dylan was a man who was adored and well-rewarded, but he was in the process of realising that he wasn't fulfilled. As the album suggested, he no longer wished to pander to a demographic he had largely created with 'finger-pointing songs'. (Tellingly, he used that phrase in a positive sense to a friend while recording *Freewheelin'*, but he would later deploy it as a pejorative.) Events also suggest that he was no longer fulfilled by folk per se, even though he had singlehandedly stretched the boundaries of the form over the previous two and a half years to something more to his liking. This left him with a dilemma: if he were to permanently abandon both folk and protest, where would he now find an audience? Debate will forever rage about whether his next move was an improvised means to extricate himself from this situation or a manoeuvre that was long-planned and cold-blooded.

•

In the eight months between Dylan's third and fourth albums, the American music world had turned on its axis. It had started in February 1964, when The Beatles hit no. 1 on the *Billboard* chart. They cemented that landmark two months later when they occupied the first five places on the same chart. This breakthrough unleashed a tidal wave of US chart hits from British rock groups. Superficially, the changes that had been wrought had little relevance to Dylan: that a four-piece from the previously little-known English city of Liverpool with curiously hirsute if neat appearances had sold back to America a retooled variant of a form of its indigenous rock'n'roll was hardly of consequence to a folk artist.

This, though, doesn't take into account that brief period before the British Invasion when in the United States folk music was the new rock'n'roll. Everyone vaguely interested in musical history knows that in the late 50s, rock was in decay: Chuck Berry was a besmirched jailbird, Buddy Holly deceased, Jerry Lee Lewis drifting into country & western, and Elvis reduced by his army stint and too frequently middle-of-the-road music into a family entertainer who commanded loyalty only because of his supreme singing gift and the occasional appearance of the ghost of his onetime insurrectionary edge. The market they had created for teenage-oriented music was now catered to by a tame variant of rock, whether it be the absurdly anodyne Pat Boone or the endless parade of bequiffed Bobbys.

The folk revival of the early 60s to some degree catered to this void, this absence of music with any sense of rebellion and unkemptness. As Dylan was the most rebellious and unkempt of any of the singers on that scene, he had in his own small way assumed the mantle of Elvis et al. He was also the most intellectually and aesthetically restless artist operating in that new folk field. He was never going to be artistically fulfilled by what Pete Seeger or Joan Baez spent a lifetime doing: positing injustice in an anthemic or catchy way. He could, of course, release high-quality and lyrically imaginative but non-political albums like *Another Side Of Bob Dylan* for the rest of his life, and his talent and track record meant that there would be at least some kind of market for them. Or he could become a painter, an ambition that he expressed to a friend in a period of disillusion with music shortly after the release of his first album. He also theoretically had the option of novelist, something he toyed with for years, but, as with painting, there was no guarantee of success in that field. In any case, would he be happy with any of these options?

What he chose to become was a pop artist.

There are two ways of viewing the decision. One is that it was a move of integrity and honesty. This kid steeped in rock'n'roll had already compromised once by switching from rock to folk, maybe twice if we are to believe his cynical rationale for starting to write protest songs. Now he was tired of pretence and was simply determined to be himself. Protest could be left in the hands of the likes of Baez, Ochs, Paxton, Andersen, David Blue/Cohen, Bob Gibson, Peter LaFarge,

Paul Simon, and oodles more contemporary singers, many of whom were embarrassingly imitative of Dylan.

The other way of looking at it, as many of his disgusted ex-fans soon would, is that Dylan wanted to be one of The Beatles. The Cuban heels (Chelsea boots, in the parlance of The Beatles' home country) that he had adopted were certainly associated with the Fab Four. His hair also got longer (although as he is one of those people whose hair grows outward rather than downward, it could never be mistaken for a mop-top, so its provenance would always be debatable). He had previously declined to don spectacles to deal with his deficient eyesight but now addressed that dilemma via wraparound plastic shades with prescription lenses, and they couldn't help but make him look like a rock star wannabe. Those things, though—just like the rest of the outfit he began to adopt in preference to his old casual-cum-scruffy image—were actually more in line with the style of Phil Spector. He and the Wall Of Sound producer become friends that year, and Spector's finely pressed, slightly antediluvian sartorial formality, offset by his shades and (for the time) long hair, was an image that appealed to Dylan.

Perhaps Spector's 'little symphonies for the kids' also did, but it had to be said that it was indeed beat groups Dylan began to seem to imitate musically, rather than girl vocal groups like Spector's clients The Crystals and The Ronettes. Dylan was no less enraptured by The Beatles than the thousands of teenage girls who screeched at their concerts. 'They were doing things nobody was doing,' he marvelled to his biographer, Anthony Scaduto. 'Their chords were outrageous, just outrageous, and their harmonies made it all valid. ... It was obvious to me that they had staying power. I knew they were pointing the direction of where music had to go.' More importantly, they were pointing to him the way *his* music had to go: 'You could only do that with other musicians ... and it started me thinking about other people.'

In addition to the 'mop-tops', another British ensemble caught his ear. The Animals were a quintet from the northern industrial city of

Newcastle who specialised in rhythm & blues rather than the Buddy Hollyesque mix of rock and pop purveyed by The Beatles. They were fronted by Eric Burdon, a small but powerful singer who somehow sounded more Black than many 'Negroes'. Although neither of The Animals' first two releases were written by Bob Dylan, they would never have happened without him.

The Animals' producer, Mickie Most, suggested that they record the song that on Dylan's debut LP was titled 'Baby, Let Me Follow You Down'. 'He had picked up a 45 in the States,' recalls Animals drummer John Steel. The single in question was a version by Hoagy Lands retitled 'Baby Let Me Hold Your Hand', with the writing attributed to Bert Russell (aka Bert Berns) and Wes Farrell. 'It was a sort of Black pop version of it. . . . We knew the song from Bob Dylan's first album, and that was okay by us, because we loved that album.' The Animals' rendition did not have much in common with Lands' soulful, female-choir-decorated iteration. As Steel notes, 'We just sort of grabbed it and kicked it around ourselves, and that's what came out.'

What came out was a pounding, breakneck recording that, although slightly shorter than Dylan's version, packed a lot more in, partly because much of Dylan's was taken up with his spoken-word intro. (The Animals' recording has a semi-spoken middle-eight.) Steel adds of Dylan's debut LP, 'And that's where we ripped "House Of The Risin' Sun" from, no matter what you hear about Josh White, crap like that. That was another fairytale from Eric. Even though Bob Dylan was really fresh and new then, as far as we were concerned it wasn't cool to say we'd pinched a song from his album. We would much more prefer it to be thought that we were delving into some really obscure stuff. "House Of The Risin' Sun" was, to us, the outstanding track of that album.'

Steel points out, 'Mickie Most didn't want us to record "House Of The Risin' Sun". It wasn't his idea. We went into the studio to record a song that would be used for the opening sequence of [pop TV show] *Ready Steady Go!* He wanted us to do Ray Charles's "Talkin' 'Bout You" or some other song. By this time, we'd worked an arrangement out for "House Of The Risin' Sun".' The band were playing a month-long UK tour on the same bill as their idols Chuck Berry and Carl Perkins, their first experience of playing theatres rather than clubs. 'We had a calculated ruse. We knew that, if we were going to stand out, we had to do something dramatically different. That was why we were working on "House Of The Risin' Sun". The reaction we were getting from that song almost immediately on that tour ...'

With such an intense response, the choice of their second single seemed preordained. If The Animals' version of 'Baby, Let Me Follow You Down' was 'nothing like' either the Hoagy Lands or Dylan renditions, it's difficult to imagine what phrase might be employed to describe the difference in their interpretation of the song that was on their record label rendered with almost comic formality as 'The House Of The Rising Sun'. The Animals' version was exquisitely exotic, starting with its length of four and a half minutes when anything over three minutes met resistance from radio programmers. It also completely unexpectedly featured neither strummed nor picked guitar work but instead leisurely arpeggios, the brainchild of guitarist Hilton Valentine, which lent it both a feeling of class and an onomatopoeic quality, the listener being put in mind of sun rays as rendered in such stylised, staccato imagery as on the Japanese Rising Sun flag.

Steel points out that the unusual length was a function of song words retooled for an audience more mainstream than that for a folk album: 'It was just the way it worked out. Eric had to get all these lyrics in. Another conscious thing about it was, you couldn't go singing about a bloody brothel, not to a sort of audience of kids, mothers, whatever. It was the way of the times. We couldn't get it played on the radio otherwise.' The narrator became a 'poor boy' who had spent his life 'in sin and misery', not the 'poor gal' who was ruined by the titular house. Keyboardist Alan Price added the coup de grâce. His beautiful Vox Continental organ solo and a final wash on the same instrument—again, possessing an onomatopoeic quality, seeming to resemble the first flickerings of the titular heavenly orb appearing over the horizon—completed a majestic recording, one captured, astoundingly, in one take.

Upon its UK release in June 1964, the single was a sensation on several levels, from the fact that Valentine's hypnotic runs quickly became a staple of guitar manuals (Steel: 'Probably everybody in the world who's picked up a guitar for the first time started on that thing') to the fact that it was a Transatlantic no. 1, albeit making the top in the States in a clumsily edited form. Dylan personally was blown away by the song not merely because of its considerable aesthetic merits but because of the prospects he saw it opening up for him. At a 1964 meeting between The Animals and Dylan in New York, he told the band of the precise moment that he first heard their record. 'He said he was driving along in his car and this came on the radio,' recalls Steel. 'He pulled the car over and stopped and listened to it and he jumped out of the car and he banged on the bonnet. That gave him the kind of connection—how he *could* go electric. He might have been heading that way already, but he said that was a really significant thing for him.'

Dylan had in a way been heading that way for some years. His journey back to the electric rock that had been his first musical format had been a staccato affair, starting with that second-ever release, 'Mixed-Up Confusion', and the band backing on the dumped *Freewheelin'* tracks. The abortive nature of that electric experimentation suggests that Dylan to some extent lost his nerve (Columbia's qualms about the album tracks being non-originals notwithstanding).

Steel's comments indicate that The Animals assisted him in finding a way to get back his confidence in that regard. Dylan's confidence must also have been given a boost in August '64—the month before the Animals meeting—when he got together with The Beatles. That the encounter saw the Fab Four—the most famous people on the planet, and among the most loved—reveal that they were fans of his must have given a psychological fillip to Dylan's percolating plans to find a way to if not necessarily tap their market then at least operate within a sphere that was adjacent to it and contained a nexus.

One instalment in Dylan's move to pop and electricity, though, is one we can probably adjudge a red herring. In December 1964, Tom Wilson went into Columbia's 30th Street Studio to overdub 50s-style rock instrumentation onto Dylan's debut album version of 'House Of The Risin' Sun'. It was clearly a move inspired by The Animals' success with the song, but it's highly doubtful that it was intended for commercial release: although the experiment works surprisingly well in that no one would know that the backing was overdubbed if they weren't familiar with the original and the whole thing is highly listenable, issuing his version of The Animals' version of his version really would have smacked of desperation and mercenaryism. Instead, it would seem to be a matter of him and/or Wilson feeling the way, finding out how his voice and style might work within the parameters of full-band music done to a rock beat.* Even red herrings serve a purpose. Whether or not it gave Dylan himself any notions or confidence, the session certainly seems to have given Wilson ideas, and it ultimately indirectly catapulted a different Columbia act—Simon & Garfunkel—to stardom.

Far more directly pertinent than The Animals' exploration of territory he had also covered, The Beatles' admiration, or the 'House Of The Risin' Sun' experiment was the activity of a five-man California band called The Byrds. This ensemble would shortly and triumphantly occupy that nexus between the markets of the likes of Dylan and the likes of The Beatles.

With their fashionably long hair (i.e., neck-length with fringes) and three-part harmonies, The Byrds superficially resembled an American Beatles. However, they were actually ex-folkies turned electric—albeit, unlike Dylan, without prior success in the folk field, baggage that might otherwise have seen them disdained as sell-outs. In the late summer of 1964, they became apprised of Dylan's song 'Mr. Tambourine Man'

---

* It was first released in 1995 as a bonus track on the CD-ROM *Highway 61 Interactive*.

because their manager, Jim Dickson, came into possession through Dylan's publisher of the *Another Side Of Bob Dylan* outtake. The version was one on which Dylan sang with that man from whom he'd once stolen so much, Ramblin' Jack Elliott. The group shortly began rehearsing it with a view to making a recording.

Lead singer and lead guitarist Jim (later Roger) McGuinn notes of Dylan's attitude toward The Byrds' version, 'He was very pleased with it. He came to the studio even before we recorded it and listened to it and listened to several other of his songs and he gave us his approval for what we were doing with his music.' Although the extraordinary quality of the song was obvious from the start, and although it had a particularly personal importance to Dylan—he later said it was the very first song he wrote that he felt expressed his views rather than what other people wanted to hear from him—he effectively gifted it to The Byrds. It may have been extraordinary generosity on his part or a hard-nosed apprehension that a group that fitted the musical zeitgeist had a better chance of taking it into the pop charts than he, or a combination of the two. Either way, his decision was more than vindicated.

Around this time, Dylan was also intrigued by an electric blues project currently being worked on by John H. Hammond, aka John Hammond Jr. The latter was a guitarist and a solo recording artist specialising in electric blues. This project—which it so happened featured Levon Helm, Garth Hudson, Robbie Robertson, and Michael Bloomfield, musicians with whom Dylan would soon extensively work—culminated in the album *So Many Roads*, released in 1965.

There was another influence—and an apparently nagging one—in Tom Wilson. 'I thought folk music was for the dumb guys,' Wilson later recalled in the sleeve notes to the 1991 Dylan box set *Biograph*. 'This guy, Dylan, played like the dumb guys, but then these words came out. I was flabbergasted. I said to Albert Grossman, If you put some background to this, you might have a white Ray Charles with a message.'

Not that Dylan necessarily needed much nagging. During the

production of *A Complete Unknown*, the 2025 motion picture about Dylan's conversion to electricity, director James Mangold was privileged to have many conversations with its subject. He revealed to Nick Hasted of *Uncut* magazine, 'Bob really illuminated for me how lonely it feels being a folk singer. You're lonely on stage, you're lonely backstage—you're all alone.' This especially applied to someone with the 'maniacal' level of focus directed at Dylan by the media and his audience. 'A band is a kind of emotional buffer—you can hang with them. It was suddenly so clear to me as Bob described it, that the idea of a band wasn't just a musical direction. It was also a really human response to the predicament he was in at that moment.'

Contemplation of all of these occurrences and activities informed Dylan's own writing and recording. The Animals were among the first outside his immediate circle to become aware of it. That New York Animals/Dylan meeting occurred just as 'The House Of The Rising Sun' was finishing its run atop the *Billboard* chart. 'That was one of the first things we wanted to do,' says Steel of the band's bucket list for the US jaunt they embarked on to consolidate their record's Stateside success. Dylan would seem to have been just as enthusiastic about meeting them. 'We got together in Al Grossman's apartment,' recalls Steel. 'It was a bit of a shock just physically to meet him, because [of] the folkie image we had of him and everything. He was a really great-looking guy. He was so fine. It seemed to me his skin was almost transparent. He had this very sharp little mohair-type jacket and shirt cufflinks. He was really sharply turned out. This wasn't what we expected.'

As for the man inside the immaculate clothing, Steel says, 'He was very nice.' Nice enough to grant The Animals the privilege of a sneak preview of his new direction. 'He said, This is what I've just recorded, and he played us "Subterranean Homesick Blues". We thought, *Bloody hell*. He said, What do you think? And we said, Oh, wow. You're doing so well with the acoustic folk stuff, you're taking a chance with that, aren't you? It sounded a little bit like Chuck Berry.'

Dylan was indeed taking a chance—the chance that he might come crashing down from his pedestal in an attempt to break through to the rock market. In the mid-60s, a folkie becoming a rocker was something that had never happened, and it had never happened for a reason: it would be perceived as an act of betrayal analogous to a defection from the democratic West to the communist East—at least from the folkies' side. Such apolitical, non-intellectual fare as rock was considered by folk fans an opiate of the downtrodden masses. It was also, for them, crassly commercial and tainted with the payola scandal of 1959—something still a vivid memory at the time—in which it emerged that broadcasters had been paid by record companies to play specific rock'n'roll songs.

While the rock/pop buyers might be less snobby or less interested in such demarcations, their tastes were also less refined. It might have been the case that Dylan still harboured an ambition to 'join Little Richard'— now perhaps transmuted by the realities of his life to be successful in the same field as Little Richard—but was this really a possibility? It being the case that pioneers don't have precedents to guide them, he had no way of knowing whether the kids who were buying The Beatles' 'A Hard Day's Night' or The Rolling Stones' 'It's All Over Now' would be able to relate to the style of a man who penned the literate, nuanced likes of 'Only A Pawn In Their Game' or 'To Ramona', or even the more populist but hardly simplistic likes of 'Blowin' In The Wind' and 'The Times They Are A-Changin''. Should Dylan fail to interest such a demographic with his new direction, being left with egg on his face would be the least of his problems: he might have no folk audience to go back to. His solution to the danger of simultaneously failing to engage his intended new demographic and being spurned by people who thought he'd sold out was to hedge his bets.

When compact discs came onto the market in the 1980s, they began the gradual process of blurring the notion of long-playing musical works divided into separate physical sides—and hence different suites, movements, or moods—that had persisted since the LP had become popular in the middle of the twentieth century as a means to disseminate multiples of songs. That blurring process was subsequently accelerated by downloads and streaming. Compact discs only had one side, but digital dissemination involves no sides or any other tangible divisions or practicable obstacles. In 1965, though, sides of music meant something, as perfectly demonstrated by the fact that when, on March 22, Dylan unleashed a clutch of electric rock and R&B tracks on his album *Bringing It All Back Home*, he restricted them to one face, lest—it has naturally been inferred—such material fail to snag the beat-group market. On the second, he gave his existing devotees largely what they wanted with almost entirely acoustic songs. It seemed the equivalent of a safety net.

If this was the strategy, it was jeopardised by the decision to release, two weeks before that album, the aforesaid 'Subterranean Homesick Blues' as its taster single. Dylan's existing fans had no advance knowledge of the apparent hedge-betting; all they knew was that Dylan's new single was loud, up-tempo rock music on which he was backed by a full band. Many were horrified and disgusted. Not necessarily by the music, which may not have been to their tastes but was competent by the genre's standards, but by the very act of issuing such product (with 'product' being the operative word). For this particular artist to release a record that sounded like Chuck Berry just seemed cheap and beneath him. For a poet and a quasi-political figurehead to adopt the rhythms, meters, and instrumentation of recording artists who generally dealt in apolitical, moon-in-June romance and—not coincidentally—shifted huge amounts of units seemed like the most pathetic, desperate form of bandwagon-jumping. The grubby optics were compounded by the question of plagiarism. The song's rapid-fire, staccato style seemed directly inspired by Berry's 1956 single 'Too Much Monkey Business', perhaps crossed with Ricky Nelson's 'Waitin' In School' from the following year. Dylan and all his folkie peers had always used other people's melodies, of course, but not ones still in copyright.

Matters weren't helped for some by the fact that the single was housed in a picture sleeve that reproduced on the back an article published the previous January in UK music weekly *Melody Maker* headed 'Beatles Say—Dylan Shows The Way'. It communicated both that Columbia and/or Dylan felt Dylan only had value if the mop-tops sang his praises and that the label and/or artist were trying to justify his new sound by invoking the spirit of the artists widely felt to be the kings of that sound.

Had his critics known that Dylan loved rock'n'roll long before he got into folk, it doubtless wouldn't have cut any ice with them. Nor would it have impressed them that, with this record, he had changed the world. Peter, Paul & Mary's acoustic but massed-vocal 'Blowin' In The Wind' had executed one shift of axis, The Animals' full-band 'The House Of The Rising Sun' another, but they were extrapolations that were matters of happenstance and circumstance, not of agenda. What Dylan quite deliberately achieved with 'Subterranean Homesick Blues' was to break through the barrier that separated folk and rock and invent the previously non-existent: a form that married folk's intellectual and sociopolitical lyrics with music possessing rock's visceral, populist power. Precisely two decades later, Dylan would tell Cameron Crowe, for the sleeve notes to *Biograph*, 'The thing about rock'n'roll is that for me anyway it wasn't enough. ... There were great catchphrases and driving pulse rhythms ... but the songs weren't serious or didn't reflect life in a realistic way. I knew that when I got into folk music, it was more of a serious type of thing.'

We'll never know for certain what type of rock songs Dylan would have written if he'd never become a folkie, but they clearly would not have gone against the rock grain: no publisher or label would have bought them or felt they could have marketed them. Folk transformed him as a composer and enriched his art. It was with that newfound approach, and the market he had created for it, that he was able to transform rock when he went back to it. In short order—following both further Dylan releases in this vein and the success of covers of his songs by

The Byrds and other beat groups—it gave rise to the media designation 'folk-rock'. This tributary in an astonishingly short course of time merged seamlessly into the main body of water constituting popular music: within the next eighteen months, as titans like The Beatles and The Rolling Stones began adopting lyrical matter in broadly the same elevated sphere (while also continuing to purvey love songs), it became a trend, and shortly thereafter commonplace. The genre demarcations accordingly ceased to exist except in very limited terms.

Such is the breadth and depth of human ingenuity, curiosity, and whimsy that if Dylan hadn't done it, someone else would have eventually married folk and rock. However, that Dylan got there first made the move a game-changer rather than something that engendered a fad or simply led to nothing much. 'Subterranean Homesick Blues' wasn't merely something new. Because of Dylan's vast talent, it was also very good, and because it was very good, it kicked off a revolution. Musical and cultural upheaval can't be effected in a vacuum: high quality virtually guarantees being exposed to millions of ears and thereby converts the uninitiated and the sceptical.

Pop stardom was just about to whisk Dylan into the stratosphere, but before his life became rarified, he was able to proffer for one of the last times a streetwise lyric, his hippest yet. The first two verses of 'Subterranean Homesick Blues' feature a cast of characters that include narcotic drug manufacturers, plainclothes cops, and characters pantingly desperate about police plants and possible busts, all couched in cool vernacular ('kid', 'heat', 'DA', 'bust') and delivered in a Kalashnikov, syncopated vocal style. A line in which the 'kid' being addressed is advised to keep away from people carrying firehoses is clearly a reference to US Southern states' police departments currently regularly seen on television screens drenching Black civil rights demonstrators, something that sets up the remaining three verses, which open out from such small-scale vignettes into a broader critique of society. The latter takes in both the low-level losers, cheaters, and users ready to pounce on the vulnerable and those higher up the rungs of power who administer a system where obedience and conformity are demanded simply in order to secure a dubious final reward ('Twenty years of schooling and they put you on the day shift').

It hardly seemed much of an issue at the time when the mere fact of electric backing was an outrage, but the instrumentation of 'Subterranean Homesick Blues', while competent, doesn't quite live up to the sparkling lyrics. Dylan's musical journey might have started in bands, but this record, as would the other electric tracks on its parent album, seems to demonstrate that during his acoustic phase, he had forgotten about the dynamics of ensemble playing. John Hammond Jr. (electric guitar), Bruce Langhorne (electric guitar), Bill Lee (bass), and Bobby Gregg (drums) provide accompaniment but not interaction. They're just there. It's not technically bad or sonically objectionable but simply featureless, and the only effect they have that Dylan's acoustic music did not is to set the toes tapping. As such, the accompaniment has no meaning beyond making the admittedly massive statement that Bob Dylan is now a rocker.

The lyrics, though, were the crux. Pop consumers listening to the hit parades on the radio had never heard anything like it. 'Subterranean Homesick Blues' made no. 39 on *Billboard*, but its rise to those not exactly dizzy heights on May 15, '65, took seven weeks, and it occupied the Top 40 for precisely one week before dropping out again. Nonetheless, it had achieved the milestone of becoming Dylan's first Top 40 US hit. In the UK, it climbed to no. 9, boosted by Dylan's contemporaneous tour. Fine records though the likes of The Beatles, Rolling Stones, and Animals *et al* made, they weren't graced with this kind of dazzling wordsmithery, scathing wit, social commentary, or gritty realism. The fact that pop consumers propelled the song so high indicated that they had a completely opposite viewpoint to those disgusted folkies who would not think of sullying their hands with it: specifically that, rather than cheapening himself, Dylan was enhancing popular music with his singular gifts.

As for the people who broadcast those hit parades, that Dylan got this stuff played without problem on censorious mid-60s radio seems astonishing, notwithstanding how square broadcasting staff tended to be at that point. There's nothing definitively censorable about it, but—for instance—had Deep South radio stations appreciated that their region was being mocked, or had, say, the Catholic Women's League known about the drug references, one would have expected at least a small public furore. One can only assume that the breathless rush of imagery confused those who weren't plugged in.

Also confused were the folkies who thought Dylan had sold out. Electric instrumentation and lack of unsubtle finger-pointing aside, if this wasn't protest music as the term was understood, nothing was. Perhaps the folkies' perceptions were clouded by the shock of the new. As well as Woody Guthrie and Ramblin' Jack Elliott, the recorded Dylan now had a little of Chuck Berry, Elvis Presley, and The Beatles about him. He was also infused with the spirits of William Shakespeare, Arthur Rimbaud, Allen Ginsberg, Lenny Bruce, Che Guevara, and Martin Luther King. His capacity for being something never seen before was apparently boundless.

•

Dylan might now be working with a far larger cast than before but, quite remarkably, he recorded his new album in the same sort of timespan that he had laid down his folk albums: sessions for *Bringing It All Back Home* were completed across January 13–15, 1965. Even as he maintained the transition to full-band accompaniment, he knocked out albums as though it were just him and his guitar. This sort of quick turnaround time would almost always characterise his career.

While the album may have been divided equally—at least vinyl side-wise—between electric and acoustic tracks, almost an entire alternate, fully electric version exists of *Bringing It All Back Home*.

The January 13 session in Columbia's Studio A in New York saw

Dylan and Wilson lay down 'Love Minus Zero/No Limit', 'I'll Keep It With Mine', 'It's All Over Now, Baby Blue', 'Bob Dylan's 115th Dream', 'She Belongs To Me', 'Subterranean Homesick Blues', 'Sitting On A Barbed Wire Fence', 'On The Road Again', 'Farewell Angelina', 'If You Gotta Go, Go Now', and 'Outlaw Blues'. There has been considerable confusion down the years about who exactly was in the studio on this first day of album sessions. Originally, it was thought that it was just Dylan and Wilson, and that all the songs laid down were solo affairs. Then it began to be suggested that John Sebastian (bass), William E. Lee (stand-up bass), Al Gorgoni (guitar), Joseph Macho Jr. (bass), and possibly others were around. However, there were certainly a lot of heels being kicked: there is bass and a second guitar on some tracks, but no drums or keyboards anywhere.

The single thing from the session to be released on the subsequent album was not a song at all but the start of a version of 'Bob Dylan's 115th Dream' ruined by Dylan cracking up after getting out only the first line. His helpless chuckling was thought amusing enough in itself to splice onto the start of a full-band rendition of the song recorded on the 15th. The acoustic versions of 'If You Gotta Go, Go Now', 'It's All Over Now, Baby Blue', 'Love Minus Zero/No Limit', 'On The Road Again', 'Outlaw Blues', 'She Belongs To Me', and 'Subterranean Homesick Blues' were ultimately discarded in favour of accompanied versions (although, in the case of 'It's All Over Now, Baby Blue', that accompaniment is minimal).

'California', 'Farewell Angelina', 'I'll Keep It With Mine', and 'You Don't Have To Do That' (aka 'Bending Down On My Stomick Lookin' West') were dispensed with completely. Admittedly, some of this material amounted to little more than a doodle. Some, though, constituted perfectly worthy songs and/or performances, as proven when Dylan allowed the release of the session's versions of 'I'll Keep It With Mine' on *Biograph* and 'Farewell Angelina' on *The Bootleg Series 1–3* (1991). 'Farewell Angelina' finds a narrator taking leave of a lover because of unspecified but apocalyptic-sounding reasons. It feels like a step backwards for Dylan, being heavily indebted to antiquated melodic and lyrical folk motifs. It would have sounded somewhat out of place among *Bringing It All Back Home*'s gritty blues and rock, as well as its more modern-sounding folk tracks. Joan Baez, however, loved it so much that she released an album of that name in October 1965.

'I'll Keep It With Mine' is more intriguing. Dylan plays the part of what is called in literature an unreliable narrator: he sings the words of a man who is attempting to reassure someone—implicitly female and a prospective lover—that he is on her side while maintaining that everybody else proffering help is seeking to take advantage of her, yet he betrays subtle signs that in fact his own motives are sinister. Although the lyric is nuanced and sophisticated, the composition is not quite rounded out enough melodically to constitute a fully realised creation. Nonetheless, when Judy Collins released it on single in 1965, it only intensified the notion that Dylan was injecting rock and pop with the spirit of fields that it had seemed only five minutes before could never inform it. In 1967, it was also recorded by Nico, who would subsequently insist it had been written about her and her baby.

Also included on *Biograph*, incidentally, was this album sessions' acoustic version of 'Subterranean Homesick Blues'. It's arguably superior and more propulsive shorn of the slightly anonymous instrumentation heard on the familiar version. Theoretically, Dylan could have chosen to include both versions on either side of the LP, à la his inclusion of slow and fast renditions of 'Forever Young' on his 1974 album *Planet Waves*. However, that might have made the failure of nerve implied by *Bringing It All Back Home*'s electric and acoustic halves just a bit too obvious.

When Dylan returned to Studio A the following day, the place was somewhat more crowded. A session that logs indicate took place from 2:30pm to 6:00pm featured the accompaniment in various configurations of guitarists Al Gorgoni, Kenneth Rankin, Bruce Langhorne, and John Hammond Jr.; bassists Joseph Macho Jr., John Boone, John Sebastian, and William E. Lee; drummer Bobby Gregg; and keyboardists Paul

Griffin (piano) and Frank Owens (electric piano). 'Those were the really good session kind of people,' says Gorgoni. 'He couldn't have done better for session guys.'

Some might disagree. Even in the by-definition quasi-anonymous field of session work, the above names are not legends along the lines of the Wrecking Crew, the now fabled loose collection of studio musos operating at that point on the opposite coast. Dylan may never have been able to repay the debt he owed John Hammond for giving him a recording contract and changing his life, but he was at least able to express his gratitude a little by giving employment to his son. However, although competent, John Hammond Jr. in truth is not a name to conjure with. John Sebastian would shortly achieve an incredible run of success as frontman of The Lovin' Spoonful, but it was as a songwriter and singer that he made his name, his prowess on mouth harp notwithstanding, rather than as a bassist. Steve Boone would join him on his Spoonful journey, but he is not a renowned virtuoso either.

Bobby Gregg's drum contributions made him the first member of The Hawks, aka The Band—one day to feature large in Dylan's legend—to work with Dylan, but his playing isn't held in the same esteem as that of Levon Helm, who would be the drummer in the definitive Band line-up.

Frank Owens is also credited with piano, although he insisted to this author that his only work with Dylan was on *Highway 61 Revisited* later in the year. On either record, he would probably have been the most accomplished musician on the date. However, the fact that a considerable cultural gap existed between him and most of the company is suggested by his proud observation about a future Tony Orlando recording session: 'I'm the one that made "Tie A Yellow Ribbon" happen, that's my lick,' as well as his declaration that 'working with Lena Horne was the pinnacle'.

Dylan could not have engaged a bigger admirer of his craft than Gorgoni. 'I thought he was a wonderful artist, and I was glad to be there,' Gorgoni says. Presumably referring to the previous day's session, he says, 'I walked in the studio—I think I was the first guy there, except for the technical people—and he was standing at one end. I went over and I actually gave him a hug and told him how much I loved him and thought he was great. I think he was surprised.'

Gorgoni wasn't so starstruck, though, that he wasn't shocked by what he felt to be the 'unruliness' of what took place at the album's sessions. Of the orderly and organised recording dates to which he and other freelance musicians were used (admittedly, usually for non-writing singers), he notes, 'There would be an arranger and you would have at least guide lead sheets for the players. If specific parts weren't indicated, at least the breaks and what the chords were, and the format of the music. It was unusual to have absolutely nothing to go by. ...It was kind of a free-for-all, and there was nobody really in charge of it.'

Gorgoni doesn't seem to attach much blame for this to Wilson, although that would seem to be because he doesn't feel that control of such fine detail was in his ambit. 'Tom was more of an executive type of producer, an idea guy, rather than a hands-on musical kind of producer. He left that to the rest of the team. He was a very bright guy, and he had some great ideas.' Instead, he lays the blame at the feet of the artist. Asked whether he felt Dylan was nervous, Gorgoni says, 'He was, yes. Because I don't think he was ever in a situation like that where he had to deal with other musicians.' He notes, 'I don't recall him actually giving instructions. He would play the songs and we sort of had to tune in to what he was playing and find out what to do to fit in with what he was doing. ... He was more of a solo artist. He would do whatever he felt, and that doesn't work that great when you have a bunch of people that you're playing with. Everyone has to have a road map to know where the stops are, how many bars are between the verses, and so forth. ... He would play the songs, and he played them different each time. His timing wasn't the greatest, but everyone had to sort of go along and catch up with him.' Dylan only ventured a suggestion when he didn't approve of something, Gorgoni recalls. 'I was playing a little bluesy kind of thing. He said, I don't want any of that B.B. King kind of thing.'

Dylan and Grossman had recently struck up a professional relationship with a photographer named Daniel Kramer, and the latter was present on all the album's dates. Although not a musician and with scant experience even of photographing recording sessions, he has a markedly different view to Gorgoni's about how much instruction Dylan was issuing. 'It became obvious to me that Bob was way more than was realised, or that he had let people know about yet, a really total musician,' says Kramer. (Kramer has died since being interviewed. As with other interviewees no longer with us, he is referred to in the present tense for reasons of stylistic continuity.) 'He had everything under control in the studio and he put together this brilliant moment. . . . He was always a perfectionist. He always wanted to get it right on everything he did. He was very smart. He could go around to each musician, and give them [advice]: do this, start on this, this could be this, let's see, and work this out. . . . The thing is, he didn't walk into that studio and suddenly say, oh look, we could do this, and I could be this. Obviously, this had to be brewing. . . . That music, the electric music, was created in that studio at that time as we were all there watching and listening. Even the musicians had to be changed on the second day to accommodate his needs and since he knew everything, and knew everyone's part and how everyone could improve, I realised that this is not a guy with a guitar, writes good lyrics—this is a guy who can do just about anything here.'

All the songs Dylan had rendered solo the previous day were tackled on the 14th. Not all were adjudged successful, but the day's full-band versions of 'Bob Dylan's 115th Dream', 'Love Minus Zero/No Limit', 'Outlaw Blues', 'She Belongs To Me', and 'Subterranean Homesick Blues' were ultimately chosen for inclusion on the album. Kramer noticed that Dylan preferred a minimal number of takes and that furthermore he took that policy to the extreme with the six-and-a-half-minute 'Bob Dylan's 115th Dream': 'That's a long piece, and he said to the control room, "You got to get this—I'm going to do it once".'

The multiplicity on the second day of guitarists (four including

Dylan) and bassists is puzzling enough, but additionally confusing is the fact that in the evening, Dylan is said to have returned to the studio for another session in the company of Hammond, Langhorne, and Sebastian. It seems odd to have had a session with four people associated with guitar and no drummer. It's thought that tapes did not roll at this session.

The next day, the band from the afternoon session of the 14th came back for another 2:30–5:30 block to wrap up proceedings, although it's said by apparently everyone except Frank Owens that Owens had to take the place of the unavailable Paul Griffin. The album's versions of 'Maggie's Farm' and 'On The Road Again' originate from this session, with the former captured in one take. However, full-band versions of the songs that would form side two of the finished album also laid down this day were deemed less successful. Instead, Dylan used versions with sparing accompaniment, discrete flecks of electric guitar decorating 'Mr. Tambourine Man' (Langhorne) and a subtle pulsing bass 'It's All Over Now, Baby Blue' (Lee). 'It's Alright, Ma (I'm Only Bleeding)' and 'Gates Of Eden' featured the traditional format of Dylan on vocals, guitar, and harmonica, although the songs themselves occupied an artistic and philosophical plateau considerably higher than even his greatest previous compositions.

•

Bringing It All Back Home kicks off with 'Subterranean Homesick Blues'. Even though the recording is of qualified brilliance, there's nothing quite as strong on the rest of the first side, which is enjoyable but also often lyrically whimsical and musically lightweight. As with the taster single, the tracks additionally suffer from the fact of sounding more like a statement than fully realised recordings, as though Dylan either didn't know or didn't care that they don't possess the instrumental interaction that is the very point of ensemble music and just assumed it was enough that he was accompanied. Where the up-tempo tracks are a largely featureless blur of sound, the slow ones have more delineated component parts but ones so discrete as to be characterless. An interesting point is that the music is less informed by the mainstream rockabilly and R&B Dylan loved as a teenager than by the blues. Even a pretty ballad like 'She Belongs To Me' has repeated verse lines like a down-home twelve-bar.

Dylan songs occasionally had titles that appeared nowhere in their lyrics, but this album marks a period where it would be a common trait, as evinced by both the opening cut and 'She Belongs To Me', which follows it. The latter is a delicate song of devotion, but of course, this being Dylan, one that sidesteps completely the gushing banalities of pop. It additionally finds the composer deploying metaphor, a device that in his hands can make a song's message intriguing and attractive at the same time as it can render it opaque verging on unfathomable. This marks the point from which many of Dylan's songs effectively became Rorschach tests, their interpretation entirely dependent on the mindset and mentality of the listener. Of course, none of us will ever know what Dylan's lyrics mean a hundred percent, and he may well be laughing down his sleeve at the way we are moved by lines he wrote as a joke or by completely off-the-wall misinterpretations. To his credit, he has never expressed contempt for what must have been wrong-headed inferences, although he has sometimes expressed impatience (for example, people concluding that the hard rain was nuclear fallout or assuming that he cynically wrote 'George Jackson' only to get A.J. Weberman off his back). In the case of 'She Belongs To Me', while his lover's sparkling Egyptian ring and collection of hypnotists may mean something to the composer, they are observations beyond definitive interpretation to anybody else, but the track's loveliness and affecting fondness for its subject make the listener disinclined to care about the impenetrability. Although the instrumental accompaniment lacks true character, it's still sweet—something that, hitherto unimaginably, also applies to Dylan's husky singing. Just as charming are Dylan's understated harmonica contributions.

'Maggie's Farm' was the only one of the album's songs that Dylan never seems to have considered recording an acoustic version of. With its cawing vocal and bobbing rhythm, it sounds superficially similar to 'Subterranean Homesick Blues', although lyrically it has a rural setting rather than the other track's urban backdrop. That rusticity, though, might well be an elaborate façade: what seems on the surface an amusing denunciation by a rebellious farmhand of his skinflint, authoritarian, and vain employers has been interpreted by some as yet another attack on the folk and protest crowd who wanted to keep the composer corralled within their preferred parameters. If this latter interpretation is true, the metaphor seems to give way to bitter grievance in a final verse in which the singer complains that he just wants to be himself but everybody wants him to be just like them, culminating in the line 'They say, Sing while you slave, and I just get bored'. The farm's retinue of grotesque personnel and list of their failings are amusing, but—as is the way of jokes—only truly laugh-worthy the first time.

The title 'Love Minus Zero/No Limit' is actually rendered as an equation on the jacket and some record labels, the forward slash used in most printed discussion actually a horizontal dividing mathematical line. It's another becoming song of romantic admiration, although this one feels like its subject is hypothetical, the qualities under discussion an idealised checklist of what the narrator seeks in a partner. In a song that oscillates between rhyme and blank verse, metaphor again abounds, with the addition of a floridity of tableaux, with its talk of madams lighting candles, statues made of matchsticks, and bankers' nieces. It's counterbalanced by the occasional recognisable scenario, insightfully described, such as a gently withering putdown of the futile judgement-pronouncing and conclusion-drawing of the average person populating and prattling within 'dime stores and bus stations.' Hovering above all this pettiness and humdrum activity is the narrator's wise, faithful, non-extreme, and surely non-existent lover.

'Outlaw Blues' is dismayingly generic, featuring a twelve-bar progression nicked from Chuck Berry's 'Memphis, Tennessee', a bog-standard melody, and a repetition of each verse's first line, with only the occasional sparkling phrase in its plodding barrage of existentialist angst ('I might look like Robert Ford but I feel just like Jesse James') lifting it out of the ordinary.

'Even the butler, he's got something to prove!' laments the narrator of the up-tempo 'On The Road Again', in which he bellyaches with some wit about the freakshow constituted by the residents of his girlfriend's home. However, no matter how amusing the vignettes of finding frogs inside one's socks or being offered as sustenance only brown rice, dirty hot dog, and seaweed, it's another song suggesting that in his new non-finger-pointing style, Dylan sometimes found only whimsy serving as his muse. His protest songs may have been preachy or simplistic, but at least they said something of substance.

A close listen to 'Bob Dylan's 115th Dream', the closing track of the original vinyl side one, reveals the presence of a percolating keyboard part. Had it been mixed higher, it would have given some point to the electric accompaniment. In fact, the backing isn't merely anonymous but probably weakens the song: a one-man version of it might have been hailed as the greatest of Dylan's hallucinatory, comedic, discursive songs thus far.

Across six and a half minutes, Dylan proffers a story that does indeed have the fractured, distorted, woozy ambience of dreams in a lyric that is consistently genuinely funny. If indeed there were people buying this album whose idea of a daring foray into unfamiliar musical territory usually extended not much further than opting for a Rolling Stones rather than a Beatles record, their minds can only have been expanded and their sensibilities invigorated by this bizarre saga, which sees the narrator beginning by vouchsafing that he was riding on the Mayflower when he spied some land. That this is not the conventional colonist's tale is immediately betrayed by the fact that his ship's captain is named Arab (pronounced in the American way, 'Ay-rab'), which seems to have a deliberate assonance with Ahab, the captain of the vessel in *Moby-Dick*, notwithstanding the narrator's statement that he has determined he'll call this undiscovered country America. He is posed with hostility problems not by Native Americans but instead by a cop who busts the crew for carrying harpoons. A sequence of events unravels involving talking Guernsey cows, placard-waving demonstrators who want bums—not bombs—banned, a French honeytrap artist, a telephone through whose speaker a foot aggressively emerges, a traffic warden who tickets the sails of the ship to which the narrator gratefully returns, and, to cap it all, Christopher Columbus coming into harbour as the narrator is heading out. Surreal gags and witticisms tumble forth continuously, whether it be the narrator placing an order for Suzette in a restaurant and appending, 'Could you please make that crêpe?', pulling down his pants when a bank asks for collateral to cover the loan he seeks to bail out his shipmates, or an unhelpful man at the US embassy responding to his gripe that Jesus was also refused assistance with the observation that he is not Him. Humour like this did exist in mid-60s society, whether it be the albums of American humourist Lord Buckley or the radio broadcasts of the British comedy troupe The Goons, but it simply did not populate the landscapes of musical recording acts, whether folk, pop, or rock. Bringing such exhilarating, madcap, risqué mirth to the masses was in a way just as revolutionary as writing protest songs or playing folk music with an electric band.

Nay-sayers to Dylan's new sonic direction may have taken succour from the fact that, revolutionary and often entertaining though side one of the album was, side two was easily superior aesthetically. The four epic songs-cum-statements it contains feature glittering and sometimes breathtaking lyrics. All of them demonstrate Dylan's increasing penchant for metaphor and simile, often surreal, sometimes hazy, but always scintillating in their deployment of language. He was still in love with Guthrie and Little Richard, but he was also clearly inspired by Brecht, Byron, and Rimbaud. There's also a tinge of the phraseology of the Holy Bible in the mix. Tracks like 'To Ramona' had unquestionably laid the groundwork, but Dylan the poet properly starts here. Some poetry lovers might turn up their noses at the penchant he still displays for double negatives and ungrammatical colloquialisms. However, others would have felt they were apposite for a verse writer striving to articulate the views and experiences of the common person. Moreover, the linguistic inaccuracies do not prohibit majesty: not only are his songs now dripping with extravagant and evocative allegory, they are making the type of grand but simultaneously complex statements for which sloganeering never gave him opportunity.

Something else that has developed impressively since his last outing is his song construction. There is no petering out of thought or arrangement here, as there had intermittently been in his catalogue so far. Each composition is carefully crafted to build to a crescendo, a capstone verse skilfully serving the purpose of underlining the observations made in those preceding it.

Not that the power of his songcraft is solely predicated on words. Although relatively bare, this quartet of recordings feel rich and layered, boasting much in the way of melodic invention, fine singing, and excellent harmonica work.

Side two opener 'Mr. Tambourine Man' has been posited as a marijuana anthem—albeit an anthem, fittingly, with a mellow rather than marching vibe. From what Dylan told Shelton ('Drugs never played a part in that song'), that's as way off as the similar interpretations of Peter, Paul & Mary's 'Puff (The Magic Dragon)'. Some have suggested that the song is about the muse, that it turns into a person the inspiration behind his compositions. There is much speculation about the real-life inspiration for the titular character. Dylan himself pointed to Bruce Langhorne. The latter, who provides the track's accompanying acoustic guitar frills, was known for bringing to sessions a large, handheld drum skin with bells around its frame.

As with so many Dylan songs, one doesn't have to fully understand it to appreciate it. It's melodically utterly lovely and lyrically replete with superb phraseology, such as a section in which the ragged-clown narrator's boot heels wander down time's foggy ruins. Promising that he's not sleepy, the narrator pledges that if the tambourine man plays him a song, he'll follow him in the jingle-jangle morning. 'Let me forget about today until tomorrow' sums up the beatific message. This sweetly lightheaded reverie is punctuated by some excellent, lung-busting harmonica work.

Although 'Gates Of Eden' shares the preceding cut's dreamlike atmosphere, it's cut from a cloth more chilling. The narrator's talk of a utopia where the wrongs and evils of the real world are nowhere to be found is never completely comprehensible, but the one thing that does come through clear and strong is a sense of despair and dread, as indicated by eerie lines like 'Upon the beach where hound dogs bay at ships with tattooed sails'. Dylan evokes a sense of global injustice and inequity, discussing people condemned to act according to custom, paupers envying each other's meagre possessions, princes and princesses pronouncing upon what is and is not real, and people trying to resign from their fates to be left free to do anything they wish to do but die. The power of the track is helped in no small measure by Dylan's ultra-intense delivery.

In August 1993, Dylan's record company mounted a concert broadcast on pay-per-view television celebrating his thirty years as a recording artist at which an all-star cast of classic and contemporary recording artists rendered versions of his songs. Dylan, of course, also appeared, and he chose to perform two songs, 'Girl From The North Country' and 'It's Alright, Ma (I'm Only Bleeding)'. It seems logical to infer that the former was chosen for sentimental reasons and the latter because he felt it to be his greatest song. If this interpretation is correct, one can't find it in oneself to object.

The subject of 'It's Alright, Ma (I'm Only Bleeding)' seems to be an extension of that of 'Gates Of Eden'. However, in addressing the causes of the human race's problems, Dylan this time doesn't offer the psychological pseudo-comfort of that composition's reference to a fictional paradise. At the start, he notes that darkness at the break of noon is something that shadows even the silver spoon, before asserting that there is no sense in trying. *Darkness At Noon* is a famous anti-communist novel by Arthur Koestler. 'Born with a silver spoon in his/her mouth' is a well-known phrase that means someone who has been privileged from the very beginning of their life. If we are to understand that Dylan is employing the 'darkness at the break of noon' phrase as a shorthand for the cruelties of communism and the silver spoon expression as a metaphor for the wild disparities in wealth that exist under capitalism, would he perhaps mean that neither capitalism nor socialism/communism offer mankind salvation? Such an interpretation helps one understand why Dylan had recently disavowed the lie that life is black and white.

Propelled by a corkscrew guitar riff and a grim vocal, the track tackles across the course of seven and a half minutes subjects—albeit in elliptical terms—never before essayed in popular song, including psychology, self-loathing, and self-deception. The composer reserves equal contempt for those traditionally characterised as oppressors and those usually placed on pedestals as oppressed, disdaining individuals reduced to small-minded callousness by their hard lives as much as he does censorious elites. He provides additional layering by rejecting the easy option of condemning only the failings of others, him full of doubt and disgust with himself. All the while, he doesn't forget to throw in instantly memorable phases ('He not busy being born is busy dying').

The side, and album, closes with a mellow, short song—relatively speaking, in both cases. 'It's All Over Now, Baby Blue' still runs to over four minutes and is almost as devoid of hope as the two previous tracks. It's also just as compelling as everything else on the side. This second-person wodge of advice could be about any of the people about whom it's been theorised it addresses, from fellow folkie David Blue (aka David Cohen) to friend Paul Clayton to an anonymous drug dealer, but it may instead be another disguised song about himself, this one a sort of sequel to 'Restless Farewell'. The person Dylan is addressing is watching his world slowly crumble and his position being usurped (a vagabond rapping at his door is standing in the clothes once worn by him). He tells the person addressed to start anew and to 'take what you have gathered from coincidence'. Underlying the scenario is the dread fact that the subject will soon be facing the wrath of those he has used and fooled. Interpretations are legion, of course, but as with so many peak-era Dylan songs, it is so supremely listenable that it doesn't matter whether or not we have taken the song the way he meant us to. Bill Lee's bass widens and enriches the sound, but it doesn't need it much: Dylan's melody, harmonica, and singing all soar to the heavens.

•

For the sleeve of *Bringing It All Back Home*, Dylan decided to go back to colour photography for the first time since *Freewheelin'*. The snapper he chose was Daniel Kramer. The two had first met on August 27, 1964. Kramer would photograph Dylan on stage, in the recording studio, in a photography studio, and on the streets for almost an exact year, by happenstance documenting a profound musical, psychological, and professional journey in the process.

Born in 1932, Kramer became aware of Dylan on February 25, 1964, when he happened to see him performing 'The Lonesome Death Of Hattie Carroll' on the TV show of the unusually hip presenter Steve Allen. He was immediately taken with the idea of Dylan as a subject. 'I wanted to photograph him because I saw in him a poet saying very special things,' Kramer reflects. 'In 1964, when you hear something like that on a general audience family show. . . . There's this guy speaking about injustices and being open about it and he's twenty-three years old, standing there naked with a guitar. . . . This young guy saying things that other people don't say publicly or musically or with that authority. I was told his name is Bob Dylan and he's a folk singer. Being a new young photographer, I wanted to have a portfolio of interesting people to show magazine editors. So, I called his office and of course, they told me to get lost. This went on for about six or seven months. And finally, one day, I got Albert Grossman on the phone because I called after hours, and his secretary was out, and he picked up the phone. He knew my name because I had written to him and I had called. He said, I'll give you one hour with Bob next Thursday at Woodstock.'

Kramer's observations of Dylan from the ensuing session were, 'He's photogenic, but he's more than that. He also has a sense of the camera.' He adds, 'When people have that sense, it's very nice to work with them. And he's smart.' He notes, 'My hour turned into five. It turned into lunch, it turned into playing chess. He said, What do you want me to do? I said, I don't care what you do. He said, I'll climb a tree. So, he climbed a tree. There he is, sitting up in the branches like a bird. Got his bullwhip. And we watched home movies, talked, and at the end of that day, we parted. I went to my studio, I developed the film, I made about a dozen or fifteen 11 x 14 prints, went up to his office two weeks later, laid them out on a table for him and for Albert Grossman. They looked at it, they walked around the table, and then Bob said to me, I'm going to Philadelphia next week to do a concert. Would you like to come? In the two-hour drive to Philadelphia, we got on pretty good terms. This was not like a commission. I just did this because I saw that this was a wonderful moment, an interesting guy and that I should keep photographing.' Kramer snapped Dylan at three concerts in that period. 'Then he said, We're doing an album, why don't you come and photograph it? So, I went to the recording sessions and they were very exciting. When "Maggie's Farm" came on for the first time, I cannot tell you how wonderful it was. And then he said, I'd like you to do a cover for this album. I said, Well, do you have something in mind? He said, No, you do something.'

Before that carte blanche scenario could be enacted, there was a hiccup when Kramer informed Columbia Records' art director that he finally had a formal Dylan photography commission. 'He said, No, you can't do it. I need a name. Bob's a star and I can't trust you with this.' During a break in the album's recording, Kramer had lunch with Dylan and Grossman at Columbia's commissary and regretfully informed them that what they had discussed was not going to come to pass. Kramer: 'Albert Grossman dragged us into the art director's office. He demanded that it be the way Bob wanted it and that I [shoot] the cover. He was a special guy in that department. That was his business. His business was negotiating and getting what they needed.'

The upshot of Grossman's insistence was—*Sgt. Pepper's Lonely Hearts Club Band* and *Abbey Road* aside—possibly the most analysed album cover of all time. It's also one of the most beautiful. In the most simple terms, the front of *Bringing It All Back Home* features a colour photograph with a large white border, atop which is the artist's name in red and the title in blue. The photo itself shows Dylan sitting with a cat on his lap in a luxurious living room while an elegant-looking woman wearing a red dress, cigarette upraised in one hand, reclines behind him on a sofa. The woman looks no less refined than Dylan, who is hereby announcing to the wider world that his previous casual at best, scruffy at worst image has been jettisoned for starch-collared, cufflinked finery. Pointedly scattered around the room are several objects and cultural artefacts. An extra layer of intrigue is provided by the fact that all of this is seen through what looks like a golden halo, a shimmering circle around the edges of the picture.

The picture was taken in the Woodstock home of Albert and Sally Grossman, the latter being the reclining lady. 'He spent a lot of time in Grossman's place in those days,' recalls Kramer. 'It's a great house. He had a room. He could write and be out of the city. It was just a really nice place to be.' Kramer detected a genuine affection between Dylan and the Grossmans. 'It wasn't just business. He was very friendly with Sally, and with her people she knew. I think they had a comfortable relationship, [he and] Albert.' The living room of this idyllic retreat was chosen for a couple of reasons. 'First, the fireplace mantle. It meant we could put things on it. Secondly, the colour of the couch was fantastic. I thought [Sally] could stretch out on it. It all worked that that was a good spot.'

Although at least one outtake of the photography session shows

Dylan with a harmonica, Kramer says there was no question of portraying him with an instrument on the final jacket front. From Kramer's point of view, Dylan was not 'a raggedy guy with a guitar' but instead 'a prince with enormous authority'. Accordingly, 'I wanted to make a regal photograph, and I wanted to show, photographically, that things revolve around him. That's why I made a stroboscopic effect of movement around him. That circle, to me, represented a record, represented the world revolving, but he is not caught up in that. He is stationary and sharp in the middle of it all.' In a world decades away from Photoshop—or even a concept of computer software—this was not an easy ambition to accomplish. 'I had to build a special rig that I used with my camera in order to achieve this effect. This was done on one sheet of four by five [inch] colour film as two separate exposures, but in such a way that Bob would not be re-exposed and the world around him could move a bit. And I'd have ten frames, and this is the one we used because this is the one in which the cat looks at the camera. The cat was less cooperative than Bob and Sally Grossman.'

There was equal thoughtfulness to Kramer's overall approach. The many interesting objects scattered around the room include a copy of *Time* magazine featuring current US president Lyndon Johnson on the cover, a fallout shelter sign, and albums by The Impressions, Robert Johnson, Ravi Shankar, Lotte Lenya, Eric Von Schmidt, Lord Buckley, and even Dylan himself in the shape of his previous album. Most people assumed that Dylan brought the items with him, but Kramer explains, 'There could be no preparation before because no one knew what I was going to do. I had planned this in my studio. I'm making tests. . . . The artefacts were in the house. He found a lot of things in the house because I needed to make something move. If you don't have little objects, then nothing will move in my effect, and Bob got onto that. . . . He didn't know my idea until I got there and showed him. I said sit here, and Sally you sit here, just sit there without anything. I made a Polaroid, showed him on the Polaroid how I could make the things move and what I had in mind . . . and that's when he knew he liked it. Then we had an hour to pull it together. He got very smart about it. He found a lot of things that interested him, brought to the picture. Too many things, as a matter of fact, so I started to then say, No, let's do this, this fits here, that fits there. We have an air-raid shelter sign in the lower left corner because it was down in the basement, dug away. There's a piece above the mantel that Bob actually made, the clown, with broken pieces of coloured glass. . . . We were just all squirrelling around, looking for things. Bob had reasons, I guess, for some of these things. They're based on his own sense of humour or things he would like to do or say. I didn't need to question that. If they worked photographically then it was fine. I chose some things that I liked, and I had to get rid of some things he chose because we have too many things, and then he might say he didn't like something I chose. It just evolved, and the way this worked out is close enough to my expectation.' It was a post-modern and self-referential assemblage when such a thing was rare.

A miracle of happenstance lent the cover a yet further and completely unintended layer. So similar was Sally Grossman's facial structure to Dylan's own famously angular visog that it gave rise to a bizarre rumour. 'For a while, I was telling people they were correct,' says Kramer. 'Someone would say to me, Oh, is that Bob in drag? I'd say, Yeah, maybe.' Kramer doesn't recall being aware of the similarity when he was taking the picture.

Although 1965 was a time when popular music was barely receiving the sober critical appraisal it increasingly deserved, let alone the artwork it came wrapped in, this album's iconic sleeve was taken seriously and endlessly discussed—something that caused Kramer to feel a certain schadenfreude regarding Columbia Records. 'I was very, very, very pleased when I was able to call the art director and the design department and tell them that we were nominated for a Grammy for album cover photography.' However, actually winning a Grammy would have probably been a bridge too far at this point in pop history: *Jazz Suite On The Mass Texts* (whatever that is) by Paul Horn (whoever he is), photographed by Ken Whitmore, took the top prize in the relevant year's 'Best Album Cover—Photography' category.

As with the last two albums, Dylan contributed the sleeve notes. For the first time, though, they are surreal narrative rather than verse. 'some people say that I am a poet' says Dylan in his untitled, grammarless back-cover text, which constitutes poems only delineated as such by the forward slashes that follow some sentences, with that slash appearing in no logical place such as the endings of lines, which themselves are not of uniform length. As ever with his sleeve notes and written verse, we are left with the feeling that if Dylan is a poet, it's only when operating within the parameters of song, where he feels obliged to adhere to the traditions of rhyme and at least a little comprehensibility and doesn't think the occasional amusing phrase or an overarching unconventional structure makes up for a hipster-speak stream of consciousness adjacent to gibberish.

The album title has been interpreted in several ways. The most commonly held assumption is that Dylan is stating to the British acts dominating his home country's charts that, following their revitalisation of an indigenous American art form, he is now taking up that mantle. Another interpretation is one involving Dylan's own personal journey: i.e., by dispensing with folk for rock, he is returning to his true musical home.

•

So far, Dylan had played what might be termed residencies at clubs and had appeared in one-off concerts in progressively larger and more prestigious venues but, quite remarkably, his excursion to England from April 30 to May 10, 1965, was his first-ever tour, domestic or foreign.

When North Americans refer to England, they usually mean Great Britain or the United Kingdom. However, Dylan's visit was indeed an English tour, taking in the cities of Sheffield, Liverpool, Leicester, Birmingham, Newcastle, and Manchester before culminating in two concerts at London's classy Royal Albert Hall, the second of which was added to placate angry punters when the tickets to all the other concerts sold out in around an hour—this in an age long before the internet.

Although his career was still quite young, Dylan already had a long history with the UK. Following *Madhouse On Castle Street*, he had also crossed the Atlantic in May 1964 for live and television work. The affinity he was building was reflected in record sales. Another trip, therefore, was logical. This one, though, occasioned pop-star-like pandemonium upon his arrival at London Airport. With the UK feeling blessed by the arrival of an exotic star at a point in history when Americans seemed glamourous to Britons by default, his current releases did far better, chart-wise, than they did in his home country. 'Subterranean Homesick Blues' entered the UK Top 40 in April 1965 and on May 26 rose to its peak of no. 9. The same position was also achieved by the now quasi-archaic 'The Times They Are A-Changin''. *Bringing It All Back Home* entered the UK Top 40 in mid-May and made no. 1 on the 29th. It was like a minor version of the Beatlemania that had been seen the previous year on the *Billboard* charts. Nonetheless, the English concert audiences were respectfully silent throughout Dylan's songs, something that mightily impressed the reporters despatched to review them, who were used to pop gigs that were sheer 'scream machines'.

The tour marked the occasion of Dylan's split with Baez. Although he had suggested she join him on the trip, there was no invitation extended to sing with him on stage, something that she—and the audiences—would have expected because it was now a tradition, and not just informally: in the States, they had shared billings since early in the year. It would also have been an appropriate quid pro quo to facilitate for her an entry into the British marketplace after she had boosted his career back home. Dylan was instead cold and dismissive toward her, to such an extent that finally she could take it no longer and walked out, a testament to her generosity of spirit being the fact that she placed a sad, fond kiss on his head as she left. Her humiliation (and grace) was captured for posterity by the cameras of D.A. Pennebaker, shooting an access-all-areas documentary.

During the English tour, Dylan and Wilson went into London recording studio Levy's on New Bond Street with John Mayall's Bluesbreakers, an ensemble that at that point included a young Eric Clapton. However, this mouth-watering prospect yielded no fruits. The main purpose was to capture a recording of 'If You Gotta Go, Go Now', but that song—famous in Dylan's repertoire at the time—was destined never to be released by him except on compilations and as a possibly unauthorised 1967 Dutch single. The lack of productivity was attributed by Mayall to Dylan being more interested in drinking Beaujolais and chatting up folk singer Nadia Cattouse than rehearsing the musicians. (He clearly didn't know that the latter was something Dylan never did.) Bluesbreakers drummer Hughie Flint snapped at Dylan, 'You haven't worked much with bands, have you?' shortly before the session dribbled to a close.

Some felt that Dylan's temporary relocation to a faraway land was a ruse both to evade the withering scrutiny of those in his home country dubious about the new developments in his career and to exploit audiences who didn't realise the depth of his cynicism. Americans who heard the news filtering back across the Atlantic that Dylan was performing in England the protest songs he these days disdained to play in his home country nodded knowingly. Any qualms Dylan had about protest not representing where he was currently at had apparently been shunted aside so as to pander to the Brits' out-of-date image of him. Had Pennebaker's documentary been released at the time, such people would have had their suspicions about mercenaryism confirmed by scenes in which Albert Grossman and British agent Tito Burns play broadcasters off against each other to obtain the highest fee possible for an exclusive Dylan television appearance.

Such fees would soon come to seem such small change that they would barely be worth such deception and haggling. Five days after the English tour's final date, The Byrds' version of 'Mr. Tambourine Man' crept into the *Billboard* Hot 100 at no. 87. Six weeks later, it was no. 1.

•

That 'Mr. Tambourine Man' was issued on April 12, 1965, three weeks after the release of *Bringing It All Back Home*, would have made many believe that The Byrds were just another bunch of opportunists, the kind of ensemble who swooped like vultures on the latest songs by Dylan—or indeed The Beatles—to put out a quick cover job in order to secure the hit that their own slender abilities would never have enabled. In fact, their recording of 'Mr. Tambourine Man' dated from January 20, just five days after Dylan's, which means that they were working on it in the same week as its composer was laying down his released version (even if well after his abortive crack at it during the *Another Side Of* sessions). Leaving that aside, though, The Byrds were no lightweights. Frontman Jim McGuinn purveyed a unique electric guitar sound via his mellifluous work on his twelve-string Rickenbacker, while fellow singer/ guitarist Gene Clark was responsible for an endless flow of top-notch compositions. Moreover, the group's trademark three-part harmonies— supplied by McGuinn, Clark, and singer/guitarist David Crosby— were beautiful and ethereal. Additionally, the fact that The Byrds' 'Mr. Tambourine Man' would shortly come to be perceived as one of the first examples of folk-rock—the most revolutionary form of music since rock'n'roll itself was birthed—was, as noted, not quite an accident.

Ironically, McGuinn—who would be the band's mainstay as its personnel churned down the years—had actually started as a rocker before drifting into folk. 'It was just a matter of being exposed to folk music at a very impressionable age,' he recalls. 'I was about fifteen, and it happened at my school. My teacher brought Bob Gibson to perform for us, and he was so impressive that I wanted to learn how to play the banjo and the guitar and the twelve-string guitar, and my music teacher happened to know of a new music school that had opened up, and she directed me over there. It wasn't a matter of anything wrong with rock'n'roll; it was just a matter of something else becoming much more interesting to me at the time.' McGuinn found folk 'more substantial', stating, 'There was more going on. The stories were more interesting. The chord changes were much more interesting. There was so much more diversity in the styles of music. It encompassed blues and gospel and bluegrass and what we call world music today, like African chants and things from different parts of the world. It broadened my horizons musically.'

The pendulum swung again, however, when, in 1964, America was smitten by a four-man ensemble who had taken the lately somnambulant form of rock and retooled it to incorporate girl group, Tin Pan Alley, and skiffle traditions to create an intoxicating new sound. 'We really wanted to be like The Beatles initially,' says Chris Hillman, bassist in the band, who were named first The Jet Set, then The Beefeaters. For him, McGuinn, Clark, Crosby, and drummer Michael Clarke, it was a learning curve. 'We were all coming from folk or bluegrass country backgrounds,' Hillman says. 'We weren't a rock band. We didn't know anything about electric music really, so it was a trial-by-error situation. We learned as we rehearsed every night.'

'We were just doing what we could do,' says McGuinn. 'We just played folkie-style guitars even when they were plugged in. The main thing we had to concentrate on was keeping a beat because that wasn't too important in folk music, but it was in rock'n'roll. The main focus at that time was trying to be a dance band. Our manager said, If they're on the dance floor and you miss a beat, they'll fall down.'

Hillman: 'Initially the first songs that Gene was writing were very Merseybeat-type things.' In November 1964, the bandwagon-jumping was completed when the band gave themselves a name that, just like The Beatles, was a misspelt animal, even if it was also a nod to jazz maestro Charlie 'Bird' Parker.

Then the pendulum unexpectedly swung again. 'The folk thing sort of fell into our lap by accident, with "Tambourine Man" being made available for us to record with Dylan's consent,' says Hillman. 'Nobody had heard the term folk-rock. After the record became successful, then of course it was labelled that, being that it was a song from folk singer Bob Dylan and here we are with drums.'

That The Byrds switched the Dylan song's tempo to rock's standard 4/4 was reasonable enough. Ostensibly controversial was their decision to strip its lyrical content down to the chorus and second verse. However, the fact that the editing had Dylan's blessing demonstrates that he wasn't precious about his material.

Not that—save McGuinn's guitar and McGuinn, Crosby, and Clark's voices—The Byrds could actually be heard on the finished record. 'We weren't really that good yet,' explains Hillman, who says that if he had been working for Columbia Records, 'I would have probably made the same decision and had studio guys play the first single.' 'We just didn't have the time and money to waste on taking a lot of takes,' says McGuinn. 'And the band they did bring in—the Wrecking Crew with Hal Blaine, Jerry Cole, Larry Knechtel, and Leon Russell—well, those guys were so proficient that they could knock off a track in two or three takes. Whereas it took Michael Clarke seventy-seven takes to get "Turn! Turn! Turn!" on the next album. ... They're the guys who played on all The Beach Boys tracks and all the Mamas & Papas tracks, on Jan & Dean, on almost everything that came out of Hollywood. They were the best, and I was thrilled to play with them.' Russell's keyboards were mixed out of the final master. In addition to Cole's guitar, Knechtel's bass, and Blaine's drums, it's said that guitarist Bill Pitman can also (just) be heard on the released record. 'They actually took what we did and did it slicker,' says Hillman, pointing out that while the memorable, elegant twelve-string guitar riff was one of McGuinn's own devising, Knechtel was responsible for the almost as prominent looping bass line. Hillman adds a caveat: 'In hindsight, it would have been interesting to see how we would have cut that and whether that would have worked too, because I think, as good a record as it is, it's awfully slick and a little too perfect in some places.'

McGuinn's vocal performance was the world's introduction to his distinctive quavering singing style. He says he was completely unaware of that quality to his voice. 'I was trying to get a mixture of Dylan and John Lennon,' he explains. 'I wanted something folky and something a little bit Beatley.' Although he admits 'it didn't really come off that way,' he also observes, 'I came up with something different.'

The whole record, in fact, was something different—a genuinely new sound: literate, mysterious, graceful, hypnotic—and electric. So new a sound, in fact, that it might be suspected to have no market. The hit parade wasn't a complete stranger to lyrical intellect and musical sophistication, but the fact of it being purveyed by teen-idol material—with the implications for its natural demographic—was an entirely new ball game. Hillman admits his high hopes for the disc were born out of naiveté: 'I thought it was a really exceptionally good record, and not really knowing how the process worked at that time to get a single on the radio and to make it happen, I thought there's no reason why it shouldn't do something really interesting.' For his part, McGuinn says, 'I didn't know what would happen.' What happened upon its release on April 12, 1965, was it becoming the first Dylan-written song to top a US chart. Not only that, but it achieved the same summit-mounting feat in the UK—at that point in history an achievement of considerable cachet because of the collapse of interest in most American music caused by the dominance of British artists. Dylan already had a certain reputation as a man whose songs could generate chart success, but this transatlantic triumph put his prestige into another league. 'Everyone was asking, Who's this Bob Dylan?' recalled New York DJ 'Cousin Brucie' Morrow to journalist Jules Siegel in 1966. 'It's the only time I can remember when a composer got more attention for a hit than the performers did.'

Not that The Byrds didn't get attention, enough in fact to become stars. To an extent, they were also national heroes: the United States was perceived to have finally provided an answer to The Beatles and thereby to have salvaged some national pride after the emasculation that was intertwined with the British Invasion.

Having done so spectacularly well with an electrified Dylan song, the Byrds camp felt it would be natural to cover another for their follow-up. Their retooling of *Another Side Of*'s 'All I Really Want To Do' was actually a fine recording, displaying imagination in the way it gave a slowish song a brisk tempo and turned one of its verses into a pop-friendly middle-eight. They also demonstrated similarly mainstream-oriented circumspection by omitting the risqué elements of the composition. Moreover, this time the entire group got to play on it. In truth, though, they would have been better advised to make their second single the track that was actually on the B-side: Gene Clark's up-tempo, embittered 'I'll Feel A Whole Lot Better' was an instant classic with 'hit' written all over it. Not only that, it wasn't liable to be pre-empted in the manner that the A-side was. Not content with pastiching Dylan's sound with the previous July's 'I Got You Babe', Sonny Bono now proceeded to lift The Byrds' arrangement of Dylan's own song. 'Sonny and Cher literally had come in and stolen that from us,' says Hillman. 'They watched us play it at Ciro's in Hollywood, and then they cut the song. They did an okay job on it, I thought, but that's probably what killed that single.' The competitor version to The Byrds' rendition—actually credited just to Cher, although with a Bono involvement in the form of his production—made no. 15 on *Billboard*, while The Byrds' template reached no. 40. (The Byrds did better in the UK, making no. 4, while Cher could only muster a no. 9 placing.) 'Dylan was mad at me that Sonny & Cher got a hit with it,' says McGuinn. 'He said, You let me down, man.'

Perhaps Dylan was joshing. It would certainly be just a little churlish if he wasn't, for the airplay and sales royalties rolling in from the success of The Byrds' 'Mr. Tambourine Man' were astronomical. Moreover, Cher had included three Dylan covers on her August album, which was actually titled *All I Really Want To Do*. More important than financial issues, though, was that 'Mr. Tambourine Man' sealed the deal for Dylan's new direction.

'When he heard us do his material in rock'n'roll format, it probably did awaken his awareness that he could do that himself,' says McGuinn. Dylan now had not just the template for the electrification of folk music provided by The Animals record but confirmation from The Byrds' release that his own songs could fully cross over to the pop market. He seized the opportunities this suggested wholeheartedly and with alacrity. McGuinn, for one, was surprised. 'He was still a folk singer, and I thought he was going to stay on the course,' he says. 'I didn't think he was going to cross over as quickly as he did.'

Hitherto, the worlds of Dylan and The Beatles had been more or less parallel: they were both recording artists, but there had been a barrier between their respective markets. 'Subterranean Homesick Blues' and *Bringing It All Back Home* had chipped away at that barrier, but 'Mr. Tambourine Man' blew it wide open. The single's success suggested there was no reason that Dylan himself couldn't storm the pop charts, regardless of whether—à la his flurry of hit parade success on his English tour—he happened to have an unusual prominence at the time by dint of being on tour in the relevant country, which itself happened to be handily small with a concentrated media.

Ten days before The Byrds hit no. 1, Dylan had recorded a song titled 'Like A Rolling Stone' that would be released as a single on July 20. He had a band backing him on it, but other than that overture to the chart zeitgeist, it felt nothing like a hit single: it was over six minutes long, was of astoundingly venomous quality, and was stamped with that unmistakable Dylan intellect, even if it was more in his vernacular than poetic vein. It was a superb record—to this day, many think it the greatest single of all time—but that such a proposition stormed up the charts was not just a commercial achievement but a cultural triumph. Not bad for a man who, not long before he wrote it, had been on the brink of retiring.

Chapter three

CHAPTER THREE

If I Was A King

'I guess I was going to quit singing,' Dylan told *Playboy* in 1966. 'I was very drained...I was playing a lot of songs I didn't want to play...but "Like A Rolling Stone" changed it all.' Such was the torn state of mind brought about by the fact of occupying the lofty positions of king of folk and voice of a generation but no longer possessing the beliefs that had given him those roles.

His agonising was brought to a halt in the spring of 1965 when he produced a free-standing lyric of twenty pages that he later likened to 'this long piece of vomit'. It was the type of being sick that's good for you. The poison of disillusion and uncertainty seemed to be ejected from Dylan's being by the brilliance and honesty of this embryonic 'Like A Rolling Stone' lyric, and the catharsis/epiphany of its creation made him see that there was a way out of his malaise. The brooding thoughts of retirement had created a realisation that—to paraphrase from 'Rolling Stone' itself—he had nothin' to lose. He was thereby given the courage to plough full steam ahead with the mission on which he'd embarked of creating music featuring the visceral excitement then never heard in folk and the poetry and intellectualism then never heard in rock and pop.

Not that 'Like A Rolling Stone' was recorded in isolation. On June 15, 1965, Dylan entered a studio to begin work on his new album, ultimately titled *Highway 61 Revisited*. 'Like A Rolling Stone' would feature on it but, amazingly, is by no means the only candidate for its best track.

All *Highway 61* sessions took place at Columbia's Studio A at 799 7th Avenue, New York. Album musician Al Kooper recalls the studios as 'beautiful' and Studio A specifically as 'gigantic'. He adds, 'They needed to accommodate any sort of session and it's very common in those days to have twenty-four strings and fourteen horns and background singers.' Within this grand environment, Dylan seems to have determined to address the fact that, fine album though *Bringing It All Back Home* was, he had to raise his game a little on this record. Judging by the results of these sessions, he seems to have apprehended that if he didn't want it to be perceived as the embarrassing efforts of a folkie who wanted to jump on the bandwagon of a musical style he didn't understand, he needed soundscapes that sounded like he was playing *with* a band, not in front of one. It seems significant that, of the musicians from *Bringing It All Back Home*, only drummer Bobby Gregg played a major part in *Highway 61*.

Assembled for the first session were Gregg, bassist Joseph Macho Jr., guitarist Al Gorgoni, pianist Frank Owens, and guitarists Al Kooper and Mike Bloomfield. According, that is, to the studio session sheets. As with any form of record keeping, various factors—in-house shorthand, human error, reluctance in a busy environment to document anything not legally or practicably necessary, etc.—have created considerable scope for confusion. Says Kooper (later a producer himself), 'It's never delineated on the session sheets whether it's a mixing session or a recording session or somebody's making acetates of songs. I've seen many people misinterpret a session sheet. That's a very common revisionism. I've had arguments with writers who tell me that there were two sets of sessions for *Blonde On Blonde*, that we went to Nashville twice. They're telling me this—and I was there.' As if to illustrate his own point, Kooper insists he wasn't present on the 15th. Ditto Gorgoni, who says he had to 'NG' (no-go) the recording date because he had an arranging job elsewhere. Nonetheless, session sheets being the only formal record we have—and by their nature reliable at least most of the time—we will have to make frequent reference to them, and *Highway 61 Revisited* being the titanic masterpiece it is—both for Dylan specifically and popular music broadly—it's worth trying in this instance to nail down who played what on it.

For what would be a timeless album, the first day of recording was an inauspicious start indeed. Three songs were attempted under the auspices of Tom Wilson, assisted by engineers Roy Halee (working on his very first studio session) and Pete Dauria (as the session sheets render it, although some other sources spell it Duryea). Nothing recorded that day was ultimately considered good enough for release. 'Phantom Engineer Cloudy' (the working title of what was eventually dubbed 'It Takes A Lot To Laugh, It Takes A Train To Cry') was attempted ten times, yielding six complete takes, three short breakdowns (studio parlance for a track that for whatever reason founders after a brief period), and one long breakdown (i.e., a take aborted a considerable way in). A track variously annotated at this stage as 'Over The Cliffs pt 1' and 'Over The Cliff' was a working title for what became 'Sitting On A Barbed Wire Fence'. There were three complete takes, one long breakdown, and two short. Meanwhile, the first studio airing for the epoch-marking 'Like A Rolling Stone' wasn't exactly a reliable portent, producing four short breakdowns in addition to an unused complete take. 'Sitting On A Barbed Wire Fence' is a drolly surreal, loping blues whose insubstantiality is something with which Dylan's lyric practically taunts the listener ('Of course you're gonna think this song is a riff'). Following these six takes, Dylan never returned to it. The other two songs would receive more attention. The utterly underwhelming versions of them from this day, to be heard on the compilation *The Bootleg Series 1–3*, prove how mood and tempo can be the difference between mediocre and brilliant. A switch in approach with both would create two of Dylan's most cherished recordings.

Wilson had a busy day. Later on the 15th, taking his own cue from his previous overdubbing work on Dylan's 'House Of The Risin' Sun', he overdubbed a full band—including some of the Dylan session's musicians—onto 'The Sound Of Silence', aka 'The Sounds Of Silence', a haunting song about loneliness originally recorded in bare acoustic style for the 1964 debut album of folk duo Simon & Garfunkel, *Wednesday Morning, 3 A.M.*, which had been produced by him. Its composer, Paul Simon, away in England being a troubadour, had no knowledge of the alteration, nor did his sweet-triller colleague Art Garfunkel, who was deep in his architecture studies at Columbia University. However, the alteration was life-changing. *Wednesday Morning, 3 A.M.* had flopped, but on the release of 'The Sound(s) Of Silence' as a single that September, Wilson's unauthorised embellishment propelled the song to the top of the US hit parade. Simon & Garfunkel purveyed what might be posited as a vanilla version of Dylan's kind of social criticism, but 'The Sound(s) Of Silence' kicked off a chart career in which the pair easily outsold Dylan, The Rolling Stones, and a whole host of other, edgier contemporaries.

The next day's *Highway 61* session would be three hours as opposed to the previous day's four (2:30–5:30pm) and was given over in its entirety to perfecting 'Like A Rolling Stone' (unless one counts an unlogged song fragment that has been given the unofficial title 'Why Should You Have To Be So Frantic'). The fact that Dylan had not only come back to this song but attempted it a further fifteen times was something whose unusualness was not lost on Daniel Kramer, taking pictures that day at Dylan's invitation. 'Three takes were a lot of takes,' Kramer notes of Dylan's normal modus operandi.

The session sheets claim that the personnel for this session were those present for the previous day's. However, from what has subsequently been established, it would seem that Owens was absent, at least from the tapes, if not the studio, and that Paul Griffin (another *Home* veteran) was present. Owens recalls of Griffin, 'We were in the studio at the same time. He would have played organ, I would have played piano.' Owens would seem to have been usurped by Griffin on piano at some point. It was a logical move for the song being tackled. Says Owens, 'Paul Griffin was known to be an R&B player. I was noted to play more in a, not classical vein, but I played with more artists that weren't of the R&B generation. So, I was set apart from them.' Although Owens possibly played elsewhere on the album, he's not sure on which tracks he appears but seems to think he played on two sessions.

Meanwhile, Kramer, familiar with Bruce Langhorne from *Home*, confirms the latter was present, even if logic and aural evidence suggest this talented guitarist was reduced to bashing a tambourine. While Gorgoni did get to the studio that day, he says, 'My name wound up on the contract, but I didn't actually play on it—I'm sorry to say.'

At least there's no doubt this time that Kooper was in the studio. His presence is now a matter of legend, his alchemic contribution creating one of the most famous of all recording anecdotes.

'I was a big fan,' Kooper says of Dylan, although he does admit, 'When I first listened, I didn't get it.' His ears were opened to Dylan's virtues by his own good friend, Paul Simon. 'Paul and I were playing a gig one night and he said, Have you listened to Dylan? I said I didn't get it. And he said, What didn't you get? I said, Well, the voice mostly. He said, Well, the guitar playing is really good, and he started playing something for me. (He was playing electric guitar.) And I said, That is good. And so he taught me a couple of things and I got into it that way, and then eventually I got used to the voice.'

Kooper says his attendance came courtesy of Tom Wilson. 'We were friends, and he found out that I was a fan,' he recalls. 'He said, Would you like to observe the session?'

'No, that's not how it happened,' demurs Gorgoni. 'I had known Al Kooper from the business, and I was going up into the studio, and I bumped into Al Kooper right in front of 799 there. He said, Where are you going? I said, Well, I have a session upstairs. He asked me who it was, and I said, Bob Dylan. And he said, Oh wow, man, can I come up with you? I said, Of course, because he was on the music scene there. It turns out he was a friend of Tom Wilson.' If Gorgoni's recollection is the accurate one, it's somewhat ironic, as the interloper ended up on the classic recording the session produced where Gorgoni didn't.

Kooper wasn't above taking advantage of what he recalls as Wilson's generosity: 'Because I was so ambitious, I thought to myself, *I want to play on it.*' This hankering was not easily fulfilled. 'I was a guitar player at the time,' Kooper reflects. 'I knew that I couldn't play the guitar on the session because of hearing Mike Bloomfield play.' Bloomfield was from a well-to-do background but had renounced the family business for music. His stinging work was currently gracing the Paul Butterfield Blues Band, although blues doesn't seem to be what the artist had in mind for these dates. Bloomfield later recalled that Dylan told him, 'I don't want you to play any of that B.B. King shit,' a variant of the instruction Gorgoni recalls being issued on the previous album's sessions.

Serendipity gifted Kooper an opportunity. 'Paul Griffin was organ originally and then they moved him to piano, and that's when I had an available slot I could take,' he says. 'Nobody was really leading the session musically—to the point where I could go out there and sit down at the organ and start playing. It really sort of continued like that.' This leaderlessness was to Kooper's benefit, for he had never played organ professionally, his work on the instrument restricted so far to home demos. Although Wilson may not have been aware of this fact, he was certainly aware that it wasn't his speciality, leading to a tense moment for Kooper when Wilson, after two rehearsal takes and just before the first take proper, noticed Kooper on the studio floor. To Kooper's relief, the producer (assisted again today by Halee and Dauria), rather than throw him out, merely metaphorically shrugged. Wilson proceeded to 'slate' the recording ('Remake, take one').

While he may not have been present for the previous day's recording, Kooper says, 'I actually have a copy of the entire session from both days.' Because of this, he feels able to identify what had been going wrong with 'Like A Rolling Stone': 'The [previous] day was spent on trying to get it in three-quarter time, and it was considered a failure. It would have gone on for ten minutes. It's a big difference. I guess that was junked because they went right into trying it in 4/4 time.' That difference was actually substantially more than the switch from a waltz metre to a rock beat. The outtakes that have subsequently seen air indicate a 3/4-time version could have worked at a certain level, but a slow, melancholy, keyboard-dominated song is not the stuff of which epoch-marking is made.

Not that Kooper was concentrating on whether the proceedings were revolutionary. He recalls, 'It was only three chords. I was a full-time studio musician, so I was able to learn it pretty quickly. There was no written music, however, so I had to learn it in my head. Because I did such a commando raid, I didn't want to be the cause of the take stopping because something was played wrong, so I kind of laid back and made sure that I was going to hit the right chord after everyone hit it first.' Adding to Kooper's anxiety were the methods employed to ensure individual instrument tracks didn't bleed into others: 'The speaker was far away, with blankets, so I couldn't even hear the organ.'

While Kooper was dancing in the dark, Dylan was playing his electric guitar like he was still a folkie scrubbing an acoustic instrument. What might appear a demerit—as well as, once again, a naïve lack of understanding of ensemble playing—is for others a highlight of the finished track. 'Oh, that's fine,' says Gorgoni. 'That's the way he played. He wasn't a lead player. He didn't play single-line melodies. He would find guitar grooves and rhythms to play, and that's how he wrote his songs, and I think they were an integral part of the songs, an integral part of the arrangements.'

Kooper goes further. 'It's actually brilliant,' he opines. 'It's a very important part of the sound of that record that is rarely discussed.' He adds, 'Bob was playing in C tuning, which is very rare, especially of electric guitar, which is the lowest of all special tunings. People keep away from it because it's complicated fingering as well.'

Meanwhile, Gorgoni suspects that the session was rescheduled when he was out of the loop the previous day, causing him to turn up late. 'When I arrived, it was already in progress,' he says. 'It would have been strange to just jump in, although I could have. Why fix it if it ain't broke? It was really something. The walls were shaking.' Having said that, he admits it did later cross his mind to feel regret over his absence from the track. 'Here I was on all this other stuff, and now it falls together and I wasn't there. But c'est la vie.' (If his story about getting Kooper on the session is correct, his pal was clearly less shy about muscling in.)

Whichever day or days Frank Owens played on the track, he has an abiding memory. 'While we were between takes, I could see Bob Dylan writing down the next verse,' he recalls. 'He had a piece of paper with him or a pad or whatever, writing the next verse for "Like A Rolling Stone". I thought that was quite curious. He was composing as he was going along.'

Of the fifteen takes that day, five were completes, nine were short breakdowns, and one was a long breakdown. Although the complete takes were spread evenly across the session—takes one, four, eight, eleven, and fifteen—it was actually take four that provided the master. Perhaps the fact that take four had not yet been subject to a final mix prevented Dylan from appreciating at its playback that he and his colleagues had just laid down an absolutely perfect recording. Certainly, something approaching blessedness attended the take, so much so that it can be difficult to adjudge whether the churning, circular instrumentation behind Dylan is fantastic by design or fluke. For instance, a collective plunge by the musicians in the last chorus produces a sensation scintillatingly akin to leaving one's stomach behind when one's car crests a hill. Additionally, while Kooper's organ was both unscheduled and—because of Kooper's nervousness—half a step behind the other instrumentation, Dylan liked it so much he demanded it be mixed up, thus giving the song one of its signature sounds. Meanwhile, an action that had prosaic origins became a dramatic curtain-raiser. Explains Kooper of Gregg's opening snare-drum bash, 'He's playing the upbeat of four before bar one—he played a pick-up into the song.' Retaining the count-in's final tap—instead of, as was standard, lopping the whole thing off—produced a truly lapels-grabbing entrée, one that Bruce Springsteen once memorably described as sounding like 'somebody'd kicked open the door to your mind'.

Dylan's alleged lover, Edie Sedgwick, Dylan's road manager, Bobby Neuwirth, and even Dylan himself have all been posited as the individual at whom Dylan directs his venom in 'Like A Rolling Stone'—named as 'Miss Lonely' and characterised as a once high and haughty individual fallen on hard times. Whatever the true target, said venom is goosebump-inducing. This figure—once inclined to laugh at the unfortunate, now not disposed to talk so loud or seem so proud and reduced (it's implied) to prostitution—receives no sympathy from a man who has written so many songs expressing concern for the socially and financially dispossessed. Instead, as the melody rises to a crescendo at the start of each chorus, Dylan howls at them, 'How does it *feel?*' It's hate of such an unadulterated nature that the listener is almost ashamed to be enjoying it.

'Stone' certainly brought an unprecedented malevolence to the Hot 100 when it proceeded to work its way up it. Because popular song was then largely preoccupied with romantic love, hurt and disdain were already part of its makeup. Not, though, this sort of spite. Yet, asked if he was surprised that 'Rolling Stone' was issued on 45rpm, Gorgoni says, 'No, because I think that's what they were going for. They were trying to make a hit with him.'

'Like A Rolling Stone' broke new ground in another way. 'The amazing thing was that it got on the radio,' says Kooper. 'It was twice as long as any record that was on the radio.' The disc's 6:06 playing time was the reason Columbia initially refused to release it. Dylan's insistence that it not be cut created a stand-off. It was ended only when an acetate was given to a New York disco that it so happened was a media haunt, prompting radio stations to request the non-existent release for broadcast purposes. Music labels simply do not decline demand for product. However, Columbia made sure stations also had access to a cut-down promotional copy of the disc. Most jocks, though, didn't bother with that and played the unexpurgated original. Although *Billboard*-centric history dictates that it was kept off the top of the American charts by The Beatles' 'Help!', 'Like A Rolling Stone' actually made no. 1 in the then just as esteemed *Cash Box* chart. Over in the UK—at that juncture in history, of course, the centre of the musical universe—there were an even greater number of competing charts. In the one published in *Record Retailer*—retroactively the most important, because it is the one referred to by the compilers of industry bible *Guinness British Hit Singles*—it made no. 2.

It's far more difficult to pronounce a single the greatest ever released than it is an album, there being so many more singles than there are long-players. Moreover, because they are individual songs, one's perception of them is far more dependent on mood than is an album, the multiple cuts of which provide—and create—a greater variety of tone and emotion. However, not many of the music cognoscenti would be prepared to enter into anything more than a half-hearted argument with you if you stated in their presence that 'Like A Rolling Stone' sits at the singles summit.

'Like A Rolling Stone' cemented Dylan's authority and pre-eminence. The Rolling Stones' '(I Can't Get No) Satisfaction'—released Stateside the month before—approached it in terms of being streetwise and belligerent, yet its ambience of dissension would have been unthinkable without the example Dylan had already set in his music. Moreover, great singles band though the Stones were, they were still a year away from being able to fill an album with their own compositions. The Beatles bestrode the world, but the polysyllabic words and quasi-psychology in the lyric of 'Help!' constituted them tentatively feeling their way out of their position as high-grade moon-in-June merchants. Moreover, their August album—also called *Help!*—showed that they weren't too grand to doff their collective cap: one of its tracks, 'You've Got To Hide Your Love Away', had a colloquialism, harmonica style, stretched melody, and bellyaching tone that fans of Dylan found very familiar. To some extent, the Fab Four extended that sound across an entire album in the shape of December's *Rubber Soul*, even if refracted through their own undisputed musical genius. Simply put, 'Like A Rolling Stone' put Dylan head and shoulders above anyone else in the rock milieu he had already greatly influenced and had now belatedly chosen to inhabit.

•

There followed a six-week gap in the sessions. It's tempting to romantically conclude that this was because the session that yielded the master of that momentous outpouring of hate left Dylan so drained that he needed to recover. However, the more mundane reality is that the interregnum enabled Dylan to write more material.

He had one gig in his diary in this period, on July 25, five days after 'Stone' was released. It was an event as epoch-marking as that record. This year, Dylan decided to play the Newport Folk Festival with a band.

The ensemble was ad hoc. 'This was a very last-minute thing of him playing electric,' says Al Kooper, who was the group's keyboardist. 'It was conceived at the festival. I didn't go to the festival to play with Bob Dylan—I went to the festival because I always went to the festival. I bought tickets. Then Albert saw me walking around and said, Can you meet us backstage tonight? Bob wants to talk to you.' Of the plan Dylan unveiled at that meeting, Kooper reflects, 'I think he wanted to sort of preview to his audience what was next when he asked us to play behind him.'

As well as Kooper, Albert Grossman recruited the nucleus of another festival act, the Paul Butterfield Blues Band: guitarist Michael Bloomfield, bassist Jerome Arnold, and drummer Sam Lay. To this trio was added Barry Goldberg on keyboards. Grossman was undeterred by the fact that Lay's experience was primarily restricted to rhythm & blues. Among his previous session clients were the illustrious likes of Howlin' Wolf, John Lee Hooker, Lightnin' Hopkins, and Muddy Waters. 'Anybody you put in front of me, I could play with them,' Lay says. 'I didn't know Bob Dylan from nobody else. He had a different style. I had never heard his style before, but I know one thing: I really enjoyed it, and I fell in love with it.'

Kooper: 'We stayed up the whole night before and rehearsed. This is a put-together band for this show, and so there was only one night to rehearse for it.' However, the events that were about to take place were for most preordained not by paucity of preparation time but by the very nature of what was being prepared. Dylan had already created some controversy at the previous year's festival by unveiling the allegedly bland, empty songs that would appear on *Another Side Of Bob Dylan*. However, Dylan had at least performed unaccompanied that day. Nineteen sixty-five was the first time the public—outside of Minnesotans in Dylan's youth—had seen Dylan playing in a band format. Dylan himself took to the Newport stage with a Fender Stratocaster strapped across his chest. Moreover, with his leather jacket and Cuban heels, he resembled the clichéd idea of a Carnaby Street mod. He looked and sounded like he had switched his affections from work-shirted earnestness to the flash and fun of the space age—something that for this particular demographic amounted to sacrilege. 'The real folk people were very narrow-minded, almost like stone jazz aficionados,' says Gorgoni. 'They're in that one niche as far as what they accept and what they acknowledge. The taste these days is way more eclectic.'

As Dylan performed 'Maggie's Farm' from the last album, his brand-new record 'Like A Rolling Stone', and what was then still called 'Phantom Engineer', sounds of disquiet and disgust emanated from the crowd. When Dylan left the stage after that trio of songs, it was to a loud chorus of boos. Shortly thereafter, he returned to play solo acoustic versions of *Home*'s 'It's All Over Now, Baby Blue' and 'Mr. Tambourine Man'. That much is undisputed. Disagreement ensues when it comes to interpretation of those facts.

Sam Lay repeats the conventional wisdom when he says, 'The people wasn't satisfied. They didn't want that band up there with Dylan, they wanted him acoustic-style. We was a loud band, and electrified at that. Bloomfield plays a supersonic sound.' He also says, 'He did "Maggie's Farm" and it wasn't played right. I had heard the record, and it didn't sound like the record.' However, Lay admits his opinion is based on what he was told after the fact ('I didn't know Dylan that much,' he reiterates). It's a version of events that is fiercely rejected by Kooper. 'He wasn't being booed,' Kooper insists. 'It's so ridiculous how history is corrupted. Bob played on the last night, so people came from all over the country and sat through a lot of music that they probably didn't care for to hear Bob play. They had all kinds of music there: gospel singers and Irish music. It was quite a compendium of folk music. And most people played on stage for between forty-five minutes and sixty minutes, and we came out and played for fifteen minutes—and we were the headliners. So, I think from what I saw that people were very upset that he only played for fifteen minutes. . . . We only learned three songs, so that's what we played. People weren't upset that he played electric— although I'm sure some people were—but I think people were going, *More, more,* rather than booing.' Kooper adds, 'There were people that had played electric instruments over the weekend before Bob came up. One of them was the Paul Butterfield band.' As for Dylan's pop-star outfit, Kooper shrugs, 'Well, I mean, let's face it, from the beginning, he didn't look like a regular folk singer. He didn't look like The Clancy Brothers.'

A further theory is that people were upset by poor sound quality, one aspect of which rendered Dylan's voice inaudible to some sections.

'He was always a quiet type of person,' says Lay of Dylan. 'You talk to him, he'll talk to you, but he just wasn't the kind to just butt in and volunteer no kind of statement.' However, asked if after the Newport performance Dylan seemed upset or downcast at his reception, the drummer says, 'No, by no means. That night we huddled up in a room where we were staying: Joan Baez, all of us, was together that night, and Bill Monroe and The Bluegrass Boys. He seemed the same.'

Crucially, though, Dylan himself seems to have assumed that the hostility he faced was due to his new sonic approach. His next gig was at Forest Hills in New York, on August 28, where he introduced an electric second set to his stage act. The event was photographed by Daniel Kramer, who recalls a troop address by Dylan beforehand. Kramer: 'I heard him say to the musicians, You might get some booing tonight. They might do that. That's nothing to do with us. We do our music and we do our bit and we let it happen.' The Newport experience also seems to have led Dylan to write one of his most bitter songs, one that he ensured to lay down upon his return to the studio.

•

When Dylan went back to 799 7th Avenue on July 29, an unfamiliar face was looking out from the window of the control booth. For a reason that has never been formally revealed, Tom Wilson was no longer the artist's producer.

A certain amount of friction between Dylan and Wilson can certainly be discerned from the last session's recordings. To a certain extent, it revolved around Kooper. When Wilson gave the instruction to start take one of 'Like A Rolling Stone', there was a hiccup when it was pointed out that the organ player hadn't located his headphones. 'You gotta *watch*, Tom,' admonished Dylan. Kooper describes such rebukes as 'sort of unnecessary', but there was another terse moment during a playback after Wilson had shown reluctance to follow Dylan's instruction to bring up Kooper's instrument in the mix on the grounds that he wasn't an organ player. 'Don't tell me who's an organ player and who's not,' snapped the artist. Asked if this incident illustrates that Dylan was trying to assert his authority over Wilson, Kooper says, 'Oh no, that's ludicrous. He could have said whatever he wanted. It wasn't like that. Tom was smart enough to not really enforce anything, and he tried to help Bob out any way he could. He didn't have politics in his blood at all, in terms of his vocation.' Kooper admits of the general atmosphere that day that 'it was tense' but adds, 'Knowing Tom Wilson prior to that, I can't imagine why.' Of the notion of any resident conflict, he says, 'I think it was between Tom and Albert Grossman, actually.'

The suggestion that Grossman may have instigated the putsch has some credence: after all, he had played a part in the installation of Wilson over John Hammond. Then there is the fact that few seem to think Wilson a great producer. Asked if Wilson was proactive in his role, Frank Owens says, 'No, he was not. He was easy-going, I'll put it that way.' Some musicians found him actively exasperating. Vic Briggs, guitarist with Eric Burdon & The Animals, recalled to this author of his group's later association with Wilson, 'Tom basically didn't use to do much of anything. He divided up his time between drawing American football plays on pieces of paper and calling up white women he wanted to screw. It seemed like he wanted to get the thing over with as quickly as possible. Occasionally he'd even listen to the music.'

Grossman, incidentally, is recalled by eyewitnesses as a constant but unobtrusive presence at the *Highway 61* sessions. 'His main presence I think in life was to be his projection of Buddha, the all-knowing, knowledgeable guy who made sure that everything went according to plan,' says Harvey Goldstein. 'He had some role in the decision-making of the music, but I would say not that much. In Dylan's case, it was pretty much his whims and his taste, but Albert was his facilitator. What Albert did up to a point was, he made the right business decisions for Bob that put him in a good place financially.'

Wilson was soon gone from Columbia, moving to MGM for what he later candidly admitted was 'more money'. Among artists he would go on to produce are The Mothers Of Invention, The Velvet Underground, The Animals, their psychedelic successors Eric Burdon & The Animals, Nico, and Soft Machine. In 1968, Wilson resigned as MGM A&R director in order to set up the Tom Wilson Organization, an umbrella company that took in several production, management, and publishing companies. He also did production work for Motown and co-wrote an R&B opera titled *Mind Flyers Of Gondwana* that was envisaged as involving Gladys Knight, Bob Marley, and Stanley Kubrick, although these ambitious plans ultimately came to nothing. Wilson suffered ill-health, Marfan syndrome resulting in a heart attack in 1976 and another, fatal one in 1978. 'His roster of people that he'd signed was pretty amazing,' says Kooper. 'I think he's overlooked quite a bit.'

Wilson's replacement was Bob Johnston. Born in Texas in 1932, Johnston was a Columbia staff producer who had started out as a songwriter and stumbled into work behind the console pretty much by accident. Nashville musician Charlie McCoy recalls, 'He was writing for the publishing company owned by Elvis. He came here to try to get songs in Elvis movies. He hired me to be a session leader, so we started doing demos of these songs of his and actually, he did get six or seven songs in Elvis movies.' Among Johnston compositions rendered by The King are 'It Hurts Me' and 'Let Yourself Go'. McCoy: 'Some of the songs that were rejected he took to New York to Columbia Records, to just pitch for whatever artist. The head of A&R there was a guy called Bob Mercy. He was impressed with the demos and he asked him, Where did you do these? He said, I did them in Nashville. He said, You produced these? He said, I did. And he said, Man, this is great, do you ever think about wanting to be a producer? He was pretty smart: he said, Of course. And the guy said, Well, we have an artist at the end of her contract and we need a hit on her. Would you like to take a shot at this? And he said, Absolutely. What's her name? And he said, Patti Page. Now, Patti Page was a big artist in America, but she was having a long dry spell. So, using his connections in Hollywood, [Johnston] found a movie that had a theme [song] and they needed a recording of it with a singer. So he got the rights to go record the song and he had a big hit record with Patti Page, revived her career. The song was called "Hush, Hush, Sweet Charlotte". After he had the hit with Patti Page, Bob Mercy said, Hey, what would you think about trying to record with Bob Dylan?'

In some senses, it was hardly a logical suggestion. 'Hush, Hush, Sweet Charlotte' was a lush production featuring a string section, the type of music of which Dylan's work was considered almost the converse. 'Well, of course, "Hush, Hush, Sweet Charlotte" was pretty much cut and dried the way it needed to be done,' says McCoy. 'He goes from an artist who actually needs a producer to these singer/songwriters who are doing their own thing, like Dylan and like Leonard Cohen. These artists were all people who were almost arranging on the spot, the way they wrote and played. If he had continued on the line with normal kind of artists like Patti Page, perhaps his career would have turned out a whole lot different, but the fact that he got into this folk-rock field with these very creative singer/songwriters, it changed everything.'

'He tells a lot of jokes,' says Kooper of Johnston. 'He was the antithesis of Tom Wilson. Bob Johnston's a country boy.' Kooper wasn't impressed by the newcomer. 'He was invisible,' he says. 'He didn't really influence anything. His key method of producing a record was encouraging the artist, saying, Boy, this is fantastic, this is the best record I've ever been involved with. I never did that when I produced records. I was the opposite. I would say, Well, that's really good, but let's go to the bridge, because we have problems here, and see if we can fix that.'

McCoy, asked if Johnston was the kind of producer who knew what all the bells and whistles were for, says, 'I think so. He was pretty sharp. . . . He was just keeping hands-off of Dylan and let Dylan go where he wanted to. On the Patti Page session, he was absolutely hands-on.' He also points out, 'Remember now, this was only the second artist he'd ever produced. So, as far as being, quote, a producer, this was so new that it wasn't like we had Phil Spector in there.'

'I don't think there was any room for Johnston to do anything,' says Goldstein. 'The only thing that was happening was in the studio. . . . His role as a producer was basic. Bob wasn't listening to him, musically. [Johnston] was a quality producer, but it wasn't that kind of thing that he could have that influence. He was basically going, Okay, take one— go. You want to try another one, Bob? But it wasn't like he was leading the session.' Goldstein adds, 'You couldn't get a better engineer than Roy Halee.' Halee would eventually work for—as engineer or producer— everyone from The Dave Clark Five to The Byrds to Barbra Streisand to Journey, and extensively for Simon & Garfunkel. 'Whatever you gave him was going to be represented,' says Goldstein of Halee. Kooper, meanwhile, adds that whether it was Wilson or Johnston in the control booth, 'Highway 61 was a very chaotic group of sessions in that no one was in charge.'

However he did it, Johnston made a palpable difference. Although nobody makes a claim for him being of the same auteur stripe as Spector, Johnston's tenure as Dylan's producer saw his client's sonic landscapes take on a significantly greater breadth and polish. The six albums they recorded together encompass Dylan's most celebrated work.

Maybe symbolically, Johnston's first day in the job was long and fruitful. Supposedly, there were two separate sessions on the 29th, one from 10am to 1pm, the other from 2:30 to 6pm. The first session was engineered by Dauria and Frank Laico and saw Dylan theoretically backed by Gregg, Macho Jr., Griffin, Kooper (invited back to play organ for the sessions' duration by a Dylan clearly pleased with his 'commando raid' work), and Bloomfield. At the second session (engineers Laico and Ted Brosnan), Macho was theoretically displaced by Russ Savakus and Griffin by Frank Owens. Yet bassist Harvey Goldstein says he played on 'Positively 4th Street', 'It Takes A Lot To Laugh, It Takes A Train To Cry', and 'Tombstone Blues', naming the three tracks recorded this day. Furthermore, although he knew Savakus and was on the sessions for almost the remainder, Goldstein says he did not clap eyes on Savakus then or afterwards. More than one Dylan chronicler has suggested that Savakus bailed out of this date because he had difficulty getting to grips with electric bass, which he had never played before. 'The upright bass was pretty much the standard in the early 60s, and then toward the middle 60s, the Fender bass started to become [dominant],' says Gorgoni. 'The more aggressive the rock started to become, then the electric bass was required. Also, the sensibility of the electric instrument is a little different from the stand-up bass. They were more jazz-oriented.' As usual, the session details don't make clear who played on which tracks or takes.

The recording sheet renders 'It Takes A Lot To Laugh' as 'Phantom

Engineers', 'Tombstone Blues' as 'Tombstone', and 'Positively 4th Street' as 'Black Dalli Rue'. The versions of the first two tracks that would appear on the album came from these sessions, as did the completed take that would turn the last-named into Dylan's follow-up hit to 'Like A Rolling Stone'.

Goldstein explains of his arrival, 'I was playing at a club in Manhattan and I got a call on a break in a burger place right next door. [It was] Al Kooper saying that Dylan was having a problem with the bass player. He's a childhood friend of mine, and he had said, I know this bass player that could be good. And so he got me onto the session. That was really my entrance into the world of pop music.' Although Goldstein notes, 'Kooper knew me because I played rock'n'roll with him, we did a lot of gigs,' he adds, 'Never heard of Dylan, I had no clue who he was. I was into jazz. The gig I was playing was a guy who was like Trini Lopez.' Recording-wise, he says, 'I hadn't done anything professionally. This put me in a whole other place. . . . It was like landing in a foreign land, adapting to what was going on there.'

Goldstein arrived at the studio alone. 'The first thing I saw when I came in was Albert. Nobody even looked at me. They were listening to a take. In fact, it might have been "Rolling Stone". It took about ten or fifteen minutes before anybody even said anything to me. Then Dylan turned around and said, Hi, man. Then basically I was just standing there, so I walked into the studio, found the bass amp, plugged in, started to tune up. Eventually, Dylan came into the studio. Kooper came in. Then Bloomfield barged into the room, started to talk . . . Bloomfield was like just a burst of energy. Running through the studio door with a Fender Telecaster on his shoulder, no case, wearing penny loafers and no jacket. . . . Then we started to noodle around. Then I met Bobby Gregg.' Of the latter—who would be his partner in the rhythm section during the album's sessions—Goldstein says, 'I measure a great drummer by how much work I have to do, and all I had to do was just kind of follow. I had a basic idea of the chord changes, so I can anticipate he could go either here or there, but I was pretty much able to just sit with Bobby on the bass drum and take his lead on the fills. A good drummer makes that happen. He drove the sound. He provided the engine.'

Adding to the stranger-in-a-strange-land vibe was the fact that what Goldstein was hearing was unlike anything he'd encountered in any musical idiom: 'I had no idea what the music was. What I knew about songs was, there was logical progressions. These didn't necessarily conform to that. There was not a guaranteed time structure or chord structure. It was in flux.' Dylan provided no help in the sense of guidance: 'His basic instruction was just, Follow what I'm doing. He never said anything about chord changes. He'd be writing some of the lyrics for the next tune as we were doing that tune. It was total impressionism. Pretty much all the songs, he would just start it off and we'd start playing it. And I think all of it was one or two takes, three takes maybe.' He noted that Dylan was not merely executing a guide vocal for the takes that could be replaced by a proper one later: 'It was for real.'

Kooper says the minimal-takes/no-overdubs policy to which Dylan has almost always cleaved derives from the fact that 'he's interested in the realness and spontaneity of everyone playing together', although he adds that a certain shyness may be behind the zero-instruction approach.

'I think it's a good method,' says Goldstein. 'It became normal. I don't mean just with Dylan, I mean generally in studio sessions.' Across the course of his career, Goldstein has experienced multiple different approaches to recording. 'Like, I did a project with Seals & Croft. We did the album that had "Summer Breeze" and "Hummingbird", and on those things we really did pre-production. We worked it out. We went over it until when we went into the studio. It was a performance of a polished piece of music. That's one way of doing it. I've done a lot of things, as with Bob and other artists, where it's spontaneous, and the excitement of the spontaneity is as valid as the pre-production, the polishing. Sometimes the performances are better because they're more urgent. If you're going to polish something, you better have good content. Bob's main thing, his type of artist, where it's lyric-based, it's the performance of the lyric. The music accompanies the lyric, but it's not the main focus. It generates a feeling.'

Dylan's college friend Tony Glover was present at this session and has recalled Dylan turning around the tempo and feel of 'It Takes A Lot To Laugh' during a lunch break. The session sheets bear him out to some extent, for they show the day's work starting with the song and then after three takes (two completes, one short breakdown) it being set aside so that 'Tombstone Blues' could be attempted, before being returned to for four more passes (two completes, two short breakdowns), the last complete take of which (and indeed the last pass) was deemed the best performance. The change Dylan made was an act of sublime inspiration, transforming a bobbing, cawing, and insufferably smart-aleck number into a slow, tender, sensual mood piece. Even the nomenclature was inspired: as was common with Dylan songs of this period, its final title is interesting in and of itself and—simply by dint of it not appearing in the lyric—mysterious.

'It Takes A Lot To Laugh, It Takes A Train To Cry' is the first— and still one of the few—Dylan tracks that can be described as impressionistic. However, although its effect is dependent more on its instrumentation and ambience than its lyric, the latter—a touching, laid-back celebration of the joys of being in love—is both plenty good and delivered by Dylan with a throat-catching vulnerability. Goldstein's bass plucking and Griffin's alternately rumbling and splashing piano work also impress highly. Over four leisurely minutes, Dylan and the band truly enjoy themselves, getting into a groove in which Dylan's harmonica roams in and out at will. Exquisite on every level, this track should be played to silence anyone who claims that Dylan cannot play harmonica or sing.

A point to be made here is that Dylan's move over to rock could easily have seen him ceasing to use harmonica, an instrument he'd thus far employed to add colour and variety to what would otherwise be unfurnished soundscapes. At this very point in time, contemporaries gifted on the instrument, like John Lennon, Mick Jagger, and Brian Jones, were audibly losing interest in it. That Dylan retained his despite now having auxiliary musicians to help fulfil his visions gave him a unique sound in the musical world: he would now habitually use harmonica where on other rock artists' recordings a guitar or keyboard solo would normally reside.

Perhaps Dylan decided to make 'It Takes A Lot To Laugh' a more benign song because he was a little spiritually weary after eleven takes of the extraordinarily vituperative 'Tombstone Blues'. Not that there's anything wrong, musically or lyrically, with this rolling, thunderous denunciation of militarism, social inequity, and the outrages perpetrated in the name of religion (with references to venereal disease tossed into the radical brew for good measure). Dylan's merciless scrutiny, however, might have left him wondering—like John the Baptist in the lyric, after reluctantly torturing a thief for a merciless God—if there was a hole handy for him to get sick in.

There were four short breakdowns, three long, and four completes, the last complete being chosen for the album. Despite its sacrilegious nature, and despite Bloomfield teasing out characteristically spiky lines throughout, there could conceivably have been a quasi-gospel flavour to 'Tombstone Blues', courtesy of a soul vocal group. Recalls Kooper, 'There was a version that we did with The Chambers Brothers singing backup vocals. I actually was sorry that they didn't keep that. They were singing the chorus every time Bob sang the chorus.'

Although some assume that 'It Ain't Me Babe' is Dylan's disguised put-down of those who wished him to remain within the protest field, 'Positively 4th Street' seems to be a denunciation of those who felt he should stick to folk stripped of any such veil. Although there is a 4th Street in Minneapolis, where Dylan attended university, few doubt that it is the denizens of Dylan's former home of Greenwich Village's West

4th Street into whom he is tearing in the other song that was recorded that day. 'Positively 4th Street' was recorded a mere four days after his bumpy reception at the Newport festival. An interpretation that the composition is his instant, shaken response to that event would dictate that Dylan is assuming that some of the people booing him there were the folkies and the radicals who had been his sycophantic admirers at 4th Street hangouts. After four short breakdowns, three long, and three completes, the last complete was chosen for the master.

Studio records state that the following day again saw two sessions, although Kooper's note of caution over their reliability/comprehensibility seems to be borne out by the fact that Savakus and Goldstein are noted as present for both, something Goldstein's memory dictates is an impossibility. Also noted as being in attendance on the first session (2:30–5:30pm, engineered by Halee and Dauria) is a pianist rendered by the session-sheet notation only as 'Arthur . . . ??' The ever-present formidable nucleus of Gregg, Kooper, and Bloomfield made up the rest of the crew. The only recorded personnel difference for the second session (7:00–10:00pm, engineers Halee and Larry Keyes) was Paul Griffin displacing the mysterious Arthur.

The recording sheets note the taping this day of 'Lunatic Princess No. 3', 'Look At Barry Run', and, simply, '???'. The songs would become better known as 'From A Buick 6', 'Can You Please Crawl Out Your Window', and 'Desolation Row'.

The first of this trilogy is an up-tempo piece of R&B that would be the final album's only real throwaway track. It was wrapped up in four takes; two short breakdowns were followed by two completes, the second of which was designated the master. It is perceived by Dylanologists to be a tribute to Sara Lownds, a divorced mother of one whom Dylan would marry in November 1965, although—as pop stars did at the time—he initially kept his nuptials secret. Its compliments are typically idiosyncratic ('She walks like Bo Diddley and she don't need no crutch'). Its slightly monotonous feel and generic chugging blues lick make it sound like it belongs less on this album than on *Bringing It All Back Home*, while Kooper's relentless organ swoops are rather suffocating. It's at least brief, being, with the title track, one of only two songs from the final album to come in under four minutes. At a time when The Beatles were still cramming fourteen songs onto thirty-five-minute albums, six of this fifty-one-and-a-half-minute album's songs clock in at over five and a half minutes, some well over.[*]

In contrast to the brevity of 'Buick"s recording process, 'Can You Please Crawl Out Your Window' was a nightmare to capture. Something about this composition's stop-start, quasi-syncopated structure led to the assembled musicians having to make twenty-one attempts to nail it, an astounding number of takes for Dylan, then or now. There was one long breakdown, five complete takes, and no fewer than fifteen short breakdowns. However, although that last complete (and indeed the last attempt of the song at the sessions) was released as a single, it was only by accident, finding its way onto the A-side of what was supposed to be 'Positively 4th Street' before the mis-pressing was spotted. The song became the follow-up to that latter single in December 1965, but only after another dozen passes at it, and with a completely new set of musicians—The Hawks—backing the composer. All this endeavour was to little avail. As Goldstein notes of its troubled gestation, 'Had it worked, you wouldn't have had all those problems.' Or, put another way, you can't polish a turd.

The session's last song was 'Desolation Row', a Dylan epic in the vein of 'Chimes Of Freedom', 'Gates Of Eden', and 'It's All Right, Ma (I'm Only Bleeding)'. Kooper recalls of this pass at the song that it was 'done very late at night. Bobby Gregg had already left. Harvey and I were just hanging out and Bob said, I'd like to cut this. Bloomfield was gone as well, so I played guitar and Harvey played bass and Bob played guitar.' Dylan ran it down (musicians' language for the demonstration

---

[*] There is an even worse version of 'Buick' released on initial Japanese copies of the album.

of the chord changes immediately prior to recording). 'He said, Here's how it goes, and then he showed us the basic song. Maybe two or three verses.'

Goldstein's reaction to this miniature preview of 'Desolation Row' was 'It was a strong song, but musically it was just repeating over and over again. ... So the [task] would be to make it interesting. Not a lot of fun on my part.' As Dylan had demonstrated only two or three verses, Goldstein had no idea the song would last nearly twelve minutes. During the single take attempted, the bassist became probably the only discerning human being ever to be bored by 'Desolation Row'. 'I almost fell asleep because it just kept going on and going on and going on,' he says. 'I wasn't that caught up in that lyric. Shortly after that, I understood more about how these things work, and I would have absorbed the lyric and reacted to the lyric more. So it was a big lesson to me.' He also says, 'The fact that he didn't use it also said to me, Well, you weren't doing something right, but I think more than that is that the bass didn't actually fit on that particular tune.'

The first pass at the song was decent enough—as listening to it on the 2005 compilation *No Direction Home* will attest—but not quite good enough to be used. 'It's completely different,' says Kooper, whose electric guitar could also be said to not fit the song. He laments, 'I wish that Bobby Gregg had stayed there because it would have been great with drums on it.'*

After a weekend break, sessions reconvened on Monday, August 2. Once more, two separate sessions are annotated—these both overseen by the production team of Johnston, Halee, and Keyes—the earliest of which ran from 8pm to 11pm, the second from midnight to 3am.

---

* Note: some sources have suggested the previous day as the origin of this recording of 'Desolation Row'. There are several further alternative versions and demos of the song—and many others—on *The Bootleg Series Vol. 12: The Cutting Edge 1965–1966*, a 2015 collection of demos and outtakes from *Bringing It All Back Home*, *Highway 61 Revisited*, and *Blonde On Blonde*.

Confusingly, Frank Owens is noted as present from 8pm to 11:30pm and Paul Griffin from 11pm to 3:30am. Even more confusingly, there's a half-hour overlap in which they were theoretically manning the same piano. Gregg, Kooper, Goldstein, and Bloomfield were all present for the duration. Newport Festival alumnus Sam Lay, meanwhile, is down as drumming from 8pm to 11pm.

Although he received no credit on the album sleeve (something he shares with Macho Jr., Bruce Langhorne, and 'Arthur … ??'), it has been suggested that Lay (listed on the session sheet as 'Samuel ??') played on the outtakes of more than one song. 'No, I don't recall doing that,' he says. 'I remember that one thing.' That one thing is the title track, of which he says, 'They kept it and they used it, and that is my drumming on there.' Even if it hadn't been merely a one-song gig, his day's work was curiously expensive, for on top of being one of the highest-paid sessioners around, Lay had to be fetched from Chicago to replace Gregg (the reason for whose absence from this part of the day's sessions is not known). Recalls Lay, 'I didn't ask no questions. I grabbed my bag and took off. I only had about an hour to get there and I made it. Just happened the flight was leaving.' Perhaps Dylan wanted something from Lay that he felt Gregg was unable to provide. Certainly, the rapid-fire work Lay executes on a track listed simply as 'Highway 61' on the recording sheet makes it the most propulsive thing on the record. There were ten passes at it, evenly divided between five quick breakdowns and five complete takes. The last complete was the tenth pass and was used for the master.

The song starts with God demanding that Abraham kill him a son and 'Able' responding, 'Man, you must be putting me on.' Merely comical though those lines may seem today, in the mid-60s, especially in the US, they were, for many, jaw-dropping in their heretical nature. 'You think that we were there listening to the words?' says Kooper. 'We really weren't. We were trying to get the music worked out.' On a similar theme, he says the album's musicians were not cognisant during the recording process of just how revolutionary it was going to be. 'And that includes me. Our mentality was to satisfy the artist and the producer, and [make sure] that they were happy with what we were playing.' However, Goldstein—who had sat glassy-eyed through 'Desolation Row'—asserts of the lyric, 'It caught my ear. It was that strong.' Not that cruelty committed in the name of a deity was all that Dylan was examining: every shyster, hypocrite, predator, and bull artist in America seems to gravitate in his lyric toward the titular motorway. The reason for Dylan choosing this as the album's title song may lie somewhere in the fact that said artery constituted his physical escape route from a Minnesota he has admitted he spent much of his formative years plotting to leave.

The musical punctuation is for once not provided by Dylan's harmonica. Instead, an amusing high-pitched whistling is to be heard. Bizarrely, there is some dispute about whence that singular sound emanated and who provided the relevant instrument. Lay recalls, 'I had a bunch of keys in my bag on a little ring with a whistle on it. Sound like a police siren with a high pitch to it. I was getting my drums put in place, and I recall taking that police whistle out of my pocket on my key ring to lay it down, and I blew that thing and you hear that on that record. He asked me, What is it?' Yet Al Kooper tells a different story. 'I used to wear this siren around my neck, and Bob asked me if he could borrow it for "Highway 61",' he says. 'It was a siren you blew into. I just used to carry it with me because I would use it at appropriate moments in my life. It was one of my trademarks.'

The day was again extremely productive, yielding masters not just of the title track but also 'Just Like Tom Thumb's Blues', 'Queen Jane Approximately', and 'Ballad Of A Thin Man'. Says Goldstein, 'That was the beef. That was the best day. Pretty amazing actually.' As if capturing a quartet of some of the most staggeringly brilliant recordings of all time was not enough, the sheets also record five passes at 'Desolation Row'—four short breakdowns and one whose result is unclear.

'Just Like Tom Thumb's Blues' memorably traces a sweaty descent into paranoia and drug dependency against an incongruously elegant backdrop dominated by pianos of both electric and tack variety. The jewel in the crown of several memorable lines has to be the divinely scene-summing and colloquial 'Because the cops don't need you and, man, they expect the same'. Although the end result is exquisite, its sixteen takes suggest it was a problematic song to perfect. There were eight short breakdowns, three long, and five completes. The fifth complete (and last pass) was chosen. Amazingly, there was an even better rendition than the one on the album: not only does what is described merely as an 'earlier take' on *No Direction Home* have a more streamlined melody, its first vocal line is in tune. The latter blemish on the familiar version would have been a simple matter to correct with a punch-in, but evidently Dylan's purism about overdubbing made it *verboten*. Reasons Goldstein, 'He was a perfectionist in the sense of, he knew when he had it. He said, Okay, this might be out of tune here, this might be a wrong note here, but I got the song, and that's what's important.'

'Queen Jane Approximately' is, implausibly, even more majestic. Some have suggested that this half-solicitous, half-mocking composition is about Joan Baez, a suspicion that partly stems from the fact that the previous year Baez had released a version of the traditional 'The Death Of Queen Jane'. However, this interpretation takes no account of the fact that, if one is to assume that Dylan is once again talking to himself in the second person, the advisers who heave their plastic at the feet of Queen Jane to both convince her of her pain and that her conclusions should be more drastic can plainly be seen as folkies and radicals invoking Dylan's previous record releases and telling him (oddly, but inescapably in this reading, the queen in question) that he should go back to the protest songs where they know his heart really lies. For Goldstein, that the song may not mean the same thing to the listener as it does to the composer is irrelevant. 'You can make of it what you want—that's his whole point,' he reasons. '*I'm just putting it out for you to hear and for you to enjoy and interpret any way you want. It's already served me by coming out.'*

While the subject of the lyric can be disputed, few would disagree with the proposition that the accompaniment is transcendently beautiful, especially the shimmering arpeggio from Bloomfield before each verse's first occurrence of the line 'Won't you come see me, Queen Jane?' The pause Dylan leaves for said broken chord demonstrates precisely the sort of understanding of the dynamics of playing with a band that had been lacking on his previous album. The artist now seems to fully comprehend that the musicians can contribute to his songs instead of being servants to them, meaning that his switch to rock actually has an aesthetic validity, rather than 'merely' constituting a cultural statement. Asked if he felt that Dylan was learning how to mesh with the group as the album progressed, Goldstein says, 'Oh, absolutely. It's a big transition to have the freedom to do what you want to do. Luckily, all the players that were playing with him to varying degrees could be flexible with him, but still, the structure was maintained on those songs. And, for him, it was another discipline to do that.' Kooper adds, 'I think that he was learning how to phrase the song based on the difference between how he wrote it and how the band was playing it. I think that's a more accurate appraisal of what was going on.'

That the arpeggio is so delightful that it's the type of thing a listener awaits with keen anticipation cannot do anything but suggest that Dylan was perfectly comfortable with the fact that he was now making recordings for whose pleasing qualities he—unlike with his one-man-and-a-guitar albums—could not always take the credit. 'He didn't have a problem with that at all,' says Goldstein. 'He's not that kind of selfish person. That enhanced him, so he was happy.'

Dylan again proves that profoundly unconventional though his singing is, it can still be in its own way perfect: he enunciates the line 'When yo-o-r *sick* of all this repetition' quite retchingly.

'It was tough to record,' says Kooper of 'Queen Jane'. 'It was tough to get everybody to play it perfectly because it has a lot of unexpected things in it—how long you hold this chord and that you'd go to this chord.' Nonetheless, the recording wasn't an example of the bitty process of endless false starts in the manner of some other tracks. Four complete takes were achieved, in addition to two short breakdowns. The last complete pass became the master.

While the above three tracks were described on the recording sheet as, respectively, 'Highway 61', 'Juarez', and 'Queen Jane', the logs unexpectedly correctly state the title of a song it would have been understandable to assume was called 'Mr. Jones'. Goldstein remembers Dylan's instructions to the musicians for 'Ballad Of A Thin Man' as 'The word *dark* or *spooky*. Dark in the sense of colour.' It certainly was those things, taking the paranoia of 'Just Like Tom Thumb's Blues' to stygian depths. A slow number with doomy piano (audaciously played by Dylan himself, despite the two distinguished pianists he has to hand) and macabre organ, Kooper notes that its music is 'more sophisticated than anything else on the album'.

He could have added that its tune was the artist's most impressive yet. Something that got lost in the furore over Dylan selling out/going electric was that he had simultaneously made the leap to writing his own melodies (or, if we are to believe his teenage musical bandmates, leapt back to it). Up until now, Dylan's effortless lyrical facility was an almost embarrassing contrast to a musical penchant for second-hand tunes. *Highway 61 Revisited* would be Dylan's first album where his listeners weren't able to observe of any of its tracks that he had deployed 'No More Auction Block', 'Nottamun Town', or some other old-as-the-hills tune as its base. Ending his practice of co-opting copyright-free melodies for his lyrical visions was by no means an insignificant development: there was no guarantee that his own melodies would be any good. While anyone can devise generic 'top lines'—especially someone like Dylan who can dazzle and distract with spellbinding words—fewer can write tunes that are actively compelling. It so happened that Dylan had that facility. In the specific case of 'Ballad Of A Thin Man', he produced a smouldering melody with a remarkably elongated, tension-building bridge.

As for the lyric, Kooper recalls, 'The first time we got a take that we could listen to, we all went in the control room, and when it finished, Bobby Gregg said, I don't know about the rest of you guys, but I can't play on a song with words like that—and just cracked everybody up, including Bob.' Gregg was joking, but the words—portraying a man stranded in a terrifyingly alien environment—were arresting even by Dylan's standards. The song is the perfect example of the fact that whatever the controversy surrounding his renouncing 'finger-pointing songs', Dylan was still a voice of dissent: his song words may lately have become more elliptical, but they remained unmistakably the product of a questioning and querulous mind, and Dylan's hipster persona only deepened the perception among the rebellious young and the left that he was somebody who was, as it were, on their side. Proof of this would be provided in September of that year, when *Esquire* magazine featured on the cover of its 'Back To College' issue, beneath the strapline '4 of the 28 who count most with the college rebels', a montage illustration of four faces: those of Fidel Castro, John F. Kennedy, Malcolm X, and Dylan. Consequently, this song's famous refrain—'Something is happening here and you don't know what it is—*do* you, Mr. Jones?'—was instantly interpreted as an attack on a bewildered pillar of straight society. In other words, 'Ballad Of A Thin Man' is widely assumed to be precursors to The Kinks' 'Well Respected Man', The Beatles' 'Nowhere Man', and The Jam's 'Mr. Clean', all songs mocking or denouncing a straight/square/conservative. One individual even took the song personally: a journalist named Jeffrey Jones claimed the composition was written as a put-down of him after he was commissioned by *Time* to write a feature whose motif would be the rebirth of the harmonica in popular music. Managing to grab a few minutes with Dylan at the Newport Folk Festival, he exasperated him with his banal questions ('It seems to be, like, very important in folk music. I mean, after the guitar, probably the second-most-played instrument. They wanted me to find out what you think'). Later that day in a hotel dining room, he found himself seated adjacent to Dylan's party, from which table Dylan mocked him by calling out, 'Gettin' it all down, Mr. Jones?'

No doubt the perennially playful Dylan was happily conscious of the fact that most would perceive the song to be an uncomplicated, self-righteous denunciation of a notional figure of convention and decorum. Jeffrey Jones, meanwhile, would seem to have encountered Dylan after the song had already been completed, with coincidence creating the inevitable piss-taking result. Dylan aficionados, let alone journalists— either conservative or radical—should know better, however, than to assume him capable of such a one-dimensional, hackneyed approach. He was by now way past such methods. The 'straight' bit, in fact, seems correct only in one sense. Homosexual allusion litters Dylan's songs, and yet strangely it is seldom picked up on by the army of people who analyse his lyrics, something that one critic—Craig McGregor—has likened to a 'conspiracy of silence'. Lines in 'Ballad Of A Thin Man' such as the one about the sword swallower approaching Mr. Jones and then kneeling seem to leave little room for doubt that this is a song exploring sexual activity outside orthodox patterns, and possibly Dylan's ambivalent feelings about such.

There were three takes: one quick breakdown followed by two completes. The second complete was chosen for the master, despite Dylan audibly almost cracking up on the line where he tells Mr. Jones that he tries so hard—another example, it would seem, of Dylan's preference for impressionistic power over formal perfection. At the same time, though, the track was subject to the album's first 'insert', something apparently done on the day. It's not known what was overdubbed, but considering the way that Dylan's voice is projected so that—uniquely for the album—it sounds as if it's directly in front of the listener's face, it would be logical to wonder whether the entire vocal track was the addition. Goldstein, though, says, 'He had a lot of gobos [screens, aka baffle boards] because it was a ballad, and they went out of their way to preserve leakage. He didn't have all the band coming into his microphone, so automatically his voice is going to have more presence, and they can also use a better quality mic. I think they used a U 47 on that one.' Kooper says that if the track was mixed specifically to achieve that effect of immediate presence, it was nothing to do with any nous on the part of Johnston. 'This was not a function of the producer, this was a function of whoever was mixing the record, like the engineer,' he asserts. 'There were some producers that are very knowledgeable about engineering, especially later on, because some of them were ex-engineers. But Tom Wilson and Bob Johnston didn't really know fuck-all about engineering. They had no idea that you could do something like that.'

In contrast to the insistence on a single take of the last album's equivalent marathon, 'Bob Dylan's 115th Dream', Dylan still hankered to perfect 'Desolation Row'. Enter famous Nashville session man Charlie McCoy (although not too famous to have his name misspelt 'Charley' on the album sleeve). McCoy was present due to the machinations of his friend Bob Johnston. 'He said to me, Hey, if you're ever in New York, I can get you Broadway theatre tickets,' McCoy recalls. 'In 1965, I had occasion to go to New York. I called him up and I said, Okay, I'm here, how about the theatre tickets? He said, No problem, but first this afternoon I'm recording Bob Dylan. I'd like for you to come over and meet him at the Columbia studios. He introduced us, and Dylan said to me, Hey, I'm getting ready to record a song. Why don't you grab that guitar over there and play along?' Asked how he found Dylan as a person, McCoy—who went on to work with him extensively—says, 'Like I found him the rest of the time: he had very little to say. He was deep in his music, and that was pretty much it.'

McCoy recollects that he and Dylan were accompanied on the remake of 'Desolation Row' by an acoustic bass player. This made it the album's only all-acoustic track. McCoy doesn't remember the bassist's name, and it is not recorded on the session sheet, but it's logical to assume that the player was Savakus. Recalls McCoy, 'They ran it once because the recording engineer was getting sounds of the bass and now an extra guitar. We did two takes. We didn't have time to do any more than two because the bass player had another session to go to.'

The strange aspect of this story is that McCoy was not a guitarist by trade but a mouth harpist. 'He knew I was a harmonica player,' says McCoy. 'I played very little guitar. If I ever did, it was acoustic rhythm guitar or a six-string bass, so I was really being challenged.' Yet the impromptu invitation to play on an unfamiliar instrument worked beautifully. That McCoy didn't make his living on the instrument didn't mean he couldn't wrest pleasing sounds from it. He proceeded to add intriguing frills to Dylan's straightforwardly scrubbed rhythm guitar. Moreover, in contrast to Goldstein's previous automaton state on the track, McCoy paid sufficient attention to proceedings to furnish the climactic final verse with appropriate flourishes. (Savakus, if he hasn't been mixed out completely, is unobtrusive, perhaps providing a sonic bed.) 'I was enjoying it,' says McCoy. 'I like to play guitar and never got to play like that in Nashville, doing a lead thing. So, I accepted the challenge.' The challenge included being—as it were—on his own. McCoy tells a familiar tale when he says, 'For that session, and the four albums that followed, I never got any instruction about anything. [When I was] session leader, I was on my own to direct the band in the direction I thought it should go. I thought, *Well, if he doesn't like it, he'll say something.* But he never said anything. Maybe he was just concentrating so hard on what he was doing that he wasn't paying attention to us. There was never any feedback from him about what we did.'

'I was doing my bad Grady Martin imitation,' says McCoy of his 'Desolation Row' contributions, describing said guitarist and mouth harpist as 'one of my idols'. McCoy states that Martin's guitar work on

'El Paso' by Marty Robbins is 'absolutely the greatest piece of session work I've ever heard' because 'the guy never repeated himself and it was always interesting.' He recalls, 'Now, I've got this acoustic guitar in my hand, and it's kind of the same thing. I'm thinking, *Oh my God, I'm going to do my best here to do something good.* There wasn't really enough time to sit around and plan things. I was just going off the top of my head.'

At this point, the picture gets slightly confusing. McCoy says he is 'absolutely sure' it's him on the album and is just as certain that he went through two complete takes from scratch with the other two musicians. This doesn't fit in with the recording sheet information for August 2, which suggests only one of the passes at 'Desolation Row' could conceivably be a complete take, while the album's final session on August 4 (1–4pm, with Johnston, Laico, and Dauria in the booth) is labelled an overdub session, not a bona fide recording date. 'Desolation Row' was recorded as three short breakdowns, one long, and four completes (including an 'incut' and composites). It's said that four (some sources say two) composites were edited together to form the track that appears on the album. (A composite of 'Tombstone Blues' was completed on the 4th, but there is some confusion about whether this was used.)

The inevitable futile attempts have been made to pinpoint a real-life source for the song's titular thrumming-but-bleak locale. Kooper, for one, has suggested Eighth Avenue, Manhattan, back in New York's scuzzy period. Dylan himself, in one of his eminently discountable 60s press conference quips, suggested in San Francisco in December 1965, 'Oh, that's someplace in Mexico. It's across the border. It's noted for its Coke factory.' However, Dylan is far more likely using a notional slummy street as a metaphor for the entire planet. Either way, the song is extraordinarily rich, seeing him cast his jaundiced eye on a locale/world where people are perennially hoodwinked by misfits, has-beens, sadists, and themselves. His eye roves across fortune tellers and death squads, the piously hypocritical and the heedlessly privileged, his pen summarising their sins pithily and pitilessly. In a work of stunning lyricism and incandescent imagery, it feels like he gradually works his way through every social issue afflicting Western society. Particularly impressive—especially for those who have detected a misogynistic streak in his oeuvre—is verse two. Therein, Cinderella is accused of being 'easy' but comfortably replies that it takes one to know one. Enter a character called Romeo who lays claim to her, only to be told in no uncertain terms by another patron that he is in the wrong place and had better leave. Mayhem, it is implied, ensues. Significantly, the only sound left after the departure of the ambulances is 'Cinderella sweeping up on Desolation Row'. There are nine other verses almost as sublime. Dylan's singing is world-weary where it's not merely sardonic, but he musters the energy to stylishly raise his voice at the yearning climax of each verse, and—as was now standard—he precedes the final verse with a soaring harmonica section.

It was done. Although mayfly-life recording times were common in 1965, the enduring esteem in which *Highway 61 Revisited* is held makes the fact that Dylan and his crew captured this masterpiece in six cumulative days little short of mind-boggling.

•

The artistic tour de force and definitive philosophical statement of 'Desolation Row' is really the only way the album could have ended, but there are more mundane reasons why 'Desolation Row' makes a perfect closer. One is that it would be difficult to imagine how to follow such a marathon. (Dylan, McCoy, and Savakus had shaved twenty-one seconds off what the Dylan–Goldstein–Kooper version had clocked up, but it is still a sprawling 11:21.) The other is that it's the only song with a 'clean' ending rather than a fade-out. It's unclear, though, whether Dylan immediately understood that concluding the album in any other way was inconceivable.

At a point near the end of the album's sessions, Johnston gave Dylan a rough mix of the LP. We know this can have been no sooner than

August 2 because the rough mix contained some of the songs first recorded that day. Its contents were, in order, 'Like A Rolling Stone', 'Ballad Of A Thin Man', 'Just Like Tom Thumb's Blues', 'Highway 61 Revisited', 'Positively 4th Street', 'It Takes A Lot to Laugh, It Takes A Train To Cry', 'Tombstone Blues', 'Can You Please Crawl Out Your Window?', 'Desolation Row', 'Queen Jane Approximately', and 'From A Buick 6'. Of course, this doesn't necessarily mean that this was the envisaged sequencing or even the final contents.

Said rough mix is mono, as was natural at a point where it would be another three years before the recording industry began to perceive stereo mixes as definitive. The songs on it haven't yet been edited down to fade-outs, meandering instead to untidy ends. 'Can You Please Crawl Out Your Window?' is the version mistakenly released as 'Positively 4th Street'. The version of 'Desolation Row' is the electric Dylan–Goldstein–Kooper version, suggesting that if there was a complete take of 'Desolation Row' on August 2, it wasn't considered good enough.

The acetate could not have been commercially released. Dylan's LP lengths in the days of vinyl were always very generous, in fact unwisely so, it being the case that when a vinyl album exceeds forty minutes, audio fidelity begins deteriorating. These eleven tracks cumulatively clocked in at an hour—an excessive running time even for Dylan. In the end, it was 'Positively 4th Street' and 'Crawl Out Your Window'—both weaker tracks—that were excised. In fact, the collection could have benefited from additional pruning: omitting 'From A Buick 6' would have improved the album and still have left it a forty-eight-minute record. (It could also have made for a symmetrical four cuts per side.) It's interesting that on the rough mix, the substandard audio quality of 'Buick' is such as to imply that it has been belatedly added from another acetate. Another thing that suggests it's an afterthought is its positioning at the end.

As usual with 60s records, there are many differences between the finalised mono and stereo mixes of *Highway 61*, almost certainly by dint of them being prepared in differing circumstances. In all likelihood, Dylan will have exercised final say on the mono mix but taken little interest in the stereo iteration. Although 'Like A Rolling Stone' appeared in its single incarnation on the LP's mono edition, it was remixed for the stereo version. The mono mix of 'Desolation Row' features a concluding laugh from Dylan—relieved, we infer, at having got to the end with no mistakes—that is barely audible in stereo. Bar the closer, all the tracks are longer in the stereo mix. In some cases, this is a matter of the fade-outs being delayed by just a few seconds, but in the cases of 'Queen Jane Approximately' and 'It Takes A Lot To Laugh', there are thirty and forty seconds more music, respectively. Also as standard with 60s records, the mono mix is fuller and packs more of a punch, partly the result of the greater care and attention invested; it was assumed that the stereo edition would be heard by only a minority, and—a big issue in the 60s—a privileged minority at that. Nonetheless, it has to be admitted that the mono version of 'Like A Rolling Stone' sounds shockingly tinny compared to the stereo version (and the stomach-stealing plunge isn't really audible at all), while the prolonging of the pleasures of the exquisite 'It Takes A Lot To Laugh' afforded by the stereo variant is highly appreciated.

Whether one loves or hates them, these variations have rather been forgotten by history: the mono albums were deleted surprisingly early (1968 in the US, '69 in the UK), and there were no mono CD editions until October 2010, when the world was finally given another chance to compare mixes upon the release of the Dylan box set *The Original Mono Recordings*. Greater music-label receptiveness to consumer knowledgeability and demand lay behind the monaural versions of Dylan's first eight albums being retrieved from history's dustbin and re-established to definitive status, but so did mammon: they were made commercially available at a premium price. For some audiophiles, incidentally, the 1992 DCC Compact Classics 'gold' edition of *Highway 61 Revisited*—mastered from the stereo mix-down tapes as opposed to compressed, equalised cutting masters—provides the happy medium between mono power and stereo breadth.

•

The sleeve of *Highway 61 Revisited* once again demonstrates that, in the 60s, Dylan put almost as much thought into his album covers as he did his music.

Not all this hard work was admirable. As he had on his last album, Dylan filled the back cover of *Highway 61* with narrative surrealism. In this case, it takes the form of passages like 'On the slow train time does not interfere & at the Arabian crossing waits White Heap, the man from the newspaper & behind him the hundred inevitables made of solid rock & stone ...' Trying to penetrate prose like this is as futile as attempting to decipher Dylan's brain-melting 1971 (but 60s-written) novel *Tarantula*. What might seem like something that would be gibberish in any guise, though, was subjected by its author to significant revision. In the UK and Italy, there were noticeable differences between the back cover text and that on the US edition. 'Savage Rose & Fixable' becomes 'Savage Rose & Openly', 'some college kid who's read all about Nietzsche' is instead 'some college kid who's read ...', and 'the barbarians jammed into pay phones' is yet to be superseded by 'Vivaldi's green jacket'. Naturally, these variations—presumably the consequence of Britain and Italy having received a rough working version—conferred instant collectability on the differing releases. The standardisation that came with the CD age has now ironed out such differences, which also extended to the photography and layout of the back of the UK edition. Regardless of variations, the photos of Dylan on all back covers are puzzlingly grainy or bad (depicting Dylan with face obscured or hidden). Whatever the iteration, the only admirable component of the album's back cover is the musicians' credits.

The names of permanent band members had of course always been printed on record releases, but with odd exceptions like The Rolling

Stones namechecking Jack Nitzsche, Gene Pitney, Phil Spector, and Ian Stewart, before *Highway 61 Revisited* a recording artist had never deigned to reveal to the public the identities of the hired hands who had assisted in fulfilling his visions and contributed to their enjoyment. It certainly seems to confirm Goldstein's assertion that Dylan was comfortable in the knowledge that people other than himself had contributed to the quality of his recordings. Within a short while, it became inconceivable in the industry not to list such contributors. (As if just to prove that rules meant nothing to him, least of all the ones that he set, Dylan left all credits off his 1975 album *Blood On The Tracks*.)

The front cover was considerably more prepossessing. The white-bordered colour photograph beneath the artist name and album title was beautiful and striking and abounding with meaning. Once again, it was set up and taken by Daniel Kramer. 'I realised that this was something that should be documented,' Kramer says of his decision to continue photographing Dylan after his first batch of work with him. 'Albert and Bob suddenly said they needed pictures for ads, for posters, for song-sheet covers, for whatnot to form his brand, his image. . . . He was doing wonderful things, and we got very friendly. Then Joan Baez came into the picture. I liked her very much. It was easy to work with them, and we travelled.'

Kramer took a widely distributed monochrome shot of an impishly smiling Dylan with his fist half-obscuring his face. It derived from the one and only session in Kramer's studio to which Dylan consented. 'He wanted to always work reportage, but I told him he has to come to the studio at least once,' says the photographer. 'I must control him, control the lights. That is the way you find this handsome, special face and person and inner spirit.' Kramer was managing to place some of his Dylan pictures in prestigious outlets. 'I went to a national family-type magazine. Bob had been published in music magazines, in folk magazines, but no one had really done a big national spread on him, [to] make him a household name. So I took a portfolio to *Pageant* magazine.

It was [a] little magazine in size, but it was like one of the big magazines in the States.' Under pressure from his fifteen-year-old daughter, the editor of *Pageant* said he would take some of Kramer's Dylan pictures and print them in a substantial spread, but he had a stipulation that displayed his naiveté. Kramer: 'He said, But Dylan has to do the captions to the pictures.' Nonetheless, on the off-chance Kramer called Dylan with the request. 'I said, Here's the thing. We could get nine or ten pages. You have to do the captions to word counts. They have spaces that they would allot to it, and that's what you have to do, and then we can get the spread. He said, Okay, we'll do it. He wrote captions to fifteen or so pictures, and they were like you would expect: one and two lines from songs that hadn't been written yet, or things in his head, and so on. That was our first national publication. After that, I did *Look*, the *Saturday Evening Post*, *Paris Match*, and everybody, and they went all over the world. People got to know Bob Dylan.'

Although Dylan had played Kramer versions of some of his new songs, the *Highway 61* shoot took place two months before recording of the album began, so the cover wasn't meant to communicate anything about its contents. Instead, says Kramer, 'It was intended to get your attention, make you think about it, stay with you.' The Beatles had been artily moody on the jacket of *With The Beatles* (1963) and the Stones sulky and spotty on *The Rolling Stones No. 2* (January 1965). *Highway 61 Revisited*'s front was in an adjacent vein. The first thing one notices is that Dylan, sitting on a low step, looks unabashedly like a rock star. He clutches in one hand the wraparound shades he is lately not seen without. His once unkempt hair is now styled and fashionably abundant. Over a tough guy's motorcycle T-shirt, he is wearing something quasi-feminine, so shiny and multicoloured that it could even be a blouse. His squinting eyes are gazing with a mixture of disinterest and hostility directly at the camera lens. As well as the mixed signals, the picture has a feeling of naturalism, the business-like air created by Dylan's lack of a smile deepened by the presence behind him of a man—seen only from the chest down—with a top-of-the-range camera dangling from his hand.

Says Kramer, 'His idea basically was, we had a very complicated one for *Bringing It All Back Home*, let's do something simple.' A day in mid-April 1965 was spent roaming New York. 'We just shot all day at different venues. We shot at a café. At one point I felt we could use a change of clothes, so we went in a men's shop and he bought a suit. We went and shot some more. We ended up back at the apartment on Gramercy Park on the steps of this brownstone. It was Albert Grossman's city apartment, and Bob had space there.' Kramer can't recall whether the memorable shirts came from Dylan's own wardrobe or the trip to the clothing store but says, 'Bob felt that he'd like to get a shot of himself in his motorcycle T-shirt—he had a Triumph motorcycle.' Kramer says that at first, he was 'a little concerned' about the satiny, proto-psychedelic shirt that Dylan wore over the T-shirt 'because if there was some sunlight it really would have been a horror show for me'.

Kramer also notes, 'I was shooting with a square camera—two and a quarter, album covers being square—and I saw that there was a hole in the background because of the square.' Kramer asked Bobby Neuwirth (now best known as Dylan's nasty tour manager in *Dont Look Back*) to stand behind and to the side of the subject to fill the space: 'Bob [Neuwirth] had a striped shirt on, horizontal stripes, so it added a little colour.' However, with Neuwirth necessarily cut off at the chest, Kramer still didn't like the composition, 'because now it looks like a mistake; like, *Why did you shoot a picture with half a person standing behind him?*' Accordingly, 'I gave him my camera to hold so that it added an element—balance—to the picture. Bob is holding his glasses; in other words, not working, he's got his glasses off. Behind him is this guy standing: he's got a camera, maybe he's going to photograph Dylan, maybe he's not, maybe they're travelling.' Kramer adds of Dylan, 'Look at his legs. They're apart. You have a crotch. This is before Madonna.' And the face? 'He's hostile, or it's a hostile moodiness. He's almost challenging me or you or whoever's looking at it: *What are you gonna do about it, buster?* ... I thought at the time that it hit all the marks.'

'I have outtakes,' Kramer says. 'We have different expressions where he's not this way, where he's actually smiling. You go through a gamut, and my job is bringing my subject into a certain alignment with the stars so it will be the right thing ... I always edit down to what I call the good ones, ones that I wouldn't be embarrassed or ashamed to have published, and then I bring them to my client. I just assume that Bob has the right to make this final choice, which he did.' Although the final image choice was Dylan's, Kramer felt he was able to influence the overall composition of the front of the sleeve. Of *Bringing It All Back Home*, he says, 'I would have had much less white. On *Highway 61* it used less white because I was always complaining, [Why] for no reason take a perfectly good picture and make it smaller?'

Many a rocker, before and after, has adopted the type of rebellious pose Dylan struck for this album's cover photograph. The contents of the disc beyond, though, showed that this rocker was not one who simply embraced the clichés, conventions, and received attitudes of rock'n'roll but was somebody intent on redefining them.

•

Dylan's half-acoustic, half-electric gig at New York's Forest Hills Stadium took place two days before *Highway 61*'s release.

The band Dylan assembled for the second half of the concert comprised Harvey Goldstein on bass, Al Kooper on keyboards, and two members of The Hawks: Levon Helm (drums) and Robbie Robertson (guitar). Those who objected to the electric set had something else about which to feel resentment in the shape of the venue itself. Thirteen days earlier, The Beatles had solved their growing popularity conundrum— the number of people who wanted to see them was always far greater than the capacity of the sort of theatre, ballroom and cinema used to host pop concerts—by becoming the first pop act to rent a sports stadium.

Although the approximately 14,000 attendees at Dylan's Forest Hills gig were dwarfed by the 55,000-plus souls who squeezed into the Fab Four's Shea Stadium concert, it still seemed vulgar to many Dylan disciples that he should play in a venue that required him to perform from a stage situated far away at one end of the venue's grass field. On top of that, his concert was preceded by hype-laden introductions by disc jockeys Jerry White and the so-called Fifth Beatle, Murray The K. For those who thought that *Another Side Of Bob Dylan* was a sign of a man losing his nerve and Newport '65 a sign of a man losing his principles, Forest Hills indicated someone who was losing any sense of shame. The fact that Joan Baez had played the venue back in '63—with Dylan as her special guest—was of no relevance to them.

'There's a photograph I made at Forest Hills that I called *The Gladiator*, in which he looks like a centurion because his hair is backlit and glowing, and it looks like a big helmet,' says Kramer. 'An electric guitar across his chest. He's on the stage, the lights and so on, and he's getting ready to be an electric rock'n'roller. That picture kind of sums up, I think, what Bob felt. He knew that there would be some headwinds, but he wanted to do this, and he had wanted to do it for a very long time. And it was to be expected. He knew that he wouldn't get a hundred percent response. He didn't get it at Newport, and he wasn't going to get it here. ... There was some booing, and there was one time when some kids ran across the stage.'

'The audience was split,' says Goldstein. 'There were a lot of vocal boos, but I think overall the audience was making the transition with him. Some grudgingly, but they were making the transition.' Of Dylan's general feeling about the controversy, Goldstein recalls, 'Bob was saying stuff like, The folkies don't get it. We're moving on. It's not that different. We're enhancing it. I don't wanna be hung up on all of this traditional stuff, because the traditional folk artists stay in the same place.'

Dylan would play another venue with Beatles connections on September 3, the band consisting again of Goldstein, Helm, Kooper, and Robertson. There, Goldstein felt progress had been made. 'By the time we got to the Hollywood Bowl, it was good,' he says. 'It was like a regular show and people were positive about it.' However, as with Kramer, his assumptions about the conversion rate should be caveated in that they are observations by someone who would not experience the immediately subsequent gigs as he wouldn't work with Dylan past this point for some time.

From here on, the other members of The Hawks would join Helm and Robertson in the electric sets that were now a permanent part of Dylan's stage act. 'Timing-wise, it just didn't work, because I was out working,' says Goldstein. 'I couldn't be hanging around waiting for something to happen.' He was informed by Grossman that the rest of The Hawks would be replacing him and Kooper. The latter had bowed out voluntarily. He said in *No Direction Home* that he became 'frightened' when he saw Dallas on the tour itinerary 'where they had just killed the President.' He explained, 'I thought, *If they didn't like that guy, what are they gonna think of this guy?*' The ensemble with which Dylan would embark on his July 24–December 19 North American tour—not to mention his infamous world tour from February 4 to May 27 the following year—would experience some of the most extraordinarily hostile crowd reactions in entertainment history. Dylan himself later admitted that the sound quality for ensembles at Sixties gigs was 'pretty archaic, really'. However, even if the sonics had been pristine, there would still have remained the burning issue of supposedly selling out. The resentment behind the ceaseless booing accompanying Dylan's electric sets would famously reach a climax on May 17, 1966, in England's Manchester Free Trade Hall. There, the cameras of D.A. Pennebaker captured outraged young Mancunians fulminating at being tricked into attending a pop concert and one particularly disgruntled audience member yelling at Dylan the word 'Judas!'

Kramer was one of those who found the whole controversy befuddling. He notes of the events following the release of 'Subterranean

Homesick Blues' and *Bringing It All Back Home*, 'He was at the folk festival in July and he was at the tennis stadium in August, but everyone knew what he was doing because they got this record in March, so there was no secret.' Yet while Dylan by this point was hardly springing anything on anyone, to the adherents of the intrinsically leftist 60s folk revival, to be partial to a populist genre like rock meant that you were buying into the consumerist values of a capitalist system that was surely crumbling under the weight of its own inherent injustices. In that tumultuous decade, millions thought this way. Epitomising the fact that it was a slap in the face to Dylan's fans that the man who had written 'The Times They Are A-Changin'' had been seduced by the cheap allure of rock stardom were the words of Izzy Young in *Sing Out!* that November: 'Dylan has settled for a liaison with the music trade's Top-Forty Hit Parade. . . . The charts require him to write rock-and-roll and he does. . . . The Polish polka will make it, and then he'll write them too.' The left who were so in favour of changing the world were deeply conservative when it came to their idol's music. It would have been futile for Dylan to respond to such charges by pointing out that the folkies had got it almost exactly 180 degrees wrong insofar as the British Invasion acts had not turned his head but rather re-ignited his passion for the rock'n'roll he had been immersed in as a kid—and, of course, provocative to state that he wasn't being opportunist by going rock because he'd already done that by taking up folk and protest in the first place.

One should not dismiss the bravery Dylan displayed in shrugging off the reaction at Newport and ploughing on with his electric visions, both on stage and on record. It's true that a large emotional comfort zone could be said to have been created for him by the fact of radios all around him blaring out The Byrds' version of 'Mr. Tambourine Man' and a massive financial comfort zone by its (then) one million sales. However, Newport had already shown him that there was a possibility he could alienate, even haemorrhage, his existing fanbase by changing direction, and, despite the chart success of 'Like A Rolling Stone', there was no reason to assume his often difficult songs would consistently generate devotion in that market.

Yet the folkies, radicals, and anyone else who didn't like Dylan—and even many broadminded pop and rock fans didn't; his voice took some getting used to—were trying to hold back an unstoppable tide. Nineteen sixty-five belonged to Bob Dylan. Everywhere music consumers looked during that year, they were confronted by songs either performed by Dylan, written by him, or inspired by him.

'Mr. Tambourine Man' and 'All I Really Want To Do' were just one small part of a tsunami of Dylan covers. In the autumn, The Turtles had a US Top 10 with their rendition of 'It Ain't Me Babe'. Toward the end of the year, The 4 Seasons (under the pseudonym The Wonder Who?) brushed the US Top 10 with 'Don't Think Twice, It's All Right'. Joan Baez's previously mentioned *Farewell Angelina* album featured, as well as the title track, further Dylan compositions in the shape of 'Daddy [Mama], You Been On My Mind', 'It's All Over Now, Baby Blue', and 'A Hard Rain's A-Gonna Fall'. The LP was a transatlantic Top 10. Her version of 'Baby Blue', released as a single in the UK, just missed the Top 20, while 'Farewell Angelina' was Top 40 in the same country. An artist of a previous generation, Johnny Cash—who to be fair was also Dylan's pal—tried to acquire some of Dylan's cachet by covering three of Dylan's songs on his album *Orange Blossom Special*, including 'Mama, You Been On My Mind'. Meanwhile, Manfred Mann had a UK no. 2 with 'If You Gotta Go, Go Now'.

'If You Gotta Go, Go Now' occupies a curious place in the Dylan canon. It was a big part of his concerts at the time, providing an interlude of levity and audacity in the way the narrator mocks a female companion's coyness about whether or not she will commit the still socially bold act of spending the night with him. It epitomised that moment in the middle of the Swinging Sixties when the young were determined to shrug off the taboos surrounding intercourse but were at the same time hesitant to do so because they didn't quite yet have access to reliable contraception. Despite it being well-known to his fans, though, Dylan never treated them to a release of the song, and it was left to a third party to exploit its topicality.

As a band who weren't quite capable of making a switch into self-reliance like their British peers The Rolling Stones, Manfred Mann would always be dependent on outside writers for their singles. The five-piece R&B combo turned pop group, named for no good reason after their chinstrap-bearded, bespectacled keyboardist, seemed to have a special affinity for Dylan's material. Their Dylan run had actually begun with 'With God On Our Side', a track on their June 1965 EP *The One In The Middle*. 'It had been a show-stopping live number around that time,' says their bassist-cum-guitarist, Tom McGuinness. 'It was six minutes long or something, and it really touched a nerve with audiences. I can't remember who suggested the song.' It wouldn't have been Paul Jones, their lead singer, who was also an accomplished mouth harpist. McGuinness: 'Paul is not a big Dylan fan still. When it was Bob's sixtieth birthday, [the] *Sunday Times* Magazine rang around sixty people to say, What would you give Bob Dylan for his sixtieth birthday? Paul said, A harmonica tutor.'

As for 'If You Gotta Go, Go Now', McGuinness explains that he and his colleague Manfred Mann (the person) happened to see Dylan performing it on television. 'Just him and guitar. We looked at each other and said, That sounds like a commercial song. I think we watched the programme on Sunday, rang up Ken Pitt, our manager, who was also Dylan's [UK] publicist, and by Wednesday, we got an acetate. We both thought it was a great song. I always thought it had a sort of humour like George Formby about it. That sort of seaside-postcard humour.' 'It was more than suggestive,' says Jones, who is now a born-again Christian. 'To the extent that I feel uncomfortable doing it these days.' McGuinness: 'It sounds innocuous now, but at the time it was banned in America on radio stations because it was too rude. Just like the Stones' "Let's Spend The Night Together". It was risqué, but it was funny as well. Paul wasn't that keen on it, but he did a great job on the vocal and it's got me clanking away on the national guitar. It was a big hit. Would have been no. 1 if it wasn't for Ken Dodd and "Tears".*

Although at the time its risqué nature was, like so many things about Dylan, cutting-edge, 'If You Gotta Go, Go Now' has dated badly. For one thing, the phraseology now seems less than consensual. An additional way the song has not weathered well is the simple fact that, in modern society, discussion of and participation in casual sexual intercourse is utterly unremarkable, making the song's delight in its own daring quaint. Dylan's decision not to release it almost seems to confirm his widely commented-on personality trait of being able to think two or three steps ahead: it's as if he had the perspicacity to realise that this composition's relevance would be fleeting, and that he should refrain from leaving a hostage to fortune.

There were many, many other Dylan covers that year as acts scrambled to shower themselves with the gold dust perceived to reside in his songs in terms of both their commercial potential and the vicarious cachet resulting from the fact that Dylan was the hottest/coolest artist in the world. At one point in '65, there were eight Bob Dylan compositions in the *Billboard* Top 100, some of them his records but most of them cover versions. Said magazine reported in September that year that forty-eight Dylan covers had been recorded in the previous month alone.

Then there were the songs that you could have sworn were by Dylan but which he had nothing to do with other than inspiration by osmosis. Simon & Garfunkel's 'The Sound(s) Of Silence' was the type of tortured and poetic rumination unthinkable in pop before Dylan's example, and Sonny & Cher's 'I Got You Babe' was an example of the sincerest form of flattery. As was 'Eve Of Destruction' by Barry McGuire, written by

---

* Dodd was a zany comedian with buck teeth and 'Tears' a very middle-of-the-road record. McGuinness: 'Everyone remembers the 60s as being a tremendously creative time, but "Tears" was the biggest-selling single that year.'

P.F. Sloan as a pastiche of Dylan's protest style (though with a rock backing), right down to its dropped *g*s. However much a piss-take, and however scattershot its denunciation of injustice, it struck a chord with the public, who sent it to no. 3 in the UK and no. 1 in the US. Britain's Dylan manqué Donovan (guitar, harmonica, cap, and protest) debuted with his own composition, 'Catch The Wind', a 1965 UK Top 5 that was a blatant mix of 'Chimes Of Freedom' and 'Blowin' In The Wind'. Donovan also hit with a cover of Buffy Saint-Marie's 'Universal Soldier', which was itself a blend of Dylan's 'Blowin' In The Wind' and 'Masters Of War'. Oh, and then there was 'A Simple Desultory Philippic' by Paul Simon. Released on his August 1965 UK-only solo album *The Paul Simon Songbook*, it was an astute satire of Dylan's style: the title alone is pure Dylan of the period, as are many of the lines. Folk-rock became such a craze that the most unlikely and uninformed jumped on its bandwagon. 'I Got You Babe' and 'Eve Of Destruction' were one thing, but the opportunism reached its nadir when Glen Campbell covered the anti-war anthem 'The Universal Soldier' while anxiously stating in interviews that he was no pacifist.

More broadly, it was becoming increasingly clear that Dylan had created a new vernacular. An entire generation of recording artists seemed suddenly to have adopted his sometimes florid, sometimes colloquial compositional vocabulary, his expansive frame of reference, his sneering style, his questioning of tradition, and his ambivalent attitude toward romance. Although this belligerence and unconventionality was not unrelated to the greaseball snottiness of Elvis and other classic rockers, Dylan's version operated on a much higher intellectual plane.

Capping it all was the fact that '65 was the year he released an album that was a new high-water mark for the long-player format. As the rock era was still in its first decade, that achievement might be said to be, relatively speaking, an easy one. Over half a century and millions of long-playing releases later, though, *Highway 61 Revisited* continues to be regarded by many as the greatest album of all time.

·

Its colossally high quality wasn't actually much noted when *Highway 61 Revisited* was issued on August 30, 1965.

Pop criticism was in a state as betwixt and between as that of the young set who had to balance their horniness with their worry about unwanted pregnancy. There was at this point in history a certain cultural inhibition about venturing the idea that popular music could constitute great art, especially that strand of pop still commonly known as rock'n'roll. Not only had rock only been in existence for a decade, the very notion of albums as the primary artistic statement in the medium was still half a decade or more into the future. This therefore engendered another reason for the general failure to recognise *Highway 61 Revisited*'s greatness. In any case, it was released into a world that had not yet developed the critical apparatus to properly evaluate it.

With *Crawdaddy* still a year away from being founded and *Rolling Stone* (partly, of course, named after Dylan's song) two years away from its first issue, most critiquing of popular music was done by either condescending newspaper critics or pop-paper writers who might not have had such a sniffy attitude but who—because it was presumed that nobody beyond their early twenties listened to pop/rock—traded in the type of banalities that were hardly up to the task of addressing the phantasmagorical qualities of the likes of 'Desolation Row'. A flavour of the shallowness and fatuousness of the music writing of the time is provided by the review of 'Like A Rolling Stone' that appeared in the UK weekly *Record Mirror*, which not only condemned 'syrupy strings' that weren't there but found Dylan's hair-raising vocals 'expressionless intoning' and overall felt the release to constitute 'the six longest minutes since the invention of time'. Penny Valentine also somehow identified strings in her *Disc* review, in the process of her more ambiguous assessment of a 'slightly monotonous, very long Dylan record completely away from the Dylan we know' about whose prospects she offered, 'I really wouldn't like to say what will happen to this as far as the chart goes' before concluding, in a feeble attempt at some semblance of praise, 'Interesting though.' Norman Jopling of *Record Mirror* could only conclude his review of *Highway 61 Revisited* on the bland point, 'Those people who liked Bob because he was basically an anti-war folk artiste won't like this. But Bob Dylan just uses musical mediums to put over what he wants to say. He used folk, now on this album he basically uses rock'n'roll and blues. It's still Bob Dylan. The possibilities are endless.'

Sing Out!, of course, took music rather more seriously—some might say too seriously, considering Dylan's recent troubles with it. Perhaps surprisingly, their evaluation of the album was sympathetic—although it should be conceded that reviewer Paul Nelson was a contributor who had always defended Dylan's direction changes. Nelson adjudged the album 'one of the two or three greatest folk music albums ever made'. It's intriguing that Nelson had no problem viewing as folk music an album that these days is viewed as quintessentially rock. But then he had no reason to: if it was true that there had never been a folk record like this, it was even truer that its soundscapes hardly chimed with the sort of uncomplicated lyrics and simple chord changes that characterised the history of rock.

Some might say that only the passage of time and the acquiring of perspective that goes with it could allow critics to start throwing around phrases like 'all-time greatest', but in fact, at least one man in the period did have the vision—and bravery—to make such a claim. Writing in *Broadside* shortly after the album's release, Phil Ochs unproblematically adjudged *Highway 61 Revisited* the most important, most revolutionary, and best album ever made. In 1970, he elaborated to Dylan's biographer Anthony Scaduto, 'Every succeeding album up to *Highway 61*, I had an increasing lot of secret fear: *Oh my God, what can he do next? He can't possibly top that one.* And then I put on *Highway 61* and I laughed and said it's so ridiculous. It's impossibly good, it just can't be that good. . . .

The writing was so rich I just couldn't believe it. . . . He's done it. He's done something that's left the whole field ridiculously in back of him. He's in his own world now.'

Dylan himself told Scaduto, 'I'm not gonna be able to make a record better than that one. *Highway 61* is just too good.' It being the case that when he gave him that quote, Dylan was not yet thirty and had a long recording career theoretically yawning in front of him, one might assume that this was a rather precipitous, even defeatist, statement. Yet while Dylan has now released over three dozen official studio albums, among which are several classic works, his assessment has proven remarkably accurate. This is essentially because he could have added to his comment, 'Neither is anybody else.'

However, *Highway 61 Revisited* is not just a great work but also an album that changed the world. This was certainly something recognised by Harvey Goldstein. 'I came out of there really feeling a part of something incredible,' he says of the recording. 'That was the next step in pop music.' The salient point here is that this 'next step' was not the type of groundbreaking that culminates in a commercial ghetto. Aesthetic achievement does not necessarily go hand in hand with pioneering, but nowhere in the history of popular music before or since—including The Beach Boys' *Pet Sounds*, The Beatles' *Sgt. Pepper's Lonely Hearts Club Band*, or The Rolling Stones' *Beggars Banquet*—has there been such a confluence of artistic inspiration and barrier-smashing as on *Highway 61 Revisited*.

Through his annus mirabilis of 1965, Bob Dylan's success and stature gave rock and pop artists—as well as folkies—permission to tackle any subject imaginable. It was something particularly underlined by the chart performance of 'Like A Rolling Stone'. The single's hit status proved to singers and bands that they would not be jeopardising sales by acquiring a harder and more intellectual edge. Its parent album completed the picture of what was now possible in popular music. Poetic lyrics, strange time signatures, unusual instrumentation—all were now mainstream instead of hived off in artists' minds as that stuff that fringe acts (or jazz artists or avant-garde types) dealt in. Every singer and band in the world now effectively had permission to write about subjects other than their 'baby', and to do so against sonic backdrops that spurned convention and even defied belief. This being the 60s, inevitably the subjects that artists chose to explore would often be seditious where they weren't merely alternative. A general sense of evolving values and morals expanded exponentially. Many recording artists were suddenly expressing sentiments that in a broad sense made them protest singers, and, with these artists being objects of mass worship, new ideas and ideals started spreading through society by osmosis. The revolution was on stream, and Bob Dylan was the man who had kicked it off.

Nor was it just music that Dylan was revitalising. As his lyrics were often indubitably poetry, and as rock/pop was the music of the masses, the record sales of Dylan and his legion of cover merchants meant that never had so many human beings been consuming poetry, not even in the early nineteenth century, when the likes of Percy Bysshe Shelley and Lord Byron had the sort of aura later enjoyed by mid-twentieth century rock stars.

Highway 61 Revisited is the album singly most responsible for transforming popular music into what we know it as today, and is a work that—albeit in a more indirect process—actually shifted societal mores and attitudes, whether society realised it or not.

•

Forest Hills was Daniel Kramer's final day with Dylan following their extended partnership.

Kramer recognised a symmetry and a narrative to his term as what might be called Dylan's house portraitist over and above the fact that it lasted almost exactly one year. 'A lot happened, and I felt that my story was finished,' he says of the aftermath of the gig. 'I did photograph Bob after that, but it isn't part of that story...I didn't know there was going to be a transition when I started, I just felt that there was something special here. And it happened, and then Forest Hills was kind of the statement. It was enough.' He reflects of his first work with the artist, 'I photographed Dylan with a guitar, with one little suitcase, with his two microphones and a rubber mat to stand on when you perform, and this Ford station wagon that he and his road manager drove in.' It was quite a contrast to a year later: 'I photographed Forest Hills with several eighteen-wheelers unloading hundreds and hundreds and hundreds of feet of big cable and speakers and wires, and we were electrified, and that was the same performer who was now bringing a whole new music, and who in that twelve months had changed the music business, who was never going to go back.'

Chapter four

4

CHAPTER
FOUR

'This Wheel's On Fire

The mid-1960s were Dylan's peak as a provider of hits for third parties, but he has never really stopped in that capacity: even into the early twenty-first century, his 1997 song 'Make You Feel My Love' joined the likes of 'Blowin' In The Wind' in becoming a Dylan song covered by anyone and everyone, from Billy Joel to Neil Diamond to Bryan Ferry to (most famously) Adele. In contrast, his own time in the sun as a singles chart artist was brief. It was not for the want of trying, though.

By the middle year of the 60s, it was clear that The Beatles, The Rolling Stones, and Bob Dylan formed the Holy Trinity of the phenomenon, indeed social revolution, that was contemporary popular music. Just as in the 1920s social libertarianism and jazz music were intertwined in the public imagination, so in the 1960s pop and rock were perceived to be the soundtrack to, and in some cases progenitor of, a new consciousness. Notions of fidelity to social conformity, moral duty, religious orthodoxy, and sexual abstinence were beginning to fray, assisted by technology—the mass media exposing people to new ideas, access to increasingly more reliable methods of contraception, etc.—and by the unprecedented economic freedom of an age set once dependent on their parents. Recording artists were only slightly older than the questioning new cohort that formed their audiences, and their simpatico attitudes were manifested in their fashions, their interviews, and their work. The Trinity weren't the only three purveyors of great music and zeitgeist ideals, of course. For instance, many would posit The Beach Boys as of equal importance to the Beatles/Stones/Dylan, and certainly with their 1966 album *Pet Sounds* they released a work widely considered the equal of anything by any of them. However, their gloopy all-American harmonies and patina of niceness always somehow served to keep The Beach Boys just outside the Trinity's edgy cachet.

The Beatles were the nice cops to the Stones' nasty cops. '(I Can't Get No) Satisfaction' may sound apolitical from today's perspective, but its unapologetically distorted fuzztone guitar riff and its bellowed condemnation of the irritants of everyday life, not to mention the sexual innuendo of its title, were things that the media and the public simply weren't used to. Nice cops serve a purpose too, however. Their cute fringes, tender songs, and charming collective public persona made The Beatles acceptable to the older generation (i.e., those in power, either as parents or politicians). While the Stones were outside the party, shouting boorishly through the windows, The Beatles were inside, enchanting their hosts and thereby lowering their defences. While nowhere near as popular as The Beatles or Stones, Dylan was at that point head and shoulders above them in terms of songcraft and innovativeness and thus influence. However, to a very large extent, he was only influential *through* other artists. Songs written by Dylan or inspired by him might be filling the airwaves, and he might be championed in interviews by The Beatles, Stones, et al, but he personally had been largely excluded from the upper reaches of the pop market by, variously, the perception of him as a folkie, his bare instrumentation, his rough voice, and his unwillingness or inability to prettify his output à la Peter, Paul & Mary or The Byrds. Even his fairly high album chart placings were deceptive: his LP sales tended to fall away soon after release and were in the long run always dwarfed by those of his British peers. As a man of no little ego—despite the fact that he has always tried to hide it—this surely rankled with Dylan. Perhaps his fabled comment to Stones guitarist Keith Richards—'I could have written "Satisfaction" but you couldn't have written "Mr. Tambourine Man"'—was a sardonic expression of this. For one brief moment, though, it seemed that the tide might turn. His 1965 multiple UK singles chart success and the transatlantic triumph of 'Like A Rolling Stone' indicated to Dylan that he could himself become a hit parade regular. In 1965–66, it would seem that he set about a concerted effort to achieve that status. It was an effort that failed.

The major reason it did is because the triumvirate of singles he released in the year after 'Like A Rolling Stone'—'Positively 4th Street', 'Can You Please Crawl Out Your Window', and 'One Of Us Must Know (Sooner Or Later)'—were simply not suited to the requirements of the

45rpm market. This was something The Beatles and Stones could have told him, had he asked: they might not yet be his equals as composers, but one thing both ensembles did understand is what the singles-buying public would lay down their money for. It wasn't even as if the golden ears of those two acts were attuned only to the anodyne strains of material traditionally associated with the lowest common denominator: before the abrasive 'Satisfaction' or the Fabs' exquisitely mordant 'Ticket To Ride' became hits in '65, nobody would have assumed such fare was commercial. In fairness, exactly the same thing could be said about 'Like A Rolling Stone', which recast the notion of hit-single material even more than anything yet released by the other two prongs of the Trinity. However, that record had a sky-high quality with which no one (bewildered music-paper reviewers aside) could argue. Dylan's immediately post-'Like A Rolling Stone' 45s were neither very good nor very chart-worthy. Not only that, but he was clearly oblivious of the fact that each of them was incrementally less interesting, even if he can't have been unaware that they were consecutively less successful.

'Positively 4th Street', released in September '65, was the first. It may seem strange to dismiss a US no. 7 and UK no. 8 as something not really suited to the single format, not least because it remains a fixture of heritage radio stations today. However, one can't escape the feeling that its high chart placings—and hence continued prominence in the culture—were a fluke, a result of a confluence of impetuses and circumstances including the novelty factor of its bile, Dylan's then general ascendency, and the willingness at that particular juncture of radio programmers to give him airtime. Although the track has several memorable moments—especially the declaration of malicious intent of its opening line, 'You got a lot of nerve to say you are my friend'—its vitriol and organ swells produce a certain deflating sense of déjà vu. As its contributor Al Kooper notes, 'That just sounded like more of "Like A Rolling Stone".' In being placed on the B-side of 'Positively 4th Street', the mediocre 'From A Buick 6' found its true niche.

'Can You Please Crawl Out Your Window' (December '65) could be viewed as the third in a trilogy of vitriol. The language of the putdowns is more elevated than that of 'Positively 4th Street' ('With his businesslike anger and his bloodhounds that kneel') and the instrumentation is slightly more pleasing (and darker). However, the track is weak melody-wise, and the overall air is inconclusive. Like 'Positively 4th Street', it was a standalone single—an unusual phenomenon in the States, where record companies and the ferocious enterprise of US culture insisted that profits be maximised by the inclusion on long-players of songs already familiar from the charts—but that status no more made it possessed of the requisites of a hit than its contents. An increasingly egocentric and highly strung Dylan legendarily threw fellow singer/songwriter Phil Ochs out of his car when he told him 'Can You Please Crawl Out Your Window' was not up to snuff, but the fact that Ochs was usually his greatest champion should have given him pause. Fittingly, these dregs from the casket—the final instalment in an incrementally declining trio—barely bothered the chart compilers. The track nudged into the Top 20 in the UK, while in his home country it could climb only just inside the *Billboard* Top 60, a curiously unsuccessful beginning to Dylan's recording association with The Hawks/Band, with whom his name is now to an extent intertwined. The single's B-side was 'Highway 61 Revisited'.

For 'One Of Us Must Know (Sooner Or Later)', released in February 1966, Dylan retained two of The Hawks—Danko and Robertson—but also ensured some of the musicians from the more smooth-flowing *Highway 61* sessions appeared in the form of Al Kooper, Paul Griffin, and Bobby Gregg. However, this highly credible backing band couldn't do much with a composition that sounded like a middle part of something else.

Wonderful though the invective of 'Like A Rolling Stone' had been, that and its two follow-ups had put Dylan in danger of typecasting himself as a purveyor of malice (itself almost an inversion of his previous protest-singer image as a voice of compassion). 'Sooner Or Later' at least stepped away from that tone. Almost certainly a song about Joan Baez, it sees Dylan or—if we must be studiously conscious of the concept that any song could be fictional—the narrator state that he hadn't meant to treat the person to whom the song is addressed so bad or make them so sad: 'You just happened to be there, that's all.' While there's a suspicion of mild mockery beneath the contrition, it's still a refreshing change from the endless nastiness of late. Not that that assisted its commercial fortunes. Once again, Dylan had insisted on releasing something as a single that didn't feel like one, this track like the previous two not only possessing none of the punch and flash of a chart song but in addition having a washed-out feeling. Organ runs and a curiously subdued Dylan vocal in which he peculiarly draws out words are the key features of a mid-tempo arrangement. That the magisterial 'Queen Jane Approximately' occupied the flip provided an unfortunate juxtaposition. Despite 'One Of Us Must Know (Sooner Or Later)' being a new Dylan song and for all anybody knew another standalone single (it wouldn't turn up on an album until the following June), it failed to crack the UK Top 30 and didn't even penetrate the *Billboard* Top 100.

Some will point to the success of 'Rainy Day Women #12 & 35' as disproving the idea of Dylan failing to become the hitmaker that he so obviously fervently desired to be. However, the fact that this April 1966 release was a transatlantic Top 10 (making no. 2 in the US, his equal-best chart placing in his home country, at least as far as *Billboard* is concerned) was down to artificial and unusual reasons. In the mid-60s, managing to get a song whose refrain was 'Everybody must get stoned'—as well as a title that was a slang term for a marijuana joint—onto the airwaves was a delicious fuck-you to the authorities that the young just had to be a part of. Meanwhile, the track's bawdy fairground instrumentation was good-timey and pleasantly off-kilter. In essence, it was a novelty record, and one doesn't have to be the voice of a generation or the poet laureate of the counterculture—or even artistically substantial—to have a hit with one of those.

It wouldn't be true to say that Dylan never had more big hit singles. However, the overarching spotty, straggling performance gradient of his other major chart entries—'Lay Lady Lay' was a Top 10 in the US and UK in 1969; 'Knockin' On Heaven's Door' was a Transatlantic Top 20 in 1973—is not the definition of a chart regular. That moment in time in which he might have become one had gone by the spring of 1966. For the rest of the decade, Dylan would continue to be the oracle to whom all other recording artists looked for guidance on how to conduct themselves or what they might be capable of getting away with in their art, but he was now destined to never haul himself up onto their plateaux of sales or profile.

One important thing came out of his failure. The staccato recording sessions in New York of the latter two of those three 'Like A Rolling Stone' follow-up singles had been immensely frustrating. Like 'Can You Please Crawl Out Your Window', 'Sooner Or Later' had required the kind of multiple takes Dylan always detested, needing nineteen attempts, only a handful of which were completes. He later said, 'It was the band. But you see, I didn't know that. I didn't want to *think* that.' He certainly knew it by the final two takes, on which only Danko and Robertson were retained, with their colleagues displaced by Bobby Gregg, Paul Griffin, Al Kooper, and William E. Lee, 1965 Dylan session alumni. Finally, he conceded to himself that he needed new musicians in a broader sense. When he did, some Machiavellian scheming on the part of Bob Johnston—at least according to Charlie McCoy—finally yielded fruit when Dylan decided to relocate his recording dates nearly a thousand miles to Nashville.

McCoy asserts that this hoped-for outcome was what lay behind Johnston inviting him to play on 'Desolation Row' the previous year. He says, 'After that session was over, they had a chat, and [Johnston] said, Hey now, Bob, don't you see how easy that was? So that's the way it works in Nashville. We go there and those musicians there will just fall right in and it'll be great. . . . That's what he used to sell Bob on coming down here. After I left, Johnston told me, Man, I was so glad you came. That went good. Because of that, I think I'm gonna be able to convince him to come to town and record. . . . I think he felt like the Nashville musicians could give another point of view to Dylan's music. Everything here is lyric-oriented . . . I don't think Dylan was really keen on the idea. I was a carrot.'

Interestingly, John Hammond claimed that he was the first in Dylan's circle to suggest that his talents could best be brought out by Nashville sessioners. He told Scaduto he said as much during the *Freewheelin'* sessions to Don Law, head of Columbia in Nashville, but that when the latter went into the studio and heard Dylan laying down 'Oxford Town', he told Hammond he was 'crazy' if the thought Dylan could record that sort of thing in Tennessee.

Some might suggest that Law's reaction was understandable. At a point in history where a credible music press had yet to establish itself, there was little public discussion about Dylan's move to 'Music Row'. However, it was extraordinary indeed that a recording artist like him should take the step of relocating his sessions to Nashville. The latter was a sociologically conservative town dominated musically by the pedestrian strains of what was then still called country & western; Dylan was a groundbreaking folk/pop/rock artist associated with political progressivism. However, with typical far-sightedness, Dylan was less interested in the local traditions and politics and in what had gone down before than he was in the proposition that the scene's session musicians were preternaturally gifted and efficient and able to enhance his art.

The results from two blocs of recordings at Columbia Music Row Studios, Nashville, Tennessee, on February 14–17 and March 8–10, were certainly hugely productive both quality- and quantity-wise. They resulted in an album that many consider superior even to *Highway 61 Revisited*.

'He knew that musicians here are really creative,' says McCoy of Johnston. 'The best way to make records in Nashville is [to] get these talented people and let them go.' Not that McCoy feels Nashville musicians were above taking advice or instruction. 'I'm a little proud of the fact that, in Nashville, if you're going to be a studio musician, the first thing you learn is that you check your ego at the door,' he says. 'We don't have time to fool with egos. It's been that way since I first came here. The old A-team guys had established that, and it's still in effect today. It's a great way to make records. Almost every musician in this town is capable of being a session leader, but they're all great followers and they have a lot of respect for each other. If you're the leader today, well then, hey, I'm on your team, I'm following you. But if I'm leader tomorrow then you're on my team.'

Not that Dylan threw himself completely on the mercy of strange musicians in a strange town. He brought with him two East Coast allies in the form of Al Kooper and Robbie Robertson. Kooper himself had a more important role in proceedings than merely contributing organ. 'I was music director,' he says. He emphasises, though, 'I didn't have anything to do with producing that record.'

Dylan would a few years hence make quintessentially country-music recordings in Nashville, but on his inaugural working visit to the city, the aural evidence suggests that he instructed the musicians to play anything but the type of sounds with which the locale was synonymous. Much of the music to be heard on *Blonde On Blonde* was in recognisable, established genres such as blues, pop, R&B, and rock. Some of it was uncategorisable by dint of being revolutionary. None of it, though, had country inflections. 'Well, you know, the people here are good about listening to a song and interpreting the song, and if it's not a real dyed-in-the-wool country song, they have a way to play to the song rather than take the song and put it in a style,' reasons McCoy. However, he does emphasise that some erroneously assume that Nashville musicians only had experience with country stylings. McCoy himself had played on the R&B-pop hit 'Oh! Pretty Woman' by Roy Orbison and on sessions by Perry Como and Cliff Richard and points out that down the years, Nashville Cats (as The Lovin' Spoonful's John Sebastian admiringly described them in song) had cut recordings with, among others, The Everly Brothers, Brenda Lee, and crossover artist Patsy Cline. He also reveals, 'We'd sit around between takes and play blues just for fun.'

McCoy says the *Blonde On Blonde* musicians received 'zero' guidance about what or how to play. 'It was up to me. I kept asking for guidance and I've asked Bob [Dylan], Well, what would you think if we would do this? And his answer to me was, I don't know, man. What do you think? So I finally quit asking. I told Bob Johnston, Look, I'm trying to get some answers. He's not giving me any. I'm just going to take it on my own. And Bob [Johnston] said, That'll be fine.'

Al Kooper, though, asserts that while Dylan continued his no-guidance policy personally, instruction was this time relayed through him. 'It was delineated that I was going to tell the guys in the band what to play,' he says. 'I had suggestions. I had a concept. See, I was the only one that knew all the songs. So I suggested to Bob that he come an hour later and I could teach some of the songs to the band each night before Bob got there so that Bob wouldn't have to sit through that. Bob thought that was a good idea. So, that's how we worked ... I didn't know these guys at all, so it could have been a very uncomfortable situation. But these guys were so nice that it was never a problem ... Robbie Robertson and I were the only people from out of town there, and they made us totally comfortable. ... It was much more civilized than *Highway 61*. *Highway 61*, to me, is a very punk album because everything is unsupervised.' He doesn't just mean the word in terms of quasi-anarchy, but also with regards to what ended up in the grooves: 'To me, it's very punky musically compared to *Blonde On Blonde*, which is very arranged.'

The Nashville musos whom Johnston assembled to record what became *Blonde On Blonde* are generally believed to be McCoy (bass, guitar, harmonica, trumpet), Kenny Buttrey (drums), Jerry Kennedy and Wayne Moss (guitar), Hargus 'Pig' Robbins and Bill Aikins (keyboards), Henry Strzelecki and Joe South (bass, with South also contributing some guitar), and Wayne Butler (trombone).

There have long been stories that some or all of these men had never heard of Dylan. 'That's not true,' McCoy insists. 'These studio guys here, they're well aware of what's going on in all music. Everybody knew who he was.' Nor was there resentment about the presence of Kooper and Robertson. McCoy: 'We all knew who they were, too. And they obviously knew who we were. It was a great kind of mutual respect, and we got along great. And, well, the result is history.'

The history-making started with a bang. The recording of the first track took place at a part of a day when work was usually long over, and in fact when even musicians are long in bed. Moreover, according to McCoy's recollections, the track in question was an ethereal number that turned out to last for twelve minutes. While studio logs indicate that 'Sad Eyed Lady Of The Lowlands' was in fact laid down at the album's third Nashville session, on February 16, the uncivil hour of the time of the recording is not disputed by anyone. McCoy observes, 'His flight was late, he came in and he said, Look, I haven't finished writing. You guys just hang loose while I finish the song. At 4am: Here we go. That was tough. . . . Everybody's trying to stay awake and nobody wanted to be that guy that made everyone else have to do it again. That was the starter.'

The actual first Nashville session was none too shabby. It saw the capturing of the masters of the sweetly comedic 'Fourth Time Around' and the phantasmagorical opus 'Visions Of Johanna'. For good measure, it also saw Dylan and the musicians make fourteen attempts to perfect the bitterly comedic 'Leopard-Skin Pill-Box Hat', but although there were at least three complete takes, none was deemed satisfactory, and it wasn't until the final day of recording, on March 10, that it was attempted again and ironically, nailed in a single take.

Emblematic of the sessions was Dylan's extraordinary ability to declaim without prompts. 'In many of those songs in Nashville, he was not using lyrics [sheets],' says McCoy. 'Of course, it's easier with your own songs to remember your lyrics, but there were a lot of lyrics and I must say, he's got quite a computer up there. That impressed us all.'

'They did something that they had never done before, which is they were booked for the entire day and night,' says Kooper of the session musicians. 'Most sessions, it's like 10–1, 2–5, 7–10. They were just booked for twenty-four hours straight. It was tough for all of us, but we all respected what was happening.'

'No, the first day we were booked from two o'clock and the rest of the week we were booked from 6pm,' demurs McCoy. However, on one thing he is in agreement with Kooper: 'It was a hard week.' One reason for that was because 'some of us were working other sessions during the daytime'. Another is that 'most people in Nashville at that time would do an album in three sessions. I think we counted thirteen. That was unheard of here at the time, absolutely unheard of.'

Despite the long hours, however, there was plenty of time to shoot the breeze, read the paper, and play cards. Kooper: 'Bob would sit in the studio with a pad and just rewrite lyrics, sometimes for six hours at a time, without budging from the piano.'

Perhaps the quintessence of Dylan's pushing at the boundaries not just of Nashville customs but any musical tradition per se was the process of capturing 'Rainy Day Women #12 & 35'. 'We're working in the early evening,' says McCoy. 'Bob Johnston comes to me and he said, Look, later on, he wants to do a song with a Salvation Army style. I need a trumpet player and a trombone player. I said, Well, does it need to be good? He said, No, no, no, it needs to be awful. I said, Okay, then I'll play trumpet, and I'll get you a trombone player. He said, Great, have him here at midnight. So, I called his buddy of mine, trombone player, Wayne Butler, and he showed up about twenty to twelve, and about 12:30 he left. It was done.' Of the track's party atmosphere, McCoy says,

'All that yelling and screaming you heard, that was going on while the take was happening. There wasn't any overdubbing there.' Those who might suspect that a little inebriation lay behind the jolly soundscape would be wrong. 'That was not tolerated.'

•

There were ultimately an extraordinary five US singles released from *Blonde On Blonde*. That there were three in the UK was in a sense just as remarkable, because in that country standalone singles were so common that twelve of The Beatles' twenty-two 45s never appeared on an album, and all fifteen 60s Rolling Stones UK singles were non-album. There again, the album featured a remarkable amount of material.

There had been double albums in the classical and jazz genres, but not in pop or rock. The very concept was slightly ridiculous. For all the sales and growing respect for The Beatles, Stones, Byrds, etc., rock was to wider society, the established media, and the business world nothing more than kid stuff. It was not something felt to possess the gravitas implied by such a grand and expensive artefact as a two-record set. There were also practical objections: if the purchasers of a product were reliant on pocket money (an allowance, in US parlance) rather than a wage, it had to be priced within their more modest means. In making *Blonde On Blonde* a double LP, Dylan—as he had so many times before—ignored precedent and practicality and—also as so many times before—was vindicated.

He was only slightly ahead of the curve: seven days after *Blonde On Blonde*'s appearance on June 20, 1966, came The Mothers Of Invention's double album *Freak Out!** Once that door was opened, others piled through it: The Beatles' eponymous double set colloquially known as the 'White Album' appeared in 1968, as did the Jimi Hendrix

---

* Produced by Tom Wilson, coincidentally enough. In another coincidence, it—like *Blonde On Blonde*—had a fourth side containing a song that was only just over half the length of a conventional vinyl side.

Experience's *Electric Ladyland*. The Who's *Tommy* followed in '69. By the late 70s, the biggest-selling album of all time was Peter Frampton's 1976 double live album *Frampton Comes Alive!*

Also unprecedented was the dressing and design. *Blonde On Blonde*'s title seems apropos of nothing. Nowadays it would be assumed to be a sexual innuendo, but in more innocent times other lines of speculation were explored, which included the fact that the initials of *Blonde On Blonde* spell 'BOB', and that 'blond' is the more common spelling in the phonetically inclined US. (At least one report at the time claimed that the title had in fact originally been spelt this way.) Various other theories have been put forward down the years, but nobody has yet to offer a convincing explanation, least of all the perennially unhelpful Dylan. Not that anyone would know what the title was by glancing at the sleeve. It was only discernible by examining the tiny lettering on the spine, the only wordage to be seen anywhere on the outside of the jacket.

The jacket was otherwise occupied only by a wraparound colour photograph of the artist's head and torso leaning against a wall. It being the case that vinyl albums were twelve inches square, opening up the gatefold sleeve provided an image fit for placing on a teenager's bedroom wall. Not that this could ever have constituted a standard pop pin-up. The black-and-white chequered scarf wrapped around the artist's neck looked quite stylish, as did his brown, hip-length coat. However, Dylan looked weird, and not just because of his increasingly long and frizzy hair. That famously angular face was blurred due to the photographer Jerry Schatzberg shivering from the cold, but Dylan's frazzled mien may have been due to something more than the pic being out of focus: this was a man living on the very edge.

Flipping that gatefold jacket over revealed photographs of Dylan and friends and associates, including a self-portrait of Schatzberg, included by Dylan without bothering to ask him and which the photographer took as an 'in lieu' for a written credit. There is also a listing of the musicians to be heard within. That specific instruments are not attributed to them, aside from Dylan and McCoy, would have been a minor issue for people never usually granted such public acknowledgement.

The consensus among Dylan fans is that *Highway 61 Revisited* or *Blonde On Blonde* are the two albums in contention for the status of his masterpiece (with *Blood On The Tracks* running a close third). Dylan himself might have told Scaduto that he wasn't ever going to be able to top *Highway 61* but he also seems to hold a particular regard for its follow-up. In 1978, he observed to Ron Rosenbaum of *Playboy*, 'The closest I ever got to the sound I hear in my mind was on individual bands in the *Blonde On Blonde* album. It's that thin, that wild mercury sound. It's metallic and bright gold with whatever that conjures up.' We should note that he isn't saying he thinks that *Blonde On Blonde* is a better album than *Highway 61*, as well as the fact that we are half a century and many albums on from even the '78 quote. All that we can comfortably assume is that *Blonde On Blonde* was special to Dylan then, and probably remains so.

Aside from being his particular sound, it's possible that he's so fond of *Blonde On Blonde* because it's such a personal work. There are no grand societal statements here along the lines of 'It's All Right, Ma (I'm Only Bleeding)' or 'Desolation Row'. He had previously made a journey from protest to personal songs and more nuanced social commentary, but he has now moved into territory that is so idiosyncratic that some of the songs can only ever be relevant or make sense to him.

Oddly, considering Dylan's triumph in refusing to allow 'Like A Rolling Stone' to be cut down for single release, the 45rpm iteration of 'Rainy Day Women #12 & 35' was only half the length of the version deployed to open *Blonde On Blonde*. The untrimmed original only serves to prove that an unimpressive play on words—'stoned' can mean intoxication or having rocks thrown at one by the disapproving—doesn't get more impressive with repetition, nor does self-conscious high spirits or studied subversiveness.

'Pledging My Time'—again present in a version half as long as its first appearance, this one on the B-side to 'Rainy Day Women'—demonstrates many of the problems with this album. The song is engaging enough for its duration, and its music is incredibly well crafted. However, at bottom, it's simply a blues. Although it doesn't repeat its first line like so many eight- and twelve-bars, and although Dylan's lyrics are naturally a cut above the norm (amusingly, he helpfully tells his lover, 'If it don't work out, you'll be the first to know') and often intriguing (after saying that a hobo tried to steal his baby, he eyebrow-raisingly appends that he then wanted to steal him), it's still all rather generic.

'Visions Of Johanna', on the other hand, demonstrates how this album can hit heights unprecedented for both Dylan and everybody else on the planet. A sumptuous seven-and-a-half-minute opus, it finds Dylan reflecting on the charms of a departed lover. The title's assonance with her first name inevitably created speculation about a certain Miss Baez, but more interesting than such conjecture is the issue of the identity of the men in the song. At the risk of putting forward yet more pointless theories—i.e., ones neither provable nor disprovable—it's possible that the song adds new layers to Dylan's normal pronoun games: although he lurches back and forth between first and third person, it does seem that when, for instance, he refers dismissively to a little boy lost, Dylan is talking about himself, the placing of a distance between him and aspects of himself being a mechanism to enable him to be self-lacerating. Meanwhile, his lyric perfectly captures the soporific, stuffy loft in which a man is entwined with one woman while his thoughts are on another. The instrumental backing is sublime, with gentle percussion and guitar arpeggios providing unobtrusively simpatico accompaniment. Dylan seals each verse with an elegant, undulating harmonica riff.

The track also establishes that this is very much a produced album. Although Dylan was still singing live vocals, and although he still cleaved to his policy of as few takes as possible, Johnston and his engineers were now creating true sound paintings with the results. The organ in this track is judiciously placed in the middle distance, not too close as to be either unremarkable or overpowering and not too distant as to be frustratingly buried, but right where it needs to be to create atmosphericness.

'One Of Us Must Know (Sooner Or Later)' closes vinyl side one, and although not a great song in any context, it feels more natural in this setting, not just because it always sounded like an album cut rather than a single but because a song about the aftermath of a breakup makes it of an emotional piece with the preceding track.

Side two opens and closes with examples of songs Dylan had shown no previous capacity for writing but of which henceforth creditable and slick examples would pepper his catalogue, from 'I'll Be Your Baby Tonight' to 'Mozambique' to 'You're Gonna Make Me Lonesome When You Go' to 'Make You Feel My Love': that is, conventional pop numbers. Or at least as conventional as such a singular mind is capable of devising. The side-opener is 'I Want You', a beautifully nimble confession of desire. A pretty tune allied to a breathless, mysterious lyric, skipping percussion and exotic, willowy sweetening make for a fine variation on standard hit-parade material. Released on single shortly before the album, the track was a transatlantic Top 20 hit. Said disc also featured what would be for many years the only officially released audio evidence of the stunning music played on Dylan's '65/'66 tours in the shape of a B-side that featured a version of 'Just Like Tom Thumb's Blues' recorded in Liverpool.

'Stuck Inside Of Mobile With The Memphis Blues Again' is a variation on nothing, which is to say nothing had sounded even remotely like it before. In retrospect, it's clearly a diary of Dylan's mental and physical descent over the past eighteen months or so, a state of chaos alluded to by the woozy logic inversion of many of the lines (eyelids are smoked and cigarettes punched rather than vice versa) or in the references to drug taking facilitated by a sinister figure with a vested financial interest in being a provider (Albert Grossman—the 'rain man'—was making sure that Dylan's overworked, flagging constitution was bolstered by artificial means in order to maintain the revenue stream of which he owned twenty percent). The music is steady-rolling, mid-tempo, and effortlessly glossy. In truth, the track makes its point by the halfway mark of its seven-minute playing time and would be stronger if it weren't so extended, unique or no.

'Leopard-Skin Pill-Box Hat' exemplifies the tension this album displays in the transcendence of Dylan's song words and the earthbound nature of some of its music. We are completely tickled by his story of a faithless lover with an affected choice of headgear from whom a doctor orders him to stay away for the good of his health, only for the MD to transpire to be resident in her abode, and we are delighted by the narrator's insane simile, 'It balances on your head just like a mattress balances on a bottle of wine.' But why cook up such a hilarious lyric only to waste it on a bog-standard blues workout?

That he's increasingly capable of so much more is proven by the very next track. Side closer 'Just Like A Woman' may well be the prettiest thing Dylan has ever recorded, and the fact that the sweetness of the melody and frilliness of the arrangement is counterpointed somewhat by his playful, subversive, and sarcastic lyric is not a demerit. The track is the essence of the way Dylan was now fully interacting with the backing musicians. The latter provide progressions and accents that perfectly complement the spirit of the song, the aural equivalent of the ribbons and bows he posits the object of his desire metaphorically divesting herself of in her ambiguous growing-up process. Some, of course, will disagree completely with this analysis and enjoy the very contrast between the rootsy and gnarly 'Leopard-Skin Pill-Box Hat' and the lacy, delicate 'Just Like A Woman' and feel it proves the breathtaking range of Dylan at this point in time. It certainly has to be conceded that nobody else was covering the waterfront of popular music in this way.

Side three of the album is the most conventional insofar as it contains five relationship songs of a standard pop length and even some fairly mainstream musical stylings, but that's about the extent of the orthodoxy on display. Ironically, it's the deviation from archetypes that actually prevents Dylan achieving true greatness on any of these tracks.

A famous, if fictional, story is attached to 'Most Likely You Go Your Way And I'll Go Mine'. 'The rumour is, and Al Kooper started this, that I played bass and trumpet at the same time,' says McCoy. 'I can, and I showed it to Al Kooper once that I could do it, but I did not do it on that take because we had Henry Strzelecki on the sessions as the bass player. So this rumour has followed me. I hate to burst the bubble, but it's not true.'

'Most Likely You Go Your Way And I'll Go Mine' is a relentlessly wry dissection of a failing relationship delivered against the backdrop of a careening, muscular arrangement punctuated by a powerful harmonica refrain. A strangely gentle-voiced Dylan offers laconic observations like 'You know you could be wrong' when his lover tells him that she's thinking of him. The odd disconnect between the propulsive and insistent music and Dylan's sardonic and elliptical lyric prevents it from being exciting; a similarly themed Rolling Stones track, for instance, would lay it on the line words-wise to far more enervating effect.

One could make the argument that it's Dylan's unique phraseology and worldview that lift 'Temporary Like Achilles' above the status of yet another standard blues (although the unusual component for a blues of a middle-eight assists, as does some attractive piano work). Some of the lines give credence to the theory that homosexual allusion litters Dylan's catalogue, with talk of a man in drag and the narrator pointedly complaining that his lover is too hard. However, while that might have been interestingly risqué in 1966, it hardly qualifies it as even noteworthy from today's perspective. Some Dylan fans desperately try to invest wisdom in the line 'To live outside the law you must be honest' in 'Absolutely Sweet Marie', but it doesn't really make sense. Nor does this track's mixture of innuendo (Dylan says he's beating on his trumpet), breakneck music, and an organ riff that threatens to become infectious but never quite manages the feat.

'4th Time Around' will have struck many of the album's purchasers as being a Beatles rip-off, but its melodic resemblance to 'Norwegian Wood', released the previous December on The Beatles' _Rubber Soul_, is—if Al Kooper is to be believed—part of a complicated story. He says Dylan had given John Lennon a tape of his work-in-progress and then been surprised to find Lennon beating him to the punch. If true, Dylan appears to have been more amused than angry, and the title he gave his own composition when he got around to releasing it seems to suggest that he is acknowledging that he himself had been indulging in some of his old magpie tendencies when he 'composed' it. Some question Kooper's account (or else the account Dylan gave Kooper) and assert that the song is a parody of the way The Beatles pastiched Dylan on _Rubber Soul_. Either way, Lennon later admitted the title '4th Time Around' had reduced him to a state of paranoia. Ironically, of the two men, Lennon did better with the tune, 'Norwegian Wood' being one of The Beatles' greatest creations. Nonetheless, Dylan's variant makes for an absorbing and amusing three minutes. When his lover asks for recompense for the sexual favours she has dispensed, the narrator gallantly hands her his last strip of chewing gum. He gets kicked out as a consequence, and, when he knocks to request his shirt back, tells her he can't understand what she's saying: 'You better spit out your gum.' It's genuinely funny. Rather unexpectedly, in the midst of all this slapstick and mockery comes a beautiful harmonica solo.

Which doesn't stop Dylan graciously giving way to Charlie McCoy on that instrument on 'Obviously 5 Believers', an up-tempo R&B track with galvanising interplay between McCoy's harp and sinewy guitar. McCoy explains that his playing was a function of Dylan's disdain for overdubs: 'It was a riff that went on behind his vocal, and obviously it was physically impossible for him to do that.' As with 'Most Likely You Go Your Way And I'll Go Mine', one can't help but feel such rockin' fare would have far more power in the hands of an artist less inclined to overthink the lyrical side: talk of the likes of fifteen jugglers and five believers feels meaninglessly ornate in the context.

Side four of *Blonde On Blonde* saw another example of pioneering: 'Sad Eyed Lady Of The Lowlands' was the first time an entire vinyl side of a popular music album was occupied by one song. All the preceding ambivalence about romance and the mickey-taking of lovers is thrown out the window in Dylan's ultimate tribute to Lownds. Whether it's aesthetically worthy in addition to being innovative format-wise is another matter.

There's nothing necessarily wrong with a twelve-minute song. After all, 'Desolation Row' is a track that simply flies by. However, that particular album closer has a universality where this extravaganza finale in some ways feels relevant only to Dylan and his new wife, right down to a title that seems to be a silly in-joke about Lownds' surname. The generosity of spirit inherent in such a worshipful creation and Dylan's tremulous vocal certainly make it touching, the gossamer accompaniment is unquestionably attractive, and the lyric undeniably boasts some lovely lines and evocative couplets (Dylan talks of his lover's silhouette becoming visible when the sunlight dims 'into your eyes where the moonlight swims'), but in addition to the overarching impression of the listener being made eavesdroppers on a couple's banal canoodling, the song is not possessed of enough general resonance to sustain fascination like 'Desolation Row'. As with 'Stuck Inside Of Mobile', we have pretty much had our fill before the halfway mark.

When it comes to double albums—excepting possibly the organic and untrimmable narrative that is *Tommy*—debate always rages as to whether they really merit their extended status. *Blonde On Blonde* is no exception, but Dylan also seems to have had at least five more songs he could have used: he told Grossman after the final *Blonde On Blonde* sessions that he had that number of fresh compositions. A session booked for March 30 at Columbia's Los Angeles studio was cancelled, presumably because Dylan felt he had enough even for a double set, although of course, a greater pool from which to select might have strengthened the final album. Also recorded at the *Blonde On Blonde* sessions—whether in New York or Nashville—were 'I Wanna Be Your Lover', 'Jet Pilot', 'Medicine Sunday', 'Number One', and 'She's Your Lover Now'. There were also half-hearted attempts to make a full-band version of 'I'll Keep It With Mine', as opposed to the Dylan-and-piano iteration that didn't make *Bringing It All Back Home*. Oddly, there was no attempt to capture a studio version of 'Tell Me, Momma', an excellent song with a syncopated arrangement that was actually used as Dylan's electric set-opener in gigs from February to May 1966. There's a case for the inclusion of some or all of these tracks on what was a fairly short double album (seventy-three minutes being enough to accommodate at least two more tracks without sound-quality degradation). However, it can't be gainsaid that the grand statement inherent in 'Sad Eyed Lady' meant it simply had to be hived off to an entire side.

'I'm more of a *Blonde On Blonde* man,' says Kooper of the *Highway 61* vs. *Blonde On Blonde* debate. Asked if it surprises him that *Highway 61* is one of the most acclaimed albums of all time, he says, 'Very much so. ... It's a very brash, comparatively simplistic record [compared] to *Blonde On Blonde* ... I prefer the yang of that yin. I think it's to Bob's advantage that thought went into arranging and that people were communicating with each other to come up with parts that were making the words even better . . . I prefer the detailing on *Blonde On Blonde*. I think it's unbelievable.'

To some extent, the climate of the times dictated that the critics and the public share Kooper's opinion that this album was an improvement on its predecessor. It's the overhang of that impetus that has given it an elevated place in Dylan's canon. Although it's now clear that 1965 was the better year for popular music in terms of classic singles and albums released, 1966 was an annum in which a combination of heightened production standards and an increasing cultural eagerness to give pop its due made it incumbent on people to accept that unprecedented quality was abroad. *Blonde On Blonde* was merely one manifestation of an impression that the titans of the industry were jockeying for supremacy with *meisterwerks*. In the same year, The Beatles released the musically gleaming, lyrically sophisticated *Revolver*, The Beach Boys' unleashed the sonically sweeping *Pet Sounds*, and The Rolling Stones proffered their first collection of exclusively self-generated material in the shape of *Aftermath*. All were milestones and superficially felt like an incremental advance. In the cold light of another era, however, 1965 releases *Rubber Soul* (The Beatles), *Summer Days (And Summer Nights!!)* (The Beach Boys), and *Out Of Our Heads* (The Rolling Stones) are more enjoyable listens. Ditto for *Blonde On Blonde*'s relationship to *Highway 61 Revisited*.

Lyrically, *Blonde On Blonde* is much less powerful in matter subject and less proficient in technique than its predecessor. Musically, it is overly archetypal. Although 'Visions Of Johanna' and a scattered few other tracks maintain Dylan's claim on the title of Poet Laureate Of Pop—at his best, no one else was even coming close to his mastery—so much of the rest of the material gives the impression of very elevated graffiti on a toilet stall wall. Nonetheless, the double album format and the variety of the contents on offer—as well as the dazzling nature of the highlights—lent *Blonde On Blonde* a sense of grandeur, one that dazzled and impeded clear perspective. Placing ourselves back in 1966 makes this album seem far more impressive. At the end of the day, it was indubitably a first on so many levels; a work full of mystery, intellectual rigour, and lyrical daring unlike anything else in popular music at the time; a sumptuous artefact; a sprawling, all-encompassing extravaganza in which pretty much all of human life could be found.

Not only did *Blonde On Blonde* legitimise double albums and continue the process of validating poetry and extended length in popular music that had been started by Dylan's previous excursions, it also provided rock and pop artists a new geographical location to record such works, one that gave them access to musicians of a different calibre and new working methods. 'I remember reading articles in *Rolling Stone* where several so-called hip writers were looking down their nose at Nashville,' says McCoy. 'But I'll tell you what, after Dylan came here, the floodgates opened. We had Joan Baez, Buffy St. Marie, Leonard Cohen, The Byrds, Dan Fogelberg, Peter, Paul & Mary, Manhattan Transfer. . . . It was incredible.'

•

Charlie McCoy may remember the *Blonde On Blonde* sessions as being unprecedentedly arduous for an individual album, and they may well have been, but from Dylan's point of view, they were done on the fly, squeezed in between dates on his world tour.

The February 14–17 Nashville sessions came after half a dozen US dates in quick succession and preceded a trip to Canada for two concerts and back to Dylan's home country for four more dates. The March 8–10 Nashville bloc preceded eight more North American concerts, after which Dylan and crew decamped to Australia (six dates) and Europe. Aside from stops in Stockholm, Copenhagen, Dublin, and Paris, the latter was really a UK tour, with Dylan this time visiting all four countries of the United Kingdom.

Dylan brought along for some European dates D.A. Pennebaker and his film crew, even though the *Dont Look Back* documentary that Pennebaker had shot of the 1965 English tour wasn't yet complete. (It would finally see release in 1967.) Pennebaker was now employing colour stock. Of course, Dylan had also changed his equipment since they'd last worked together in that he was now backed on stage by an electric band in the second half of his concerts. The final result of Pennebaker's 1966 filming, filtered through Dylan and Howard Alk's idiosyncratic editing, was *Eat The Document*, intended for broadcast on the American ABC television network but rejected by them as incomprehensible. It was first publicly shown in 1971 and aired once in December 1978 before shortly disappearing from circulation. Many years later, some of Pennebaker's footage would pop up in Martin

Scorsese's Dylan documentary *No Direction Home*. It features several unforgettable scenes, the most famous of which is the Manchester Free Trade Hall 'Judas' incident. However, there is an even more powerful as well as revealing scene when a disturbingly hyper Dylan babbles to a doctor that he doesn't want to continue with his tour and just wants to go home. The context of this is three albums, one of them a double, recorded in not much more than a year; oodles more songs that Dylan had written but not recorded and/or issued but which were good enough to be released by, and often secure success for, others; and a touring schedule that was psychologically punishing for more than the reasons of a packed schedule and no support acts—i.e., he was playing some of the most remarkable music ever heard on a concert stage but consistently being booed to the rafters.

Then there was the god-awful chore of media obligations. Dylan might be injecting a higher consciousness and expanded vocabulary into pop and rock, but his public persona was becoming ever more intellectually unforthcoming. It was something of a defence mechanism. In his protest and folk days, he had sometimes attempted to answer questions helpfully and articulately. However, the kind of journalist he began to encounter as he moved into the pop sphere had a much younger and less sophisticated audience and accordingly traded in inanities of a type almost designed to infuriate a sophisticated mentality like Dylan's. With comical regularity, they asked him the sort of questions whose answers could be found in his press handout ('Where are you from?') or which anybody already knew the answer to ('Did you change your name?'). To keep himself amused, he began responding in surreal—and often very amusing—ways. Press conferences and interviews would be peppered with exchanges like:

Q: 'Do you have children?'
A: 'Every man with medical problems has children.'
Q: 'What are your medical problems?'

A: 'Well, there's glass in the back of my head and my toenails don't fit properly.'

Q: 'What does [Mister Jones] do for a living?'

A: 'He's a pin boy. He also wears suspenders.'

Q: 'Is it true that you changed your name? If so, what was your other name?'

A: 'Kunezevitch. I changed it to avoid obvious relatives who would come up to me in different parts of the country and want tickets for concerts and stuff like that.'

Q: 'Was that your first or last name?'

A: 'That was my first name. I don't really want to tell you what my last name was.'

The public had become used to the irreverence and jocularity that The Beatles had pioneered in media relations, but this was something altogether different. Although probably not intended to do so, it only served to heighten the perception of Dylan as inhabiting a plateau of wisdom above most human beings. However, while his own growing enigmatic cachet might have tickled him on a superficial plane, it was yet another thing causing him frustration on an intellectual and emotional level.

The means by which he was able to maintain this unholy and spiritually unrewarding work schedule was indicated by another piece of Pennebaker footage that shows a wiped-out Dylan disappearing into a room with Grossman and shortly re-emerging as fit as the proverbial fiddle. Not for nothing is the *Bringing It All Back Home / Highway 61 Revisited / Blonde On Blonde* triumvirate referred to by Dylan's fanbase as the Amphetamine Rock Trilogy. Of course, Dylan's intense ambition and egocentricity made him to a very large extent a willing participant in his abuse. No one held a bullet to his head to sign contracts or take drugs when either was put under his nose, nor did he ever turn down any of the big cheques that poured in as a consequence of them, but

Grossman was in no way whatsoever honouring his duty of care to his client.

This, note, was all just the preamble to the release of Dylan's new album and the media circus bound to follow *that*.

The start of the media circus, of course, was the reviews. By '66, rock writing was just beginning to yield evaluations that were something more than trite, quite possibly because journalists were realising that if the kids could appreciate the like of Dylan's craft, they were also in the market for intelligent evaluation of it. Accordingly, some of the print appraisals of *Blonde On Blonde* are actually worth quoting. Norman Jopling of *Record Mirror* was still marooned in the dying age as he cavilled about the lack of value for money being offered the kids who were shelling out fifty shillings. 'An entire side is taken up by one track,' he brooded. 'As most sides of Bob Dylan records last about twenty-five minutes one would expect this track to be of the same length. ... It is just over twelve minutes long—one minute more than "Desolation Row", which had three other tracks on the same side.' However, *Crawdaddy!*—launched by Paul Williams four months previously as the first professional magazine to seriously analyse rock and its culture—demonstrated the new critical consciousness when it said, 'Whoever decided it would sound best alone on a side, instead of with songs before it and after it, deserves a medal for good taste.' Williams observed of *Blonde On Blonde*, 'The songs are still a swirl of imagery, but it is a gentler, less cyclonic swirl; more like autumn leaves. The nightmares are receding.' Pete Johnson of the *Los Angeles Times* gave that newspaper's readers—many of whom will have been middle-aged, which in those days largely meant completely uninterested in or even hostile to rock—a good precis of both the artist and his latest work. Few would dispute his assertion that 'Dylan is a superbly eloquent writer of pop and folk songs with an unmatched ability to compress complex ideas and iconoclastic philosophy into brief poetic lines and startling images', even if his succeeding caveat—'Coupled with his writing talent is one of the worst voices in the annals of high fidelity'—screams old-school thought processes. He continued, 'He draws his imagery from mythology, history, psychiatry, philosophy, folk sources and literature, easily juxtaposing jarring elements with the pungency of a nightmare.' Stating that Dylan's current style was somewhat at odds with his early efforts, Johnson concluded, 'Pretty songs with ironic overtones, such as "Blowin' In The Wind" and "Don't Think Twice", have fallen prey to a more metallic method of satire, but he has not lost his poetic ability.'

Whether or not one subscribed to the idea that *Blonde On Blonde* had severe failings, and whichever side of the fence one came down on as regards his heretic status, Dylan's ascendancy continued unabated. That he was still the figure to whom the rest of the musical world looked up was demonstrated by the fact that, that summer, Stevie Wonder made 'Blowin' In The Wind' a hit all over again (no. 9 in the US, no. 36 in the UK). His contemporaries continued to deport themselves like dogs slavering around his dining table. On July 29, 1966, two covers of 'Just Like A Woman' were simultaneously released in the UK, one by Manfred Mann, one by Jonathan King. As Dylan's avowed favourite cover artists (even if they now had a new singer in Mike d'Abo), it was fitting that it was the former who should triumph in this chart competition, reaching no. 10 while King stalled outside the Top 40.

July 29 had another significance. It was on that day that Dylan crashed his motorbike when he hit an oil slick while riding on a quiet Woodstock back road. Consequently, the wider world saw and heard nothing of him for almost a year and a half. Remarkably, though, during that interregnum, his legend and influence became even greater.

Chapter five

I Shall Be Released

In late 1967, Mike d'Abo, Tom McGuinness, and Manfred Mann (the person) were walking down Wardour Street in the West End of London. They were on their way to the offices of B. Feldman & Co, Bob Dylan's British publishers, to hear some acetates of new, previously unheard songs by Dylan with a view to their band, Manfred Mann, covering them. It was an exciting prospect: recently so omnipresent in the culture, Dylan had been mysteriously absent and silent for an entire year. Moreover, their group had done very well before with his songs.

'There was a guy ahead of us and I thought, *Wow, he looks weird,*' recalls McGuinness. 'He was in a grey business suit and he had long grey hair coming over his shoulders. You didn't see people looking like that. We stopped to have a pastry or a coffee or something, and when we got into Feldman, there he was.' The fact that Albert Grossman was dressed in conservative clothes while rocking a bohemian hairstyle was not the only odd thing about the meeting. 'Albert Grossman started playing demos,' says McGuinness. 'He played us "I Shall Be Released", "You Ain't Goin' Nowhere", "Mighty Quinn", "Please Mrs. Henry". After about three demos, Manfred said to Albert Grossman, Why does Bob get this terrible singer to do his demos? Albert Grossman looked at him with a sort of *you're-putting-me-on* look. When he realised he wasn't, Albert Grossman said, That *is* Bob.'

During his time away from the spotlight, Dylan's bark-cum-growl had turned into something much more smooth and rounded, with only the familiar whining undertow remaining of the voice that had caused pleasure and disgust in equal measure. Even more startling a tone, though, was that of his songs. His new cache of compositions suggested that the scathing hipster had been transformed into somebody profoundly more mellow, modest and philosophical. Dylan's songcraft, though, remained audibly intact. So did, it transpired, his ability to revolutionise music and culture: these recordings would have a seismic effect on the industry from which he'd almost completely cut himself off for reasons that would only become apparent over the course of the next several years.

•

During 1966, it would seem that Bob Dylan came to the realisation that if you lie down with dogs, you're going to get fleas. The dog in question went by the name of Grossman.

When in June a drained Dylan made his way back to his home country at the end of his four-month world tour, he was amazed and appalled to be informed that Grossman had set up an imminent new American tour comprising sixty-four gigs. It was to some extent understandable, as the just-released *Blonde On Blonde* did need to be promoted, and some dates were quite exciting prospects, such as the one at no less a venue than Shea Stadium (albeit with Dylan sharing headliner status with Peter, Paul & Mary). However, Dylan was also required to deliver to Macmillan a book (the one much later published as *Tarantula*) and to ABC a documentary (what would be *Eat The Document*, whose task of editing he had taken on). While Columbia wasn't expecting another album immediately, he would in the natural course of things fairly soon have to start the process of writing it. Dylan's workload desperately needed decreasing, not increasing. However, failing to fulfil signed contracts could get him sued, which scenario might only worsen a state of mind that people were increasingly noting was precarious. When a year or so before Robert Shelton mentioned to a friend that he was writing a Dylan biography, the friend replied, 'You better hurry.' Dylan later seemed to describe his situation in the song 'This Wheel's On Fire', in which he implored a third party to contact his next of kin to inform them that the rolling, flaming wheel he constituted 'shall explode'. Fate—in the form of that oil slick—gave Dylan a way out of a situation in which he was either going to end up mentally and/or physically damaged or dead.

His motorcycle accident was a scrape, but—with the aid of the same quick brain that had devised so many great ideas and lyrics—he realised he could aggrandise it into a calamity necessitating a rest cure. There is some evidence that genuine injury was occasioned: at least one person reported seeing him in a neck brace shortly afterwards, and it's said he was in bed for a month. However, there's no evidence whatsoever that the physical harm to which Dylan came—cracked vertebrae and concussion—justified him sloughing off all work for the next seventeen months. It's a testament to what a fragmented world it was even as recently as the late 60s that, during this hiatus, a comparatively high number of people for a relatively long period of time thought Dylan was dead, something assisted by the dramatic way the press reported the story. (With grisly timing, three months after the accident, Paul Simon's Dylan piss-take 'A Simple Desultory Philippic', now subtitled 'Or How I Was Robert McNamara'd Into Submission', finally appeared on a Simon & Garfunkel album, featuring on their third LP, *Parsley, Sage, Rosemary, And Thyme*. The gentle mockery now seemed like cruelty. Moreover, what had previously been a perceptive pastiche now became slightly crass and obvious with the insertion of lines like 'It's all right Ma, everybody must get stoned', 'I've lost my harmonica, Albert', and 'Folk-rock!')

When *New York Daily News* journalist Michael Iachetta tracked Dylan down to his home in Woodstock in May 1967, nearly a year after his accident, he couldn't help blurting out, upon seeing his familiar hexagonal-chinned face through the grille of his door, 'It's great to see you're up and around and the rumours aren't true.' Nowadays, the instant global communication accessible to pretty much all the citizens of the world would make such myth and rumour impossible: Dylan's whereabouts and condition would have been known within hours. It would also have made impossible, sadly, the privacy in which Dylan enveloped himself during his recuperative period. In 1966–67, though, being able to claim injury with no real means for that claim to be challenged meant that the line of people who wanted product from him was obliged to leave him alone.

Dylan exploited Iachetta's unexpected intrusion to unburden

himself. Inviting him in for a coffee, he told Iachetta that in his period of self-imposed exile, he had agreed to see only a few close friends, while 'readin'' little about the outside world, porin' over books by people you never heard of, thinkin' about where I'm goin', and why am I runnin', and am I mixed up too much, and what am I knowin', and what am I givin', and what am I takin''. He also took the opportunity to issue what in retrospect seems nothing less than a coded threat to Grossman: 'Songs are in my head like they always are. And they're not goin' to get written down until some things are evened up. Not until some people come forth and make up for some of the things that have happened.'

Dylan could also have mentioned that he had other priorities these days. His and Sara's first child together, Jesse, was born in January '66. (Dylan adopted Sara's daughter from a previous relationship, Maria.) The couple would have three more children by 1969. It's difficult to continue to be—or even want to remain—a rebellious rock god when you're trying to raise a brood.

Nineteen sixty-seven was an incredible year for popular music, with The Beatles releasing their game-changing masterpiece *Sgt. Pepper's Lonely Hearts Club Band*, Mick Jagger and Keith Richards of The Rolling Stones cementing their social outlaw status by being imprisoned on drugs charges and then following public outrage spectacularly having their sentences reduced or quashed, and the brave-new-world ethos of San Francisco's Haight-Asbury district being given a far-out soundtrack by the likes of Jefferson Airplane, the Grateful Dead, Big Brother & The Holding Company, and Quicksilver Messenger Service. Meanwhile, the staging of the three-day Monterey International Pop Festival demonstrated that the 'Love Crowd'—as participant Otis Redding called pop's increasingly flamboyantly dressed and philosophically pacific demographic—was an ever-growing, ever more important societal presence. Yet, the vibrant, fecund, insurrectionary music scene that he had transformed through his groundbreaking and genius was one from which Dylan completely absented himself.

Yet despite his non-participation—he wouldn't re-emerge until the very last week of the year—both happenstance and his previous importance kept his name very much alive. Leaving aside the fact that his absence and—more importantly—silence only caused him to become even more shrouded in the mystique that his gnomic utterances and poetic song words had already conferred on him, it so happened that there was quite a lot of new Dylan merchandise around. Columbia was seemingly thrown into a state of panic by their inability to market new product by their star. Two albums and several singles (possibly including standalone ones) per year were still considered de rigueur if a recording artist was not going to be forgotten about by his fans. As such, the label decided in March '67 to issue *Bob Dylan's Greatest Hits*, despite the fact that Dylan hadn't actually had many hits, and despite the fact that much of his fanbase was guaranteed to despise such a conventional, mercenary measure. Using lateral thinking, the label included as well as Dylan's bona fide hit-parade entries his original versions of songs made famous by others, such as 'Blowin' In The Wind', 'It Ain't Me Babe', and 'Mr. Tambourine Man'. Despite its desperate and dubious origins, it couldn't be denied that the album was a great collection of music and a good introduction to the artist. The most kaleidoscopic best-of yet released went to no. 6 in the UK, where it enjoyed a mammoth eighty-two-week chart run, and no. 10 in the US.

There was also a book of photographs by Daniel Kramer and the belated appearance of Pennebaker's documentary of the 1965 English tour. Titled *Dont Look Back* (no apostrophe, like it came from a Dylan sleeve note rather than the refrain of 'She Belongs To Me'), it captured Dylan as the persona he had been when it was filmed—trendsetting, acerbic, creatively fired up—but which, unbeknown to everyone except intimates, he had since completely outgrown, even in effect repudiated. In it, he is seen humiliating his imitator Donovan, *Time* interviewer Horace Freeland Judson, and science student and part-time journalist Terry Ellis.

Asked about Dylan's gentle cruelty to him, Donovan says, 'I don't find it so now, looking at the film. In fact, he was pissed off more with the drunk who was sitting next to him and there was a lot of people in the room going crazy. He was a little bit sharp and, like John Lennon, he doesn't suffer fools gladly, and he was very sort of opinionated and giving out to the press and putting them down and sharp language, but that was a very New York thing. When you study the film closely, you see that he says, You wrote that? Meaning, That's cool. And he said at one point, He don't play like me, he plays like Jack Elliott. So, when I look back now, he was very supportive, and Joan Baez told me at the time he was a little bit shocked that there was another guy—me—who came out of the folk tradition, who had studied Woody Guthrie as much as Bob had. There's lots you didn't see in the film. I suppose the film points out the conflicts that Bob was going through at the time. He was very kind to me. When the cameras weren't rolling, we became quite close, and I played him other songs and we hung out a lot at that hotel, and it was Bob that introduced me to The Beatles.' Such innocence and generosity of spirit were perhaps the sole attributes Donovan had that Dylan did not.

The main thing that kept Dylan's legend going, though, was the first publicly available evidence of his continued creativity. This was not even something that was commercially available, and—covers aside—none of it would obtain an official release until 1975. It still, though, had a profound effect on those who were privy to it and—as those privy were mainly recording artists—an effect on the industry and hence the public, one that was as substantial as would be expected when it came to Bob Dylan.

Located in upstate New York's Ulster County, Woodstock was a hamlet with a permanent population of six thousand that ballooned to twenty-four thousand in summer. Dylan, though, was no tourist. He'd first used the place as a refuge—whether from fame or, as time went on, to escape the wrath of the Greenwich Village set as they became disgruntled with his changes of style and allegedly of values. He had liked its quietude, as well as its in parts bohemian and artistic vibe (Tim Hardin, Van Morrison, and Frank Zappa were fellow residents), and had graduated from his section of Grossman's house to one of his own. Ensconced there after the accident, for several months he did something he hadn't done in years: he wrote no songs at all, or at least none he was prepared to show his manager, whose nearby home it's doubtful he continued to be a regular visitor to.

While he was gradually extricating himself from Grossman's influence, the opposite was true of The Hawks, who were now morphing into the entity that would be professionally known as The Band. The latter were domiciled in West Saugerties, a fifteen-minute drive from Woodstock, having rented a house which because of its outlandish colour scheme was nicknamed Big Pink. They were shooting supplementary footage for *Eat The Document*. They were also strengthening their ties with Grossman, who would be their long-term manager. The diametrically opposed views of Grossman on the part of Dylan and The Band didn't come between them: their harrowing shared experience on the world tour had been a remarkable bonding experience.

The fact that Dylan eventually proceeded to write songs and then began to lay them down on tape was another manifestation of Grossman's avarice. Dylan later spoke darkly of certain parties—implicitly Grossman and/or Columbia and/or publishing companies—'pushing' him to write. This may be true, but in any event, the inactivity involved in recuperation was going to be a boring matter for a naturally prolific artist, even a man enjoying the first flush of marriage and fatherhood. Additionally, he was able to record without straying far from home comforts, and he was accorded the opportunity to be creative both without being beholden to a deadline and in the company of mates and allies: The Band would back him on the recordings of his new songs. Significantly, he later said, 'That's really the way to do a recording—in a peaceful, relaxed setting, in somebody's basement, with the windows open and a dog lying on the floor.'

These activities began as undocumented jams sometime between March and June 1967. When they turned into recordings, they took place at Dylan's house and at the house of neighbour Clarence Schmidt but primarily in the basement of Big Pink. As such, they assumed the umbrella, colloquial title 'The Basement Tapes'. Dylan and his colleagues have always claimed that they were never meant to be publicly released. Giving some credence to this idea is the fact that Dylan doesn't bother embellishing the songs with harmonica, as well as the fact that no more than two passes were made at any song.

Yet if this was so, it might be asked why Dylan was apparently assiduously schooling the band in the ways of folk material during this period (The Hawks were pure rock'n'roll). It might also be asked why he would need a band behind him in the first place—wouldn't a one-man-and-guitar demo be just as effective for selling his songs to other artists, the stated reason for getting them down?

Then again, perhaps their presence on the recordings is the very proof that Dylan wasn't thinking in terms of a commercial release. He had thought enough of The Hawks as a live proposition to embark with them on that extraordinary odyssey that had been his electric world tour, but his recording experiences with them thus far had been failures. Whatever the reason for Dylan deciding to do full-band demos (maybe he thought that more fully fleshed-out demos than usual would maximise take-up from other artists?), the simple fact of The Band's proximity could be the mundane explanation for his working with them on his new songs. To paraphrase the man himself, they just happened to be there, that's all. Meanwhile, the fact that he had never thought much of The Hawks' recording prowess might itself be the proof that the recordings were not meant to be released.

Mickey Jones had drummed on the world tour but was no longer part of the situation. Levon Helm, though, only returned to The Hawks/Band's drummer's stool after a period in which the participants had to work around the lack of a proper percussionist. It wasn't the only thing that had to be worked around. It turned out all right for everybody, though. In the kind of happenstance and occurrence that can never be legislated for, what emerged was a unique cache of recordings. The Big Pink basement had concrete walls, resulting in the musicians becoming careful to not turn up their instruments too high. Basements also tend to be sonically close, as later evidenced by The Rolling Stones' claustrophobic *Exile On Main St.*, famously largely recorded in the bowels of a French mansion. Moreover, Dylan and The Band's recording equipment was very basic. The overall result was intriguingly and atmospherically quirky and musty. Interleaved with that is Dylan's singular state of mind and what emanated from it.

In the time that Dylan spent hidden away from the world, he seemed to undergo an almost complete personality change. Photographs of him from the period show a man in almost parodically simple and humble dress: white shirt, white slacks, flip-flops, and a bumpkin hat. Someone whose shades, Cuban heels, head-to-toe black threads, and scabrous personality had until recently rendered him the hippest man in the world now looked totally square and, moreover, someone who couldn't care less about it.

Rock had always been about self-aggrandisement, partly because it had thus far been the music of teens and twentysomethings, an age group that tends to put itself first, and partly because rock was then intertwined with social revolution—something that necessitates a certain assertiveness. Dylan's previous music had reflected that. No more. As well as now being a parent, with the discovery of the virtues of sacrifice and selflessness that goes with that, Dylan seems to have been in a peculiarly vulnerable, reflective frame of mind. His new songs were humble, penitent, patient, remorseful, and many other things not usually associated with post-Elvis popular music. Although there is anger and resentment to be discerned in his new lyrics, it does not at any time manifest itself in venom along the lines of 'Like A Rolling Stone'. The closest he seems to come is in 'Nothing Was Delivered', but the keynote line in this composition of recrimination is 'I tell this truth to you not out of spite nor anger'. The reason for such a dichotomy is that his sudden perception of the fact that his manager (the presumed subject of the song) may not have been an altogether benign actor and influence on his life and career seems to have been arrived at pretty much at the same time as Dylan acquiring sufficient self-knowledge to realise that his own behaviour in recent years had not exactly been exemplary or morally consistent. Perhaps also he was regretting his ruthless, cold-blooded exploitation of folk, protest, and rock music and the way it meant him discarding entire belief sets and friendship circles as he embraced each genre and market. This, of course, is all speculation, but it seems reasonable to believe from the available evidence that the cool, wisecracking, ultra-talented but rather nasty persona that he had been since his rise to public prominence—and captured at its nadir in *Dont Look Back*—was something on which Dylan was now reflecting ruefully.

Not that the Basement Tapes are all doom and gloom. There is much humour in evidence, alternately whimsical, merry, and surreal. There's also the possibility that Dylan is taking the piss: resentment at the fact that he was having to write these songs at all seems to manifest itself in throwaway lines that, it just so happens, end up sounding like surreal genius. If some of the lyrics come across now as well-read gibberish— the type that is now commonplace in pop—it should be pointed out that then it was a novelty. The songs also drip with sex: that Dylan and Sara were newlyweds is glaringly apparent in the ribald likes of 'Apple Suckling Tree', 'Please Mrs. Henry', and 'Lo And Behold!' On top of that, in tracks like 'Quinn The Eskimo' and 'Sign On The Cross' there are the very first stirrings of a religiosity that would later deepen profoundly, albeit carefully disguised, lest it alienate the counterculture audience that formed his fanbase and was deeply hostile to organised deity worship and the moral authoritarianism perceived to go with it. One of those religion-informed compositions, the seven-and-a-half-minute 'Sign On The Cross', is incidentally one of the few long songs.

Dylan generally eschews the epic lengths that had become an increasing feature of his music for disciplined exercises of two or three minutes.

There is also a new vocabulary. The world was used to the plain but clever speaking of his protest songs and the metaphor-packed poetry of his mid-60s compositions. Somehow, that same brain was now yielding up a new, eccentric phraseology to paint scenarios that felt distinctly olde-worlde and down-home. Talk of characters called Henry, Skinny Moo, and T-Bone Frank, and discussion of clotheslines, levees, and a daughter disrespecting her father, make the listener feel s/he has wandered into a dislocated, indeterminate time zone that possesses more in common with an American Western frontier town in the 1860s than the Eastern Seaboard and the Swinging Sixties.

Wherever it came from, this new approach to language perfectly complemented the musty, muted timbre of the music caused by the particular sonics of Big Pink's cellar and the fact that The Band's drummer was absent for much of the proceedings. It was as if this was what rock'n'roll would have sounded like if the technology and culture of the Old West had enabled it. It was an accidental but perfect marriage, one that created a unique twig on the pop branch of the great tree of music.

There arises a question of precisely what the Basement Tapes are. They number over a hundred songs (and there are theorised to be several lost or undisclosed reels), but should the many covers recorded—most of them old folk tunes—be counted? Should the warm-ups, false starts, scraps, and whimsy? Official releases were staccato and piecemeal and occurred in diluted, redacted, and sometimes controversial circumstances. The Band released what might be termed one-step-removed versions of three of the songs on their 1968 debut album, *Music From Big Pink*, but re-recordings by everyone originally involved except Dylan himself were hardly the real McCoy, if valid and enjoyable in their own right. Several of the songs were released commercially by others, and some became big hits that proved that Dylan's fairy dust remained active even as his words became ever more opaque and idiosyncratic. It was only in 1969 that some of the wider public got to hear Dylan's versions of some of the songs when seven of them appeared on *Great White Wonder*, rock's first bootleg. Not many knew where to find such illegal releases, however, and it wasn't until 1970 that most people first got to hear Dylan sing Basement Tape songs when he made the decision to release mediocre live versions of a couple of them—'Quinn The Eskimo', by then made famous by Manfred Mann as 'The Mighty Quinn' in a hit cover; and the obscure 'Minstrel Boy'—on his bizarre project of self-sabotage, *Self Portrait*. He was trying to say something about himself—however inarticulately, however Machiavellian—on that album. What, though, was he attempting to communicate the following year, when he exploited the Basement Tapes' mystique to boost sales of his second greatest hits compilation, other than that the man so opposed to mammon for its own sake that he refused to have a fan club was now a bread-head? The three Basement Tape songs included on *Bob Dylan's Greatest Hits Volume II*, while very good, were new, polished renditions emanating from a state-of-the-art studio. The world still waited for the real deal, and the fact that Dylan included the lyrics of twenty-one Basement Tape songs in his 1973 book *Writings & Drawings* only whetted the appetite for an official release.

That may never have seen the light of day if it hadn't been for the fact that his January 1975 album *Blood On The Tracks* was universally hailed as the creative renaissance of a man who had seemed unable to match previous heights for at least half a decade: issuing great material from the vaults would have otherwise seemed a desperate measure and underlined the perception of him as a has-been. (Another possible cause for the belated willingness to release the Basement Tapes is that Albert Grossman, despite becoming Dylan's ex-manager as of August '69, received publishing royalties from his songs until 1973.) In June '75, finally, came the release of a Dylan-sanctioned *Basement Tapes*. A double album, it initially seemed like the Holy Grail, yet it transpired that even this was far from the genuine article. It was certainly a great listen, and it provided a representative flavour of the original recordings, but the collection—dubious from the start because of song selection that left off some of the highlights—was gradually exposed as a semi-fraud, whether because of the overdubs supervised by Robbie Robertson or the fact that it transpired that the five tracks by The Band sans Dylan were new recordings not related to the Big Pink sessions but aurally muddied to sound like they were. (By remarkable coincidence, The Band owed Columbia five songs at the time.) In the twenty-first century, technology and the changed market finally enabled Dylan's camp to unload the entire and unadulterated set of surviving recordings onto the world in the form of *The Bootleg Series Vol. 11.*

The fourteen songs that initially saw daylight through the acetates played to the likes of Tom McGuinness and co were heard initially by only a select few. However, for the purposes of a text examining Dylan's 60s work and influence, those are the relevant parts of the Basement Tapes. They were the ones included on the so-called Dwarf Music Demos, one dating from October 1967 and a second from January 1968 that appended four songs to the first's ten. Their contents were copyrighted to Dwarf Music, the publishing company owned in equal parts by Dylan and Grossman and set up in 1965 upon the expiry of the Witmark deal. It so happens that the '68 Dwarf Music Demo cuts to the heart of the Basement Tapes. At the time, Dylan owed Columbia a fourteen-track album as the last instalment of his current contract, and the collection would have made a very respectable LP if commercially released, even if its sonic qualities were not of conventional standard, and even if the takes included of some songs were, in the opinion of many, not the best ones. It would have been both a more honest representation of the Basement Tapes than the 1975 official album of that name and a superior listening experience. However, Bob Dylan has never thought as much of the Basement Tapes as others, being clearly too close to the songs to see them as anything more than a work in progress, psychologically as much as musically. 'People have told me they think it's all very Americana and all that,' he once sniffed. 'I don't know what they're talking about.' (The fact that if you dig deep enough in the quote faults you can find some favourable Dylan comments about the Basement Tapes is merely a predictable indicator of his perennial—and quite annoying—contrariness and playfulness.)

'Million Dollar Bash' is a song in which the comedy running through the Basement Tapes is evident in the narrator looking at his watch on his wrist, then punching himself in the face with his fist. Perhaps he was chastising himself for being late for the titular occasion, at which was present a big dumb blonde whom we're informed has her wheel in the gorge, and her friend Turtle, notorious for forged cheques. Meanwhile, the Basement Tapes' exceptional lexicon—like the English language put through a tumble dryer—is in evidence in the observation, 'The louder they come, the bigger they crack'.

The line 'The comic book and me, just us, we caught the bus' in 'Yea! Heavy And A Bottle Of Bread' gives a flavour of both the odd phraseology and the often eccentric and endearing mood that characterises the Basement Tapes. Across the recordings, Dylan isn't making any grand statements about the world or caustic observations designed to please his stylish circle. In tracks like this—indicated by its befuddling title and talk of slapping a drummer with a pie that smells—he is writing nonsense verse of which Edward Lear would be proud, and exhibiting an engaging mellowness. That a lot of the lyrics make no sense is something Dylan indolently but consistently communicates he cares nothing about.

'Please Mrs. Henry' sounds like the sozzled lament of a lodger who imagines he is put upon by his landlady. It's stuffed full of phrases that sound suspiciously like filth, with the narrator boasting he can slam like a drake, threatening to fill up Mrs Henry's shoe, and speaking of his fear that his crane is going to leak. The sense of ribaldry hidden behind broken-up English is intensified by the way Dylan almost cracks up when declaiming it.

The apocalyptical imagery of 'Crash On The Levee (Down In The Flood)' is another seam in the Basement Tapes, a subset of the occasional religiosity. The narrator is warning the person he is addressing that she will have to find a new best friend when the foretold disaster occurs, yet doing so in a sad voice bearing little relation to the vindictiveness of the sort-of similarly themed 'The Times They Are A-Changin'', 'When The Ship Comes In', or 'Like A Rolling Stone'.

The tapes' unexplained disconnection from modern urban life finds its fullest expression in 'Lo And Behold!', in which the narrator travels in a vehicle never stated as being a stagecoach but which in the context of a lyric couched in antediluvian language and packed with decidedly uncontemporary-sounding event seems more than likely to be; the narrator gives his name and then hangs his head in shame and speaks of buying his love a herd of moose. He's also heading for San Antone, the title of a famous western. Sex, of course, is not restricted to any era: he asks one Molly what's the matter with her 'mound'; she asks what's it to him while addressing him as 'Moby-Dick'.

'Tiny Montgomery' shows how Dylan was populating his current landscapes with characters who, while not being particularly glamorous, feel either larger than life or like people who derive from American mythology, right done to their handles: Skinny Moo, T-Bone Frank, and Tiny Montgomery himself. Mr. Montgomery gives the message that he says hello while relaying instructions that are gibberish even for these songs: 'scratch your dad', 'nose that dope', 'gas that dog', 'flour that smoke', etc. It could all be another Dylan distancing technique—talking about himself or those close to him through a hall of pseudonymous mirrors and disguised reference to prevent exposure while enjoying the therapeutic effect of expressing his grievances—and, short of a Dylan confession, the listener will never be any the wiser. All we know is that we're left with an intriguing slice of life-but-not-as-we-know-it, propelled by acoustic guitar and decorated oddly prettily by chirruping backing vocals and organ warbles.

The happy and relaxed atmosphere of the Big Pink recordings seems to be demonstrated by a couple of separate anecdotes about Dylan turning up with a sheet of lyrics and asking others to write a melody for them. He'd never before had the creative luxury of being able to lean on others or such an atmosphere of communitarianism. The identity of the songs in question is in that sense irrelevant, although it so happens one of them is 'This Wheel's On Fire'. This marriage of a baroque but tortured Dylan lyric ('No man alive will come to you with another tale to tell') and a haunting Rick Danko melody created a classic. The Band's bassist was possibly completely oblivious of this fact as he 'set' the words, but the condition that the lyric describes is crucial to the whole genesis of these recordings: without Dylan's exploited, exhausted state, the Basement Tapes would never have come about.

'This Wheel's On Fire' is one of the few tracks with drums, as is 'You Ain't Goin' Nowhere', which boasts additional ticking percussion. A composition in which a chorus ostensibly celebrating the comfort and stability of marriage is undermined by verses with a more mordant, uncertain tone and indeed a title refrain in which the narrator seems to be admonishing himself for kidding himself that he can still be free while betrothed. A variant of this song issued by Dylan on *Greatest Hits Volume II* amended the lyric to have a pop at Roger McGuinn for some reason that may be related to a recent interview in which the Byrd suggested Dylan had let down the music scene and counterculture by turning his back on them.

The exclusion of 'I Shall Be Released', one of Dylan's most powerful—and most covered—songs, may be the most inexplicable and dubious aspect of the 1975 iteration of the Basement Tapes. Admittedly, it was by then one of the few songs of which Dylan had already treated the world to a version, but to omit the track from the long-awaited official release of what was by now a legendary cache was wrong not merely because of its aesthetic strength and cultural fame (it had been covered by The Tremeloes, Marmalade, P.J. Proby, Joe Cocker, Nina Simone, The

Hollies, Rick Nelson, Bette Middle, Earl Scruggs, and many others) but because of its keynote status. Some interpreted the composition in a literal, jailbird's-lament fashion, such as The Tom Robinson Band, who in 1977 added a new verse about getting a prisoner out of prison and to hell with waiting for a new judicial enquiry. The release Dylan discusses is clearly a spiritual one, although it's difficult to judge whether it's an escape from his former self, his demons, his obligations, or even something more elevated. Dylan talks of seeing his light come shining 'from the west unto the east', an Abrahamic religious motif that crops up repeatedly in his songs from hereon, whether it be the narrator of 'Isis' (1976) saying, 'I came in from the East with the sun in my eyes', or the narrator of 'No Time To Think' (1978) stating that starlight in the East means he is 'finally released'. It would certainly chime with the religiosity to be discerned in 'Quinn The Eskimo' and 'Sign On The Cross' (the latter addressing Dylan's complicated relationship with Judaism and Jewishness). One doesn't, of course, have to buy into or even fully understand any of this to enjoy what is, whatever else it may or may not be, a melancholically anthemic and moving creation.

Dylan is clearly vexed about something on the keening 'Tears Of Rage', a co-write with Band pianist Richard Manuel, but it's expressed from behind his usual wall of elaborate metaphor and allegory, thus denying it any potential power even as he intrigues us with what seems the perspective of grievously disappointed parents as he talks of a daughter who waits upon her parents hand and foot while always telling them no. The thought strikes that the song might be Dylan putting himself in the shoes of his own mum and dad, who were so bewildered by their eldest's effective disowning of them and denial of what they had thought was a happy home via his I'm-a-runaway interviews. This would be a real psychological, personal breakthrough if that is the case, but one thing is certain: this song is territory previously unknown to popular music. It was also absolutely out of kilter with the times. At a point in history where the establishment was being challenged like never before in modern history, it strikes an absolutely contrary tone in which it takes the non-youth side in a generational war, even if this particular war is a localised one.

With its clearly defined barrelhouse piano, ringing electric guitar, and vocal harmonies, 'Too Much Of Nothing' has among the most conventional sonics of any of the demos. 'Too much of nothing can make a man ill at ease' is the sort of sentiment found in the verses of what is a song expressing a downcast state but specifying no precise cause. They're counterpointed by a catchy chorus with pretty harmonising but which itself—with its talk of saying hello to Valerie and Vivian and sending them a salary on the waters of oblivion—might possess meaning only in an impressionistic sense yet also serve to turn a dirge into something approaching a pop anthem. Sharing management with Dylan is probably what enabled Peter, Paul & Mary to become the first artists to cover a Basement Tapes song, their version of 'Too Much Of Nothing' appearing in November 1967.

Dylan has claimed that 'Quinn The Eskimo' was inspired by the 1960 Anthony Quinn film *The Savage Innocents*, but while that might be part of the truth, it's clearly far more meaningful than that. Talk of a world in despair that will jump with joy upon the arrival of the titular character, and people stepping on each others' toes transformed into a population that merely wants to doze, would seem to be nothing so much as a Second Coming allegory. The chorus demonstrates that Dylan's by-now finely honed songcraft can shine through both his depressed state and the compromised sonics of Big Pink's basement, the 'Come all without, come all within' refrain the cherry on the singalong cake.

'Open The Door Homer' is also catchy if incomprehensible, right from the fact that it's Richard, not Homer, being implored to allow access in the lyric to its observation that one must always flush out one's house if one doesn't wish to house flushes—a piece of wisdom vouchsafed by a friend who never blushes. The combination of a mirthful lyric and plaintive melody inexplicably works well. *Writings & Drawings* insists that in the correct lyric, it is Homer being addressed. Perhaps Dylan temporarily changed it during the recording as a whimsical reference to 'Open The Door, Richard' a 1947 single by Jack McVea and Don Howell based on a famous vaudeville routine by Dusty Fletcher and Don Mason in which a drunkard arriving home after getting thrown out of a bar calls in vain for his flatmate, Richard, to let him in. The casual dropping in of obscure cultural references like this is the kind of thing a songwriter does when in a carefree mood. As such, 'Open The Door Homer' is a song that probably exemplifies the fact that there are crannies of the Basement Tapes that will never be understood by the vast majority of people who hear them.

In 'Nothing Was Delivered', not only does Dylan—we may as well dispense with the term 'narrator' for what are obviously such intensely personal songs—emphasise that he is complaining not out of spite or anger, but he also devises a curious chorus in which he returns to a theme explored in 'To Ramona', one in which he states that nothing/nobody is better or best. He also implores the person he is addressing to take care of himself and get plenty of rest. Yet for all that, the situation depicted has the language of a hostage scenario: the object of his grievance is told more than once that he cannot leave until matters are resolved. Those 'matters' are stated to revolve around theft and broken assurances. It's natural, of course, to assume the subject of the song is his estranged manager, and how must Grossman—not a stupid man—have felt as he touted around these veiled condemnations? Leaving that aside, how remarkable it is that Dylan had achieved such personal growth within two years of the way he expressed bitterness in the likes of 'Positively 4th Street'. Whether the result is worthwhile—outside of human interest, the fascination of Dylan fans with his private life, and the fact that yet again Dylan is reshaping the boundaries of what popular music can express—is another matter: the two complete released Dylan versions are not a great listening experiences, being competent but glum. Nor could The Byrds (who rather inexplicably covered it) make it any more fun.

Fun or no, as so many times previously, Dylan had with the Dwarf Music Demo delivered unto the world songs—and, in this case, recordings—the like of which nobody had ever heard before. What is unique about this material is that nobody ever really would again. They are casual but considered, knocked off with no thought to anyone ever hearing them, yet agonisingly wrought because they are the product of a man with demons to cast out and matters to get off his chest, both compromised and enhanced by their recording venue. They are Americana, Dylanalia, and a snapshot of a human being at a particularly vulnerable and whimsical moment in time. They are, in summation, something that because of psychological circumstances and physical happenstance can never be revisited by Dylan or replicated by third parties.

•

It was inevitable that among those invited to the exclusive Wardour Street preview of Dylan's new material were representatives of Manfred Mann.

In the winter of 1965, they had been cited by Dylan himself as his favourite of the many, many interpreters of his material. In a televised San Francisco press conference, Dylan was asked by a reporter, 'Of all the people who record your compositions, who do you feel does the most justice to what you're trying to say?' Instead of one of the scornful, smart-aleck non-answers he was frequently apt to come out with, he provided a thoughtful and candid response. 'I think Manfred Mann,' he said. 'They've done the songs—they've done about three or four. Each one of them has been right in context with what the song was all about.' His count was awry—the group concerned would end up doing four but so far had recorded just a Dylan brace—but even so it was highly gratifying for them. Not that everyone agreed with it. 'In one of the long-defunct papers like *Sounds* or *Disc* they did a thing about it,' says McGuinness. 'Someone wrote in the next week and said, How dare

Bob Dylan say that Manfred Mann interprets his songs best of all. The Byrds are obviously much better. I love the idea of someone disagreeing with the writer.'

Paul Jones had departed Manfred Mann's ranks in 1966. 'One of the reasons I left was, I was afraid that the Manfreds were morphing into a Bob Dylan tribute band,' he says. Perhaps the Manfreds were at the point of his departure already discussing a cover of 'Just Like A Woman'. Certainly, after some agonising, they opted to use it to inaugurate the chapter of their career in which they were fronted by Mike d'Abo. 'We heard the *Blonde On Blonde* album before it was released and thought that would make a good song for us,' says McGuinness. '[Feldman] knew we were into the idea of looking at Dylan songs. We got into a duel with Jonathan King and the radio play was split between the two versions, so it wasn't as big a hit as we hoped.'

The Feldman connection came in handy again the following year. McGuinness: 'I think it was Grossman who made the connection . . . Feldman said Albert Grossman was bringing over some Dylan demos, did we want to hear them? Well, of course we did.' Of those tracks they heard at Wardour Street, d'Abo was convinced of the hit potential of 'This Wheel's On Fire', but Mann felt 'Quinn The Eskimo' had the best chart prospects. Of the latter, McGuinness recalls, 'We recorded it and then it got shelved. In particular because Manfred said, No, it's not working.' A visit by Lou Reizner, head of Mercury Records, rescued it from its stalled status. McGuinness: '[He] said, You haven't had a hit in America with this line-up. Is there anything in the can? Michael played him "Quinn", and he said, That sounds like a hit to me. Michael rang us all up the next day, and we all went over. He had an acetate of the rough mix and he put it on and we were listening and Manfred went over to the piano and he said, Michael, your record player's running fast—it's up a semitone from the key we recorded it in. So we went back into the studio. Klaus [Voorman] added a piccolo flute, doubling the flute line. Michael added some tablas, and we sped the whole thing up a semitone—and that was it. If Lou Reizner hadn't heard it, we might never have finished it. We just made it sound a bit brighter.'

In d'Abo's opinion, 'Basically, we made a non-melody into a melody.' Although the song can be read as a second-coming parable, it can also be perceived as a meaningless slab of whimsy, but either way is infectiously anthemic, especially in the Manfred Mann iteration. It made no. 10 Stateside, the only US hit for the d'Abo Manfred Mann line-up. In the UK, it was a chart-topper. 'I sold my acetate quite recently for a lot of money to a collector,' says McGuinness of his copy of the Basement Tapes material.

The component parts of Manfred Mann continued to do well with Dylan songs. The 1972 album *Lo And Behold* by the post-Manfred Mann quasi-supergroup Coulson, Dean, McGuinness, Flint took to the max the idea of covering little-known or unreleased Dylan songs.[*] Manfred Mann—the person—also maintained his connection to Dylan. His succeeding group Manfred Mann's Earth Band would cover 'Please Mrs. Henry', 'It's All Over Now, Baby Blue', 'Get Your Rocks Off!', 'Father Of Night', 'Quit Your Lowdown Ways', 'Mighty Quinn', 'You Angel You', and 'Shelter From The Storm'.

Grossman taking the trouble to cross the Atlantic with the Dwarf songs was a success in the sense of securing cover versions of his charge's latest creations. However, his other objective in personally, physically delivering the material, for reasons of confidentiality, failed completely. He was clearly concerned to ensure that only the right sort covered the newly copyrighted—and hence legally recordable—material. A proven hit artist like Manfred Mann was a better bet than some obscure combo seeking to jump on the Dylan bandwagon. However, what he didn't count on was that staff at B. Feldman & Co would dub onto quarter-inch tape the acetates he had brought and matter-of-factly distribute

---

[*] Track listing: 'Eternal Circle', 'Lo And Behold', 'Let Me Die In My Footsteps', 'Open The Door Homer', 'Lay Down Your Weary Tune', 'Don't You Tell Henry', 'Get Your Rocks Off', 'The Death Of Emmett Till', 'Odds And Ends', and 'Sign On The Cross'.

them to interested parties. They also took it upon themselves to play them for UK music journalists. Norman Jopling of *Record Mirror* and Nick Jones of *Melody Maker* were two journos granted possibly unauthorised access to the Dwarf material, and they promptly wrote up reviews, if that term can be used about a non-existent product. Thus interest in the recordings was piqued further. Back over on the other side of the Atlantic, Jann Wenner of *Rolling Stone* wrote a front-page article titled 'Dylan's Basement Tape Should Be Released' in which he averred of the recordings, 'If this were ever to be released it would be a classic.' Such was the interest in what the reclusive Dylan was up to that everyone on the 'scene'—what would soon be termed the rock aristocracy—soon had these recordings. Their effect was profound.

What resulted from even the Dwarf Music demos' limited exposure proved that Dylan was influential by default. He had probably never intended to revolutionise folk with his rock'n'roll attitude nor to revolutionise rock with his intellectual lyrics; he was just doing what he wanted to do, but doing it so artistically incandescently and commercially successfully that a legion of others took his cue. That inadvertent Pied Piper quality now pertained to the Basement Tapes. Rock and pop had come on hugely in the past three years in terms of the subject matter its artists felt able to address and accommodate. Now, Dylan was taking it a step further with these arcane, mysterious, reflective, horny, and spiritual songs. However, this time his singular song words were actually less influential than the overall sound—that unique, rootsy, musty, unmodern timbre, which seemed like a complete repudiation of the current fashion for vast and distorted soundscapes. Ironically, it was all something of a misunderstanding.

Dylan spent the decade dissenting, but while it's true that he was dubious about the current vogues among his peers—the Summer Of Love and psychedelia—the Basement Tapes weren't a manifestation of that disapproval. Yet while lo-fi quality and unfussy instrumentation had been merely a function of their 'demonstration copy only' origins and the primitive circumstances of their recording, Dylan's peers reacted like the hordes looking in the wrong direction for a messiah in the Monty Python movie *Life Of Brian*: just as those misguided legions read significance that wasn't there into the likes of a lost sandal, so Dylan's contemporaries were dazzled by the fact that this material went totally against the grain of everything into which they had invested energy, craft, and credibility over the past year. In an age of virtuoso musicianship—exemplified by the extemporisation-oriented San Francisco bands—and larger-than-life studio experimentation—exemplified by The Beatles' *Sgt. Pepper's Lonely Hearts Club Band*—Dylan had delivered what seemed a flat-out rejection of such excesses. It seemed to chasten and chivvy his contemporaries in equal measure. As such, even those of Dylan's peers who didn't record cover versions of the Dwarf material were inspired into a wave of copycat behaviour.

The spirit and sonics of the Dwarf Music demos informed the scruffily acoustic tone of The Rolling Stones' *Beggar's Banquet* (1968). It—along with The Band's *Music From Big Pink*—also brought about Eric Clapton's decision to dissolve Cream—one of the world's top groups—as he embarked on a quest to make similarly simple and rootsy music. Before he did, he made sure to pointedly title one of their albums *Wheels Of Fire*. The Byrds' rustic *Sweetheart Of The Rodeo* seemed to owe more than a little to the Basement Tapes, not least because their immediately previous LP, *Notorious Byrd Brothers*, was seamlessly space-age. By 1969, The Beatles were making a virtue of music caught in the moment with their no-overdubs *Get Back* project (even if it was botched and ended up as the very-much-overdubbed *Let It Be* album). Following the lead of these titans were a hundred and one other acts who were suddenly unenamoured with polish and appendage.

The rock aristocracy seemed to feel liberated by the permission the back-to-basics qualities of the Dwarf demos—as well as *Music From Big Pink* and Dylan's December 1967 effort *John Wesley Harding*—gave them to end the 'far-out' studio arms race. That the influence of the Dwarf Music material was to blast away the penchant for the gleaming and the gargantuan that had informed rock in the latter half of 1966 and throughout 1967 and reintroduce small scales and acoustic instrumentation to the medium is more than a little ironic: Dylan was the man who had attracted opprobrium for embracing electric rock, but he turned out to be the death knell for what might be posited as its *in-extremis* form.

Chapter six

6

CHAPTER
SIX

I Am A Lonesome Hobo

There was actually an overlap between the Big Pink recordings and the writing and recording of Dylan's next official album, which he had finally agreed to make following a massive hike in his royalty rate, negotiated by Grossman, who was still clearly good for something.

The last set of Dylan-written Basement Tape recordings comprised 'Odds And Ends', 'Get Your Rocks Off', 'Clothesline Saga', 'Apple Suckling Tree', 'Goin' To Acapulco', and 'All You Have To Do Is Dream'. Drums aside, they sound of a piece with the other Basement Tapes songs, which itself is slightly unsettling. That they seem to have been made after Dylan laid down *John Wesley Harding* sheds a slightly unfavourable light on the Basement Tapes. It bespeaks a compartmentalisation, revealing them to be less the spontaneous work and frozen moment in time they winningly appear to be and something more self-conscious and cynical.

For those Dylan fans who had not heard the Dwarf demos— i.e., the vast majority of them—the visible comparison points in his development were *Blonde And Blonde* and *John Wesley Harding*. It was quite a juxtaposition. Rarely has there been such a contrast between an artist's consecutive official releases as those two albums. *Blonde And Blonde* was grand, stylish, often callous, very electric, and decidedly Godless. *John Wesley Harding* was small-scale, antediluvian, penitent, humble, very acoustic, and unquestionably religious. That they sound like the work of totally different artists even extends to the fact that (the first time the wider public was apprised of this fact) Dylan's singing voice had fundamentally changed.

This new cache of songs was—uniquely—written lyric-first, Dylan making a break with the technique to which he has otherwise always adhered by only setting them to melodies after the fact. They were recorded in Nashville in late 1967: twelve songs, no outtakes, in three separate sessions on October 17, November 6, and November 29. He laid them down as part of a trio, his acoustic guitar and harmonica augmented by Charlie McCoy on bass and Kenny Buttrey on drums. Apart from some piano from Dylan, the only embellishment of that skeletal setup was the pedal steel provided by Pete Drake at the suggestion of Johnston on two tracks recorded at the last session. Dylan's use of these men would suggest that he was still unconvinced that The Band were the right studio musicians for him, but he wasn't keeping his Woodstock colleagues at complete arm's length. Between the second and third *John Wesley Harding* sessions, he reportedly asked Robbie Robertson and Garth Hudson about providing overdubs, but he was persuaded by them that the collection sounded fine just as it was.

'He was the same old guy that wasn't saying anything, but the music was definitely different,' says McCoy. 'When he came back for *John Wesley Harding*, it seemed like he had a change of style of writing or something because I thought *John Wesley Harding* moved a little more toward country.' There was another thing that hadn't changed. 'There was never any guidance or anything.' Dylan was also back to minimalism in numbers of takes. 'We would always do one, two, sometimes three takes on a song,' says McCoy. He adds, 'We just tried to get it tighter and just a little better. We never really changed anything.'

Some hailed the album as Dylan's return to folk (although a perplexing number, like McCoy, detect far more country on the album than it actually contains). It certainly didn't resemble rock or pop, and the feeling that, as with so much folk, it derived from times long past was only intensified by the archaic timbre of Dylan's new phraseology. It was a different antique timbre to the one found in the Basement Tapes. There's none of the humour or horniness of the Big Pink material, but its references to things like watchtowers and fair damsels make it sound even more pre-modern than that.

Dylan also had a new brooding set of obsessions. The lyrics of *John Wesley Harding* are full of outlaws, jokers, thieves, drifters, landlords, tenants, hobos, immigrants, and messengers—many of them in opposition to each other—but it's clear that none of these roles are literal, and that the professions and situations are metaphors: all of these characters seem to be the artist himself. The songs confirmed even more than had the Dwarf Music material—and for a much wider audience— that Dylan was no longer the cocksure figure of yore who was deliciously apt to dispense 'babes', sermons, and witticisms, but instead an individual who was castigating both himself for his egotism and glory-seeking and those who had ruthlessly facilitated that egotism and glory-seeking for their own pecuniary advantage. In the final two songs, the torment is ostentatiously cast aside for a new role: in place of the figures torn by anguish in the preceding tracks is a man concerned only with romantic love and the salvation it provides from conflict, vanity, and temptation.

The emptiness of Dylan's former life and image seems to be laid bare by the first, title track, in which he sings of what seems to be an Old West character known for his good deeds. (He added a *g* to the name of a real-life cowboy, and a man with a considerably less benign image, John Wesley Hardin.) These good deeds are spoken of in such vague terms ('And soon the situation there was all but straightened out') that one can't help but conclude that he's trying to communicate the message that Hardin's reputation for heroism is completely underserved, which itself buttresses the deduction that the character is a metaphor for a certain countercultural icon closer to this end of history.

This is a relatively playful creation compared to the chilling nature of much of what is to follow, no more so than the following track. 'As I Went Out One Morning' is genuinely eerie. Dylan's harmonica work is superb throughout the album, and he adroitly sets the scene on that instrument here with some portentous swipes before launching into a tale about a man who goes walking around the abode of Tom Paine—a totem of freedom and enlightenment, plus, of course, a man whose legacy Dylan had a few years before slightly besmirched with his boorish behaviour when collecting an award named in his honour—only to run into a maiden who takes him by the arm when he only offers her his hand and promises that after she secretly accepts him that together they will fly 'south'. The exchange is interrupted by a desperate Paine, who dashes over and blurts out his apologies for what this woman has done.

On that note, the song ends without ceremony, an abrupt close that will be a feature of several of the tracks. It's thought-provoking, haunting, even disturbing stuff. Once again, Dylan is taking popular music down avenues no one ever previously had.

'I Dreamed I Saw St. Augustine' is not the relatively straightforward religious song that 'Quinn The Eskimo' or 'Sign On The Cross' is. Just as the details of the life of the real John Wesley Hardin don't tally with the Dylan song with his name in the title, so neither of the two real-life canonised Augustines was put to death, a fate this song's narrator sees in a nightmare. It is certainly, though, a creation featuring the sort of contrition associated with the devout. Before his killing, a distraught, screaming Augustine is shown 'searching for the very souls whom already have been sold'. The narrator awakes from his dream angry, alone, terrified, and tearful. No further explanation is provided as to what this means. The world had become used to opaque Dyan lyrics over the past three years, but the ones on this collection rise to a new level of enigmaticness.

Most enigmatic of all is 'All Along The Watchtower', which ends on a cliffhanger when it's announced that outside in the distance a wild cat is growling, the wind is howling, and two riders are approaching. Prior to this, the joker and the thief—who may well be two aspects of the same personality, and that personality may well be Dylan's—have been engaging in philosophical discussion, with the former complaining of people who exploit his property (perhaps intellectual property?) without appreciating its worth, while the latter tries to reassure him that this is nothing over which to get unduly vexed. This fretting is set against imagery that feels both historical (there is talk of princes and barefoot servants) and biblical (as well as being an ancient-world military observation post, a watchtower is a word associated with Jehovah's Witnesses). It's easy to assume that the joker and the thief are atop the watchtower, but in fact, Dylan never states whether they are inside or outside the city walls. If the latter, then they could be the two riders. While the lyric is fascinating, equally compelling is the music, which despite its spartan setup has a surprising sweep and grandeur.

On *John Wesley Harding*, Dylan is saying a great deal but, as with the Basement Tapes songs, doing so with unusual brevity. Half of its songs are less than three minutes long and only two of them exceed four minutes. Just one goes past the five-minute mark, 'The Ballad Of Frankie Lee And Judas Priest'. Ironically, the latter's inordinate timespan contributes to its power because its circular guitar and percussion patterns become ever more unsettling the longer the track continues. Adding to the composition's disquieting nature is Dylan's deadpan recounting of the bizarre exploits and exchanges of the titular characters, who may be the same people as the joker and the thief and may be exploring the same conflicts as essayed in 'All Along The Watchtower'. It also, as in the way of a dream, makes no sense: when Frankie Lee needs money and Judas pulls out a roll of tens, Frankie sits down to contemplate which one of them he'll take; Judas takes his leave, and Frankie has no sooner sat back down when a passing stranger alerts him to the somewhat large and dramatic development that Judas is stranded in a house nearby. Beyond the studied nonsensicality is something sinister: when Judas tells Frankie he can find him in 'eternity', or as he might call it 'paradise', Frankie says he doesn't call it anything 'with a voice as cold as ice'. The house to which the stranger refers transpires to feature great temptations—represented by a woman's face in each of its many windows—and over the course of sixteen days, Frankie succumbs to them all before, on the seventeenth day, dying in Judas's arms—of thirst. None of us will ever know precisely what this all means, but we certainly get the gist: the Dylan of recent years was seduced by things he now recognises he shouldn't have been.

Vinyl side one ends on a slightly underwhelming note with 'Drifter's Escape', which explores the same territory as the preceding tracks but without their eeriness or sonic power. The slightly monotonous tune conveys a story of a wretch on whom judgment seems imminent. It contains no memorable imagery or phraseology. However, the possibility that the bolt of lightning that enables the drifter's escape from his confused trial is a metaphor for Dylan's motorcycle crash and the psychological and careerist consequences it unleashed is certainly intriguing.

'Dear Landlord', which opens side two, is a variant of 'Nothing Was Delivered'. Slightly different in texture to the surrounding material courtesy of some bassy and surprisingly nimble Dylan piano work, it's another song of grievance couched in contradictorily temperate, even submissive, terms. 'If you don't underestimate me, then I won't underestimate you,' notes the narrator in language a million miles removed from rock'n'roll atti-tood. It would be easy to assume the landlord figure is a Grossman metaphor (and not even necessarily metaphor—Dylan had until recently had a room at more than one of his manager's homes) or even an Abraham Zimmerman simile, but it seems far more likely that the figure to whom the narrator is beholden—and who fills his life up with things that he can see but just cannot touch—is Dylan's corporeal presence, with the narrator being his spirit.

'I've served time for everything 'cept begging on the street' is the telling revelation of the narrator of 'I Am A Lonesome Hobo', a man whose failure to trust others and to accept blame has left him with no family, friends, or money, and who has across the course of his life tried his hand at bribery, blackmail, and deceit. Facing the end of his bleak existence, he has reached a state of enlightenment that enables him to inform others that if they wish to avoid his fate they should steer clear of petty jealousy, live by no one else's code, and hold their judgment for themselves.

'I Pity The Poor Immigrant' is the story of another wretch but told from an objective perspective. Or—third-person narration notwithstanding—should that be subjective? The 'immigrant' wishes he had stayed 'home', and at some point during this 'journey' falls in love with wealth itself. For the second time in the album, Dylan sings of 'the glass'—the man who had a dream of St. Augustine bowed his head and cried against said object.

Thus far, the songs on side two have been decent but not exceptional. 'The Wicked Messenger' both ratchets up the quality and takes us back to the disturbing timbre of 'As I Went Out One Morning' and 'The Ballad Of Frankie Lee And Judas Priest'. The most up-tempo item on the record, it assumes an almost unbearable intensity via a doomy descending bass line and a headlong, insistent melody whose verses all end on an ominous rising inflection. The wicked messenger despatched by Eli—a biblical figure who failed to properly discipline his sons—is clearly a mendacious and deceitful individual: dashing hither and thither, his mind multiplying the smallest matter while his tongue is unable to speak without flattery. One fateful day, he exclaims in some alarm that the soles of his feet are burning. Catastrophe seems to fall upon the land as a consequence of the messenger's behaviour, and he is repeatedly confronted by its inhabitants, who finally tell him, 'If you cannot bring good news then don't bring any!' Once again, it's a track that ends abruptly. This time, though, what follows gives this suddenness an air of resolution.

Anyone by this point in doubt that the messenger is Dylan himself—ditto all the other characters featured in the tracks—would surely have to take heed of the fact that what follows is indeed good news: no tortured landscapes, no tales of wretches facing judgment, but just two sunny, life-affirming love songs. That *John Wesley Harding* is a concept album is not remarked on much, but the way it concludes with 'Down Along The Cove' and 'I'll Be Your Baby Tonight' arguably makes it no less a narrative song suite than The Pretty Things' *SF Sorrow* (1968) or The Who's *Tommy* (1969).

If one thinks about it, it's almost a shock that aesthetic considerations even come into this project at this point—Dylan has clearly been on a hell of a journey in recent years, and on this album, he's taken us on one too in relating it—but, for the record, one of the brace of concluding tracks is mediocre and one is great. 'Down Along The Cove' is pleasant enough, a bobbing country-blues celebrating the joys of strolling along in public with one's true love. However, it's also banal. 'I'll Be Your Baby

Tonight' trades in the same kind of generic material but does so far more musically adroitly and lyrically wittily. Dylan significantly, playfully says 'Bring that *bottle* over here' before one of the renditions of the title line, and in the middle-eight cheekily rhymes 'moon' and 'spoon', leaving only 'June' out of the usual litany that mocks Tin Pan Alley clichés. Subversiveness aside, the track is great country-inflected pop and would have surely been a hit had Dylan not issued an edict to Columbia that no singles be released to promote the album.

The sleeve of *John Wesley Harding* is slightly amateur-looking. The front features a small monochrome photograph within a sea of beige in which a bearded, behatted Dylan poses gormlessly with people apparently chosen for their superficial resemblance to Native Americans (two Bengali houseguests of Grossman's and a local craftsman), which fatuously fits in with the Old West theme generated by the title and Dylan's Stetson. Turning the front cover upside down and peering closely at the bark of the tree before which Dylan and companions are situated reveals—among other tiny faces—the *Sgt. Pepper*-era visages of The Beatles. (The latter is much less discernible on CD editions.) Regardless of his seclusion, Dylan was still taking some sort of interest in the 'scene', not least because he was mates with George Harrison.

The back cover features cryptic Dylan sleeve notes that mention a 'plate glass window', presumably related to the glass referenced in a brace of the songs. The notes find three kings visiting one Frank, possibly one of the protagonists of 'The Ballad Of Frankie Lee And Judas Priest', possibly a punning metaphor for candidness. One monarch with oversized shoes and a wet and lopsided crown says, 'Mr. Dylan has come out with a new record. This record of course features none but his own songs and we understand that you're the key. . . . Could you please open it up for us?'

'And just how far would you like to go in?' responds Frank.

After looking at the others, the monarch ventures, 'Not too far but just far enough so's we can say that we've been there.'

What has been interpreted by some as Dylan's scorn for critics might be said to be justified by some of the laughable appraisals of the LP—released on December 27, 1967—in a music press that while it was moving toward intelligent analysis still clearly had one foot in triteness and cloth-eared literalness. '"Dear Landlord" must be the most impassioned plea against eviction ever heard,' Charlie Gillett amusingly opined in *Anarchy*, while *Record Mirror*'s Norman Jopling could only offer of the exquisitely eerie 'As I Went Out One Morning', 'Spontaneous laughter from everyone who listened to this with me. ... Dryly amusing in parts.'

The eighteen months between albums—unprecedented for a major star—only made the appetite for Dylan's new work the keener. Despite both the absence of a taster single and it having a release date in a retail calendar dead spot, it became Dylan's biggest seller to date, reaching no. 2 in the US and topping the chart in the UK. The rock cognoscenti had an idea of where Dylan's music was these days through having heard the Dwarf Music material, and the wider public at least had a conception of the state of his mind through the covers it had generated. Everyone, though, was still surprised that at the close of the loud, multi-coloured, effects-drenched year of 1967, Dylan should proffer a quiet and sepia-toned non sequitur to current musical trends.

He had done it again: ploughed his own furrow and pushed popular music forward another incremental, unexpected step. Reception to the record was therefore even more reverential than its artistic excellence would have already made it. Just at the point where his art indicated he was no longer interested in being atop any sort of pedestal, Dylan's genius and uniqueness were causing his fanbase to worship him all the more.

•

John Wesley Harding was a comeback, but it did not herald Dylan returning to his previous furious productivity or high visibility. He made a sentiment-motivated appearance with The Band in January at the Woody Guthrie Memorial Concert at Carnegie Hall. (His onetime hero had died in October.) Aside from that first public outing since 1966, he ducked out of 1968 completely.

In that year, the music-loving public was treated to The Small Faces' *Ogdens' Nut Gone Flake*, The Rolling Stones' *Beggars Banquet*, The Jimi Hendrix Experience's *Electric Ladyland*, The Beatles' eponymous 'White Album', The Byrds' *The Notorious Byrd Brothers* and *Sweetheart Of The Rodeo*, The Kinks' *Village Green Preservation Society*, Van Morrison's *Astral Weeks*, and The Band's *Music From Big Pink*. Some or all of these acclaimed and groundbreaking works had been influenced by the Basement Tapes and/or *John Wesley Harding*. *Sweetheart Of The Rodeo* features covers of 'You Ain't Goin' Nowhere' and 'Nothing Was Delivered'. As touched on previously, *Music From Big Pink* contains three songs either written or co-written by Dylan, 'This Wheel's On Fire', 'I Shall Be Released', and 'Tears Of Rage'. Meanwhile, in December, Joan Baez released *Any Day Now*, a double album comprised entirely of Dyan songs. (Not even psychological awkwardness could prevent her from expressing her admiration for Dylan in this way: at least two of the selected songs were about Rotolo, one about Sara, and one possibly about her.)

Singles-wise, as well as Manfred Mann's 'Mighty Quinn', Dylan continued to provide hits for others. *Electric Ladyland* featured a cover of 'All Along The Watchtower' in which the Experience took what had been a fine pencil sketch and turned it into a glorious oil painting. Released as a single, it secured for the trio a UK no. 5 and a US no. 20. Dylan loved it so much that he subsequently consistently performed that larger-than-life version in concert. 'This Wheel's On Fire' was taken into the British Top 5 by Julie Driscoll, Brian Auger & The Trinity. This was the same year that Fairport Convention proved that even Dylan in French had a magic touch: their Gallic version of 'If You Gotta Go, Go Now' scraped the UK Top 20.

As for Dylan himself, the only creative thing he did publicly all year was the cover painting for *Music From Big Pink*. He was far more interested in his artwork than making music and virtually doted on his

Woodstock neighbour, an artist named Bruce Dorfman, from whom he took daily lessons. Consequently, the sixteen-month gap between *John Wesley Harding* and his next LP was almost as long as that between *Blonde On Blonde* and *John Wesley Harding*, and without any of the previous extenuating circumstances. Moreover, although he returned with an album that, as per usual with him, did the unexpected, it was—for the first time—unexpected in a mostly bad way.

The front cover of *Nashville Skyline* features no words, merely a colour picture shot from low down of a smiling, Stetson-tipping Dylan brandishing a guitar in an image similar—deliberately or otherwise—to that on the Eric Von Schmidt album cover seen on the sleeve of *Bringing It All Back Home*. Dylan had occasionally smiled in pictures before, but never so gormlessly. There was something familiar about the brown coat he wore: it was the same one seen on the fronts of *Blonde On Blonde* and *John Wesley Harding*. However, the man inside it had been transformed yet again, and it wasn't merely the change in his voice, which had completed a softening journey that started on the Basement Tapes and continued through *John Wesley Harding* so that it was now a bland if slightly congested croon. (He claimed it was the result of what turned out to be a brief halt of his prodigious smoking habit, but people who knew him in his university days insisted that this was how he sang before he became enamoured of Woody Guthrie.)

Joining him in the February '69 session that created the album were Norman Blake (guitar, Dobro), Fred Carter Jr. (guitar), Charlie McCoy (guitar, harmonica), Charlie Daniels (bass, guitar), Bob Wilson (organ, piano), Kenny Buttrey (drums, bongos, cowbell), and Pete Drake (pedal steel guitar). There was also a separate band on 'Girl From The North Country', comprised of W. S. Holland (drums), Bob Wootton (electric guitar), Marshall Grant (bass), and Johnny Cash (vocals and guitar). Several of the above were contributors to one or more previous Dylan albums, but the results here were nothing like what any of them had laid down with him before. *Harding* had possessed a country tinge in

240

parts, but this record—from title to cowboy cover to Johnny Cash's liner note and guest appearance—was pure C&W. Not that Dylan would ever do anything so straightforward or vulgar as to issue a do-it-down-home edict. 'Nobody said anything,' says McCoy. 'They just played the song and let us go.' However, McCoy and colleagues could plainly see that these songs did not have rock chord changes. 'And, you know, *John Wesley Harding* was kind of a bridge.'

Dylan loved country from way back. Not only was Hank Williams his first idol, but he had gorged on Echo Helstrom's mother's country 78rpm records. University friends have also testified to how he loved the genre. In the 1960s, though, country was problematic. It was no less roots music than folk but its mirror-opposite politically. The counterculture—of which Dylan, whether he liked it or not, was still perceived as a leader—hated the 'rednecks' who consumed it. The north-located longhairs who were in favour of progressive legislation loved rock, the Deep-South located Stetson-wearing good ol' boys who thought there was nothing wrong with segregation favoured country. These might be esoteric issues outside the US, but a barometer of just what a burning issue it was Stateside is provided by the fact that the year before, independent segregationist presidential candidate George Wallace obtained ten million votes, 13.5 percent of all ballots cast. Most of them were obtained in the Deep South.

Nor was *Nashville Skyline* the street-cred, raw country of a Hank Williams or the recent fusion experiments of The International Submarine Band and The Byrds. This was the airbrushed, platitude-stacked country that rock fans despised as whiny (those godawful pedal-steel guitars) and musically identikit. Dylan himself had seemed to suggest he bought into this perception with a line in 'Visions Of Johanna' in which he said that a country music station was playing softly but there was nothing to turn off. None of this would have mattered if this album's music was as clever as 'I'll Be Your Baby Tonight', but whereas that country song's lyric mocked clichés and banalities, these ones traded in them unblushingly. The domestic bliss explored by just about every one of its tracks explains why: this was now a human being who put loving his wife and raising his children far above all other priorities, and that included artistic ambition.

That blunted ambition manifests itself in ways other than aesthetic mediocrity. One of the Dylan songs here isn't even new, while another is an instrumental. More than one of the others sounds like a glorified doodle and/or jam with a lyric half-interestedly plastered over the top. As well as half-engaged and lazy, the album additionally has an overarching flimsiness: its playing time is a paltry twenty-seven minutes at a time when the rock/pop audience was just learning to feel short-changed if it wasn't given forty minutes for its money.

Insubstantial and tossed off as the album's writing sounds, slightly more work went into its recording than normal for Dylan: in February 1969, three days of basic-track work (standard) was then augmented by three days of overdubs (for this artist, very much not standard).

The LP kicks off with a revisit to *Freewheelin'*'s 'Girl From The North Country' in the form of a duet with Johnny Cash, a bona-fide legend of country music. The latter writes sycophantically in his liner note that there are those who are beings complete unto themselves and that herein is someone who is a hell of a poet and lots of other things. Cash's involvement was for many Dylan fans the most provocative thing about the whole project: Cash was a supporter of the Vietnam War, an issue that was currently in danger of tearing the United States apart. The track itself is an interesting variant of the original: a full-band, glossily produced iteration, although the two men's harmonising is somewhat sloppy.

That a new version of a six-year-old song is followed by the first-ever instrumental on a Dylan release is confirmation that this album is hardly going to be ambitious. The bluegrass-flavoured 'Nashville Skyline Rag' shows how those slick Nashville Cats can turn something approaching a pig's ear into something in the vicinity of a silk purse—and it becomes even more impressive when one is apprised of the fact that it's actually a studio warm-up—but merely agreeably filling up space is not what made Dylan's legend. One also has to raise an eyebrow at the solo Dylan writing attribution, it being a long-established recording-industry tradition that the publishing on instrumentals is shared out among all the recording's participants on the grounds that each contributed as much as the other. Albert Grossman must have been proud.

'Is it rolling, Bob?' Dylan asks his producer at the start of 'To Be Alone With You'. The phrase subsequently became semi-iconic. It's the only thing about this smoothly done piece of fluff that can be said to approach that status. Whereas 'I'll Be Your Baby Tonight' was able to simultaneously employ and mock classic conventions, here there is no post-modernism, but more importantly no wit or cleverness. 'I Threw It All Away' is cut from the same country-pop cloth and has slightly more gravitas in the narrator's expression of regret over the way he has hitherto taken love for granted, bolstered by the adroit use of echo. In contrast, 'Peggy Day' has no substance whatsoever. The poet laureate of popular music now seems perfectly comfortable declaiming that he loves to spend the night with Peggy Day and—even worse—then nonsensically turning it around and telling us he loves to spend the day with Peggy Night. Some listeners might think the following line, 'By golly, what more can I say?', is a twinkle-eyed meta move. Others might conclude that they are being treated with contempt.

With the last track on side one, Dylan gives the world a fleeting reminder of his great craftsmanship, if not the poetic genius that made his name. Dylan claimed that 'Lay Lady Lay' originated in a commission from the producers of *Midnight Cowboy* but that it was written too late to be included in it. It's difficult to see how this track could have fitted into that celebrated gritty 1969 movie, even if its sexual theme and 'Lay across my big brass bed' refrain (somehow more dirty-sounding than it is) would have chimed with its frank timbre. Its matter-of-fact attitude toward sex shows how far the world had moved on—courtesy of the contraceptive pill—in the half-decade since Dylan had explored in 'If

You Gotta Go, Go Now' the coy, conflicted rigmarole that surrounded intercourse. Johnston raises his game to match Dylan's temporarily elevated songcraft, giving the track resonating guitars, a ticking cowbell, bongos, call-and-response between voice and guitar, and epic, rolling drums, the widescreen production all culminating in a spiralling pedal-steel guitar that takes things to a clean end.

Having proven to us he can still do it if he tries, Dylan infuriatingly proceeds over the following three tracks to not exert any discernible effort at all. The lonesome and raw 'One More Night' is vaguely Hank Williams-like. The paranoid 'Tell Me That It Isn't True' gravitates closer to the Nashville Sound, the corporate country strains that post-dated Williams. Both are reasonably agreeable but essentially songwriting-by-numbers. One also can't help wondering how much worth they would possess if denuded of the little frills and flourishes provided by the backing men. There was a time when musicians' licks and accents were a nice extra to Dylan's mesmerising song words rather than something approaching the track's entire guts. Then there is 'Country Pie'. A tribute to the titular musical genre, it's as inane as 'Peggy Day' and—in the fact that it unexpectedly fades out when only just past the one-and-a-half minute mark—even more flimsy-feeling.

Depending on their mood, Dylan fans would either be given hope by the album's closing track or roused to a state of fury by another reminder that he can do so much better if he can be bothered. 'Tonight I'll Be Staying Here With You' is another gem on a level and in the vein of 'Lay Lady Lay' (and indeed the similarly themed previous album closer, 'I'll Be Your Baby Tonight'). In another cleverly constructed pop-country love song, the narrator decides to abandon his travel plans to stay home with his one true love, tossing his train ticket through a window and shrugging that if there's a poor boy beyond it, 'Let him have my seat.' Impressively, realising he was short of content, Dylan hurriedly wrote the song in a couple of days.

With *Nashville Skyline*, released on April 9, 1969, Dylan took to the extreme the premise of the last two tracks on *John Wesley Harding*. Those songs celebrated romantic love in preference to the hateful avarice and egotism described in the tracks preceding them. These ones had no such mitigating and clarifying context, nor for the most part any redeeming artistic quality. Nobody listening to this LP who was previously unfamiliar with Dylan's work—and its high sales would suggest there were many such people—would suspect that this was an above-average writer let alone the supreme lyric-writing talent of all time. The figure whose music and influence had in the space of less than five years taken rock music from inoffensive banality to a state of barricade-storming profundity was now proffering the kind of cliché—lyrical and musical—that his songwriting had so recently threatened to make a thing of history.

The *New York Times*'s Mike Jahn wrote, 'Is he kidding? Possibly, but I don't think so…*Nashville Skyline* is a warm, friendly album. In voice and in words, Mr. Dylan has mellowed, calmed down, grown up. It isn't that he has forgotten how to be alienated. He just seems to have learned how to be happy.' Ritchie Yorke of Britain's *New Musical Express* agreed, saying, 'Dylan is carefree and careless. Gone is the bitterness of Dylan's early work, the sharp-edged satire of other albums.…At twenty-seven, married with a son, Dylan seems to have found whatever it was he was searching for. His seven years of writing, singing and the ensuing world idolatry, appears to have gone full circle.' Lou Goddard of *Record Mirror* declined to go along with the wave of praise. 'Were this the debut album by some unknown Western wailer, I fear it could not make its way out of a ten-gallon hat,' he said. 'The fact that it is Bob Dylan and a familiar face calls a different outlook to attention.…Anything he produces found to be disagreeable is simultaneously considered to be only temporary and excusable.…It falls below the lyrical standards of a humorous poke at obsolete wording and appealing sloppiness.' Goddard was certainly showing far more perceptiveness—and self-knowledge—than Carl Oglesby, until recently the president of the prominent 60s activist group Students For A Democratic Society. Oglesby desperately suggested that

Nashville Skyline was nothing other than 'Dylan becoming interested in the white working class at the same time the Movement did'. He opined, 'The Movement was getting turned on to the alienated, displaced white hillbillies in Northern cities and more and more convinced that if we didn't reach the white working kids there would be no future. . . . It is a conscious manipulation of a stereotype . . . Dylan as strategist, Dylan making a decision to reach another constituency.'

Mind you, in the interview he granted *Newsweek* to promote the album, Dylan was guilty of some disingenuousness himself. 'These are the type of songs that I always felt like writing,' he insisted. 'The songs reflect more of the inner me than the songs of the past. . . . There I felt everyone expected me to be a poet so that's what I tried to be. But the smallest line on this new album means more to me than some of the songs on the previous albums I've made.' The idea that Dylan would have been able to write masterpieces like 'The Times They Are A-Changin'', 'It's Alright, Ma (I'm Only Bleeding)', or 'Desolation Row' from a position of insincerity is clearly nonsense.

In a way, if *Nashville Skyline* had been his final long-player, it would have been a perfect ending to Bob Dylan's career. For him to have never been heard from again would have been a symmetrical, logical conclusion to the personal, musical, and sociological story arc traced across his ten 60s albums (including the Basement Tapes). However, it would also have ended that saga on an unfortunate note—one that suggested that he had been so beaten down by life that he had ended up reverting to the complacency, conservatism, parochialism, and timidity that he had spent so much of his adulthood kicking against, as well as reduced to an artistic mediocrity. In any case, such tidy conclusions only happen in myth and fiction, not in the messy, nuanced, stubbornly persisting thing that constitutes the course of a life.

Chapter seven

Changing Of The Guards

For *Nashville Skyline*, Dylan returned to something approaching a pop star's normal visibility.

Very unusually, he made a TV appearance to promote the album, appearing on the first episode of the US ABC network's *Johnny Cash Show* in May 1969. His visual appearance was startling. He still couldn't bring himself to wear in public the spectacles necessary for his chronic shortsightedness, but with his short hair, thin beard, and everyday jacket he looked nothing like an insurrectionary or a poet, or even the Bob Dylan everyone remembered. It was a Dylan of which UK ensemble The Hollies reminded the public that very month with the release of *Hollies Sing Dylan*, an enjoyable collection of covers of his songs spanning his entire career. The very fact that a band who had been hitmakers for half a decade and were formidable songwriters themselves should consider such a project a commercial move was a microcosm of how Dylan's name had over the decade become synonymous with artistic prestige and commercial gold dust. (The fact that Graham Nash left the band in disgust at what he considered to be a retrograde move doesn't undermine the point too much.) Two months later, British folk band Fairport Convention released their third album, *Unhalfbricking*. It featured three Dylan songs: 'Million Dollar Bash', 'Si Tu Dois Partir' (their French version of 'If You Gotta Go, Go Now', which that year gave them the only hit they ever had), and 'Percy's Song', the first cover of that 1963 Dylan composition.

In June, Dylan seemed to be attempting to rachet up his own preferred I'm-nothing-special image with an extraordinary interview he granted *Rolling Stone* publisher/editor Jann Wenner. All his professional life, Dylan had operated in an atmosphere where he and his kind were not treated with due reverence: the established media did not take popular music seriously and the pop press traded in banalities. *Rolling Stone* had helped change all that, covering and analysing rock with knowledge and respect and quickly inspiring others by their example. It was supremely ironic, then, that arguably the first interview Dylan had done in which his interlocutor had questions for him that were both well-informed and deferential took place at a point in his life where he did not want to give serious answers. He repeatedly pretended he didn't understand questions he found discomforting, frequently used Wenner's first name in the sort of ostentatious friendliness familiar from the corny showbiz types he had once mocked; employed euphemisms like 'passed away' that the old Bob Dylan would have laughed at (his dad had died in May 1968); bizarrely claimed that when he had once named Smokey Robinson as one of his favourite poets, he had been mixing him up with Jean Arthur Rimbaud; and, more than once, peculiarly stated he had no aim in life other than 'staying out of people's hair'. In retrospect, it can be seen as a surreal exercise in throwing people off the scent by a man who didn't want to be pestered by those who still perceived him as the leader of the world's counterculture. In this last year of a decade he had done so much to influence and define, Dylan was self-consciously trying to reinvent himself, basically as the gormless, grinning, unengaged bumpkin on the front cover of *Nashville Skyline*. However, if the combination of the interview and the well-crafted emptiness of *Nashville Skyline* was his way of conveying the fact that his days of dissent were over and that he was finally, definitively repudiating the notion that he was the voice of a generation, it failed.

The first manifestation of that failure was the simple fact of the success of *Nashville Skyline*. This album may have contained neither of the two elements that had made his reputation—insightful, poetic lyrics and musical sophistication—but that didn't stop the public sending it to no. 3 in the US and no. 1 in the UK. That it sold more than any previous Dylan album was partly due to the fact that it spawned a huge hit. 'I Threw It All Away' reached a mediocre no. 30 in the UK and just no. 85 in the US when released as the album's first single, and neither did this particularly matter for a man who had been perceived as an albums artist when that concept barely existed. However, it came as a very nice bonus when the pop smarts of 'Lay Lady Lay' made it a transatlantic Top 10. ('Tonight I'll Be Staying Here With You' reached no. 50 when released as the third US single.) The parent album's sales swelled accordingly. Interestingly—and suspiciously, for some—the album appeared nowhere on country music charts, even though a) it was obviously country and b) it had clearly outsold many contemporaneous country albums. It seemed a variant of the resistance he had encountered in the past, with the difference that no official body had ever tried to stop him succeeding in the folk or rock fields.

This ridiculous success for a mediocre glorified EP proved that Dylan's legend was more important than the reality of his current abilities. He had a legion of fans who would buy anything he released to see where he was currently at, and he was acquiring more fans who had heard of him by osmosis and were intrigued to see what the fuss was about.

Another part of the reason that Dylan failed to cease being 'a great youth leader'—as Wenner told him people considered him to be—was his continuing status as inadvertent revolutionary. With *Nashville Skyline*, Dylan changed the world yet again. If there had been a Berlin Wall between the folk and the rock audiences, it was nothing compared to that which existed between the country and rock crowds. The days were numbered for country being perceived as the music of people of reactionary and callous values. In making the album and in achieving such success with it, Dylan demystified and decontaminated the genre. *Nashville Skyline* gave permission for the young and the left to enjoy country music just like Dylan had previously enabled folkies, beatniks and leftists to admit to themselves the merits of rock and pop. It also gave permission to recording artists to make music inflected with country. Not many rock artists could bring themselves to embrace *Nashville Skyline*'s undiluted country sound, but the album had an effect far deeper than The Byrds et al's recent country-rock experiments: country was now out in the light. The C&W-oriented Poco, Nitty Gritty Dirt Band, and Kris Kristofferson were among the biggest stars of the immediately following era. The Eagles—the quintessence of the amalgamation of country and rock—are among the biggest stars of any era. It's difficult to imagine any of them achieving the success they did without the path having been beaten by *Nashville Skyline*.

Another example of Dylan serving as an accidental Pied Piper was his unknowing creation of the bootleg industry. One of the reasons Grossman crossed the Atlantic in '67 in person with the Dwarf Music material was almost certainly because of a worry that the goods he was touting might be copied. Bootlegs as we know them didn't exist in 1967, but the fact that illicit tapes of Dylan concerts were traded among fans, and by, 1966 being sold to them (the last date on his world tour was made available for cash and found almost sixty thousand willing customers) had caused the artist to ban tape recorders from his gigs. In July 1969, such activity took a significant step further courtesy of two people whose identities were then shrouded in mystery but who are now known to be young Los Angeles residents Ken Douglas and Michael 'Dub' Taylor. Said pair realised that there was serious money to be made from Dylan's dilatory approach to officially issuing great material—which of course well predated the Basement Tapes—and produced an unlawful but commercially available double vinyl album originally unnamed but later titled *Great White Wonder*. This double LP actually only contained seven Basement Tapes tracks, the remainder being comprised of miscellaneous material that went as far back as a December '61 home recording made in the apartment of Dylan's girlfriend Bonnie Beecher and came up to as recently as the June 1969 Johnny Cash TV show appearance. It was the beginning of a million-dollar business feeding on the public's unceasing thirst for anything and everything recorded by their idols and fuelled by the astonishing ability of bootleggers to obtain unreleased material no matter how obscure or well-guarded. Many other artists would suffer the same fate—watching helplessly as third parties issued material they'd never wanted released and made fortunes by doing so while failing to pay them a penny—but Dylan, because of his legend and his idiosyncratic/wasteful methods, has always been the most bootlegged of all recording artists.

He could live with that to an extent. Less easy to come to terms with were the hippies, freaks, and rubberneckers who continued to insist on beating a path to his door regardless of his studious change of image. Once he came home to Woodstock to find a post-coital couple in his bed. On other occasions, he would be stalked when out driving, a particularly concerning activity on Woodstock's underpopulated roads if he was with his family and/or it was night. Police were for a while encamped in Dylan's home when a man claiming to be an ex-convict rang up and said he was going to kill him. The sense of being invaded must have reached a crescendo with the announcement of the 1969 Woodstock Festival, whose originally planned location was deliberately designed to tempt him back on stage. A distressed Dylan's response was to place three thousand miles between the hordes expected to swamp the area by taking up an offer to play at the concurrent Isle Of Wight festival in the UK.* The Isle Of Wight gig was Dylan and The Band's first visit to Blighty since the '66 tour, and whereas back then they had been booed while making some of the most extraordinary music ever heard, their lacklustre and slightly bizarre set at the festival was greeted rapturously.

In the end, Dylan became so exasperated by those who insisted on seeing him as their leader and mentor that, in a ruse to make them finally leave him alone, he set about a concerted effort to dismantle his legend. He recalled to *Rolling Stone* in 1984, 'I said, fuck it, I wish these people would just *forget* about me. I wanna do something they *can't* possibly like, they can't relate to.' Accordingly, he assembled a double album comprised of bizarre interpretations of traditional songs, substandard and incongruous covers of contemporaries' compositions, a handful of barren new originals, and live versions of some of his classics so slapdash as to seem to deliberately degrade them.

McCoy played on the album, mainly bass. 'That was me and the drummer overdubbing to Dylan's guitar and keyboard vocals,' he says.

---

* Ironically, the Woodstock event didn't take place there, having to be moved to Bethel, fifty-eight miles away, after town officials banned it.

'That was another deal. He wasn't here for that. I may be wrong, but what it appears to me is that Bob Johnston wanted to get one more album with him. Apparently, he and Bob were not seeing eye to eye and Dylan had already indicated he wasn't going to work with him [again]. Johnston had access to all these guitar/piano kind of demo things, and he says, Hey, I can put some musicians on this and have one more record.' Demos? 'You might better classify them as work tapes or something— the recording was good because it was done in a regular studio.' Dylan may have approached the album with the contempt its bizarre nature or his subsequent comments about it imply, but for his and his colleagues' parts, McCoy says, 'We were doing our best. And some of it was tough because some of his tempos weren't that steady. We would never go deliberately trying to play bad. We were doing the best we could with what we had to work with.' However, he does admit that it struck him as a little strange that the preeminent writer of his generation should be doing other people's material. 'But, whatever. We had a job to do.'

Kooper also worked on the album. 'I thought it was bizarre, but I was there again to try and play as best I could,' he says. He dismisses the notion that Dylan as a human being had changed almost beyond recognition since *Blonde On Blonde*, the last album on which the pair had collaborated. 'Only in style and looks. The Bob that you dealt with was the same Bob.' However, several of the tracks were swamped in the type of syrupy string-and-brass overdubs one couldn't imagine the old Dylan having anything but distaste for.

Dylan put on the cover a quasi-grotesque picture he'd painted of a familiarly octagon-chinned face and titled the album *Self Portrait*. Few people played it more than twice after buying it on its June 8, 1970, release. Not even the people who kidded themselves about the quality of or impetus for *Nashville Skyline* could pretend that this was anything other than dreck. *Rolling Stone* published a symposium featuring the bewildered and appalled opinions of a half-dozen writers. Greil Marcus's review therein began with the words 'What is this shit?' Writer Ralph

Gleason airily stated that the public should boycott Dylan's records because 'a contract exists between us. And that is simply never to accept anything less than their [sic] best.'

Contempt for Dylan and the conviction that he was negating everything for which he had once stood was confirmed for many when, the day after *Self Portrait*'s release, he accepted an honorary doctorate in music at Princeton University. It wouldn't be true to say that Dylan had never succumbed to the blandishments of fame, but while exulting in (well-deserved) idolatry is understandable on a human level, him engaging in one of those dubious ceremonies whereby a random seat of learning seeks to gain youth-culture kudos by awarding one of those worthless, meaningless, unearned degrees—despite, it is fair to impute, its governing board members not having the slightest interest in popular music—was something that was completely bewildering. Unless, that is, it was part of his campaign to get the counterculture off his back.

This time, Dylan blinked. He seems to have been shaken by the tidal wave of derision that swept over his legend in the wake of *Self Portrait*'s release. Bizarrely, he also seems to have been bewildered by just how bad people thought it was. A short time later, he seethed to Scaduto in a comment that well predated the I-wish-these-people-would-just-*forget*-about-me quote, 'It's a great album. There's a lot of damn good music there. People just didn't listen at first.' It was assumed at the time that this derision accounted for the alacrity of the release of his next album: *New Morning*—produced by Al Kooper, although Johnston helmed early sessions—hit the shops on October 21 the same year. However, most of that album was recorded before *Self Portrait* had been issued. Which of course doesn't rule out the possibility that Dylan had lost his nerve over the aim of *Self Portrait* before it came out, not least because he later said that it was lying around for a year or so before it was released.

Whatever its motives, *New Morning* was a partial return to form—i.e., all the songs were Dylan's, and it was better than *Self Portrait* and *Nashville Skyline*, even if that's not saying much. This was a pop—as opposed to rock—album of mostly good, sometimes high-quality material, albeit one with the feel of a blandly pleasant and occasionally suffocating summer's day. It contained several paeans to marriage, one to Elvis Presley ('Went To See The Gypsy'), and two to God ('Father Of Night' and 'Three Angels', both surprisingly moving). The waltz 'Winterlude' and the jazz-scat 'If Dogs Run Free' are the only tracks that veer away from pop convention.

Some critics tried to convince themselves and their readers that *New Morning* was a great comeback but, in retrospect, it was obvious that the old Bob Dylan was gone forever. His music was no longer an elemental thing. He was now a jobbing musician, not somebody who lived only to express his worldview through his art. In any case, his worldview was limited to the end of the driveway of the home in which his wife baked and his children caroused. His universe had no room for hate directed toward the Mr Joneses of this world but only love directed toward his family.

And yet…When he sings in 'Sign On The Window' of marrying a wife, catching rainbow trout, and having a bunch of kids who call him 'Pa'—to which he appends, 'That must be what it's all about'—it sounds as if he's trying to *convince* himself, something emphasised by the fact that he then repeats that appended sentiment. Moreover, although his expression of contentment seems genuine enough when he intones, 'Ain't no reason to go anywhere,' why is the title and refrain of the song from which it comes 'Times Passes *Slowly*'? That these are cracks in the façade of a dream in which Dylan was trying with some effort to invest belief seems confirmed by something he later said to a journalist about *Nashville Skyline*: 'You had to read between the lines. I was trying to grasp something that would lead me on to where I thought I should be, and it didn't go nowhere.'

Meanwhile, his self-sabotage might have made him a laughing stock with some, but it didn't shake off the fanatics. He had been so hounded in Woodstock that in late 1969 he actually moved back from that ostensibly unreachable idyll to the bustle of Greenwich Village. There is also some evidence that he—almost paradoxically—wanted to get back into the loop of the music business. Back in New York, though, he found new problems, chief among which was A.J. Weberman, a man who had parlayed his status as a Dylan fan (he founded the Dylan Liberation Front) into a profession via his courses on Dylan at the Alternate University Of New York. Weberman took it upon himself to mount a campaign to persuade Dylan to return to protest music, part of which involved demonstrating with groups of his students outside Dylan's house. These days, the threat of a civil suit against Weberman's employers and a restraining order against Weberman himself would have quickly solved the problem, but back then Dylan could only resort to planting mousetraps in the dustbins Weberman's disciples rooted through and—ultimately, it has been theorised—releasing a protest record to placate him. In November 1971, Dylan issued the single 'George Jackson', an elegy to a Black Panther killed the previous August while attempting to break out of San Quentin prison, where he was being held prior to being tried for the murder of a correctional officer. 'George Jackson' itself was curiously ambiguous and simplistic, but some have attributed Weberman's laying off Dylan to that record, as well as Dylan's surprise appearance at the star-studded benefit concert for Bangladesh in August 1971.

'George Jackson' is now a largely forgotten release, partly because it was a standalone single and partly because it has never been played by Dylan in concert. At the time, though, it achieved a remarkable amount of coverage and praise, and that coverage and praise were clearly intertwined with a joy that 'We've got Dylan back again', to quote the headline of a famously misguided review of *New Morning* by Ralph J. Gleason. In fact, if anything, it drew a line under the old Dylan. He would write a song that was recognisably 'protest' again at least once—'Hurricane' (1976)—but any hope that he was reclaiming his position of king of the counterculture gradually dissipated.

One positive thing that could be extrapolated from the grisly

Weberman affair is that the teaching of a course on Dylan proved the growing respect for popular music in a culture that had once dismissed it as ephemera. Nor was it restricted to 'alternate' universities. By 1977, it was estimated that more than a hundred courses on Dylan's lyrics had been taught in US universities. In the same vein, as Dylan had been the first person to prove that rock could be a grown-up medium, it was absolutely fitting that he became the first ever recipient of a biography that took a rock figure as seriously as a classical composer or a novelist. Anthony Scaduto's *Bob Dylan* (1971) created an entire industry. The process of acknowledgement of popular music and Dylan's worth reached its crescendo in either 1976—when American presidential candidate Jimmy Carter quoted Dylan on both the campaign trail and in his nomination acceptance speech—or 2016, when Dylan was awarded the Noble Prize For Literature.

For over three years after *New Morning*, Dylan released no long-playing records. 'George Jackson' came more than a year after that LP. That and the five 'new' songs on the same month's *Bob Dylan's Greatest Hits Vol. II* (three re-recordings of 'Basement Tapes' numbers; 'Watching The River Flow', a June 1971 Dylan single; and 'When I Paint My Masterpiece', a Dylan song already released by The Band) would be the last the world would hear of Dylan for a further year and eight months. Meanwhile, concerts there were none. Dylan settled back down to raising kids and staying out of people's hair. Possessing, unusually, a years-based rather than recordings-oriented contract, he had the luxury of not having to go in the studio if he didn't want to. He was to some extent ensconced in the music industry, socialising with new talent, producing records, and making plentiful cameo appearances on other people's recordings, but such was his low visibility that journalists began calling him the Greta Garbo of music. 'Watching The River Flow' stated it quite frankly: 'I don't have much to say.'

In July 1973, he broke his silence, but in a way that frustrated his fans because it just seemed another tentative move or cul-de-sac. His soundtrack to the Sam Peckinpah Western *Pat Garrett & Billy The Kid* was, like most soundtracks, only intermittently interesting, even if it did contain the brilliant, brooding 'Knockin' On Heaven's Door', a minor hit. Dylan had a small role in said film but, though a movie lover, his acting career since has been highly sporadic. *Creem*'s Dave Marsh filed an on-set report in which he suggested Dylan was 'a has-been, reduced to playing bit parts on his friends' records, and now, appearing in their movies in minor roles'.

It wasn't until November 1973 that Dylan started recording a new long player of his own. Discounting the Basement Tapes, *Planet Waves* was and is his only full studio album with The Band, an arresting statistic considering how intertwined are their names. It was also his first LP (of two, the other a live set) on Asylum Records (Island Records in the UK) after he briefly left Columbia. For an album that was slapped together simply because Dylan now found himself in an era when a tour was always expected to be something that promoted new product, *Planet Waves* is impressive. Although shot through with that soporific sunny-day quality that afflicted *New Morning*, it's a solid, absorbing effort, and if Dylan's domestic notes would never make as interesting a subject matter as his previous general broadsides and global observations, he at least was now sidestepping his recent banalities. Even better, there were two additions to the body of Dylan classics. One was 'Going, Going Gone', a sad farewell with some fiery guitar work from Robbie Robertson. The other was 'Dirge', an ominous, tortured number detailing the disdain Dylan now felt for the way he was once entranced by the trappings of stardom.

Yet even as he sang the latter song's lyric, Dylan was preparing a return to full-blown stardom as he and The Band got ready for their massive 1974 tour, Dylan's first since '66. While *Planet Waves*' closer, 'Wedding Song'—an unambiguous celebration of Sara—seemed to confirm Dylan's fulfilment through domesticity, it would in fact be the finale to that stage of his life (and, judging by the bitter divorce that followed, could have been complete self-denial).

The tour was a triumph. The live circuit to which Dylan was returning was now very different to what it had been when he was last on the road. Rock was no longer the poor relation of the entertainment business. The 650,000 souls who took in his forty concerts in twenty-one American cities from January 3 to February 14, 1974, did not witness ad hoc gigs with poor acoustics in cinemas and ballrooms but professional, slick arena concerts expertly set up by a large road crew. Accordingly, fans were happy to pay good money for them. It grossed around five million dollars (over thirty million dollars today). Dylan and the band being presented as equals may have rankled with some, especially those who agreed with Band members' suggestions that Dylan was doing them a favour by using them as backing on this tour when he could have had anybody behind him, but the fact is that The Band's output over the last few years had been much more impressive than his: their eponymous 1969 album is considered a classic. Not only were the venues different, the reception was also a contrast. Booed to the rafters the last time they had toured together, Dylan & The Band were greeted orgasmically.

His fans may not have liked the (then) artistic nadir that resulted from Bob Dylan's domestic-bliss years, but during that time he was actually doing with his art what he had always done hitherto: reflecting people's lives. Most of Dylan's generation had followed exactly the same journey from youthful activism through to settling down. Many of them would also, sadly, go through Dylan's subsequent experience of the traumas of divorce, articulated so harrowingly on his next album, *Blood On The Tracks*.

In the early 70s, Dylan's reclusion, low productivity, and negligible artistic standards were spoken of in terms of a national crisis—that is, a crisis for what had (ironically enough, considering his angry non-participation in the titular festival) now become known as the 'Woodstock Nation'. People wrote songs about it: David Bowie's 1971 composition 'Song For Bob Dylan' ('Give us back our unity'), Joan Baez's 1972 track 'To Bobby' ('You left us marching on the road and said how heavy was the load'). The fact is, though—and only with passing years can this be properly appreciated—what was happening to Dylan was the consequence of an immutable fact of life: people grow older, and their priorities change. Even people from a generation that kicked over the traces like no other. Gradually it dawned on his followers that the artistic ambition, creative hyperactivity, and ethical commitment of his twenties were a thing of the past, as was his zeitgeist factor. The trajectory traced by his eponymous 1962 debut album through to *Nashville Skyline* constitutes a full circle—a journey in which he went from a scuffling, ambitious nobody to a cultural icon to a willing background figure. Although domesticity was ultimately not for Dylan, those years were a crucial and merciful escape for him. The image he had—wittingly or otherwise—created during his Decade Of Dissent was something he simply could not live with. Meanwhile, the work rate that went with it could quite bluntly have killed him.

Of course, that image would have eventually and naturally evaporated anyway. Growing older makes one less relevant to younger people, who have their own idols. *Blood On The Tracks* is a beautifully written and played album, and (something seldom discussed) the first album by Dylan's generation of artists to prove that a career did not have to follow what was now becoming a familiar pattern of early peak and long slow decline. However, its lyrical power derived from its acute dissection of middle-age problems rather than anything to which a teen or twentysomething could relate. Moreover, the very fact of his being a spokesman was meaningful only for his cohort; the chasm that existed between the values of the young and old in the 60s pertained less to subsequent generations, whose parents were weaned in a less divided, more tolerant age. Quite simply, increasingly liberal and progressive Western societies have fewer injustices against which to rail than existed in Dylan's day. Even as far back as the early 70s, Scaduto was writing, 'It's difficult to write of Dylan and his decade as a force among the young without making it all sound an exaggeration. He touched the young, deeply.' If the perception and knowledge of Dylan's societal influence was evaporating even then, by the time of Janet Maslin's essay on him in *The Rolling Stone Illustrated History Of Rock & Roll* (1981), Dylan's impact and importance for those who weren't there at the time was assuming the status of something that could only be understood by reading history books. She spoke of the 'scant effect he now has on audiences who weren't with him from the first' and emphasised how critical was timing in his ascendency ('the appearance of a charismatic, messianic singer, articulating an entire generation's feelings of outrage').

This process of diminishing cultural relevance hasn't been helped by things that can far more plausibly be posited as 'betraying values' than can abandoning protest or going electric, such as Dylan during his late 70s/early 80s Born Again Christian phase ranting from the stage about the sordid behaviour of homosexuals, or a middle-aged Dylan in the 80s adopting undignified modish clothing like spandex trousers, or Dylan in 1996 allowing 'The Times They Are A-Changin'' to be licensed for a bank commercial—all moments when one could only concur with the observation in 'It's Alright, Ma (I'm Only Bleeding)' that not much is really sacred.

In Dylan's career there have been long absences and comebacks of variable quality, classic albums and terrible ones, even works whose high quality no one could bring themselves to admit because they couldn't get on board with the manifestos they contained (i.e., at least one of his Born Again trilogy). Since the genuine artistic renaissance marked by 1997's sparkling *Time Out Of Mind*, he has assumed or been granted a position as venerated old man of music, one that it seems will see him out for the rest of his life. The artist who at the peak of his powers disdained to record and refused to perform live now issues product regularly and since 1988 has been engaged in what his fans and the media have dubbed the Never-Ending Tour. In 2020, his imperishable status was confirmed when he became the first artist to achieve a *Billboard* Top 40 album in every decade since the 1960s.

'I think he's most comparable to Shakespeare,' says Al Kooper.

'Every verse of "Desolation Row", it's like a great American short story, condensed. "Masters Of War" is an amazing piece of work. "Hard Rain's Gonna Fall" is an amazing piece of lyrical work. There's really no one that did that after Shakespeare as strongly and uniquely as Bob did ... I think when hundreds of years go by that he will be held in the same view as Shakespeare is held today.'

Inevitably, many young music lovers today either don't know or care that they are negotiating a world whose soundtrack and to a large extent cultural values have been made possible by Dylan's music and image. Few of the artists loved by the present-day young, though, can dream of matching Dylan's achievements in the 1960s when—regardless of personal sales levels—he was the most important artist in popular music, something that in a decade when music was so culturally crucial necessarily made him one of the most important individuals in Western society. His sociological and musical barrier-smashing might be irrelevant for those with no experience of the era in which he operated, his voice of dissent meaningless now that the things to which he was objecting have evaporated, improved, or morphed into different forms. Great music, though, is not dependent on cultural context. Classic songs dot even the lesser albums in Dylan's 60s catalogue, whether they be 'The Times They Are A-Changin'', 'The Lonesome Death Of Hattie Carroll', 'Lay Lady Lay', or 'Tonight I'll Be Staying Here With You'. Meanwhile, *The Freewheelin' Bob Dylan*, *Another Side Of Bob Dylan*, *Bringing It All Back Home*, *Highway 61 Revisited*, *Blonde On Blonde*, the Basement Tapes, and *John Wesley Harding* will—in part or in whole— move and enthral as long as human beings listen to music.

Bob Dylan's priceless recordings from his Decade Of Dissent are forever.

Acknowledgements

My grateful thanks to the following people for speaking to me about Bob Dylan or Dylan-related matters: Vic Briggs, Harvey Goldstein (aka Brooks), Al Gorgoni, Chris Hillman, Paul Jones, Al Kooper, Daniel Kramer, Sam Lay, Donovan Leitch, Charlie McCoy, Roger McGuinn, Tom McGuinness, Frank Owens, John Steel. Interviews with the above were originally conducted for magazine features or other books, but most of the quotes used in this text have not previously been published.

Selected Bibliography

Baez, Joan, *And A Voice To Sing With* (Century, 1988)

Bauldie, John (ed), *Wanted Man: In Search Of Bob Dylan* (Black Spring, 1990)

Blake, Mark (ed), *Dylan: Visions, Portraits & Back Pages* (Dorling Kindersley, 2005)

Cott, Jonathan (ed), *Dylan On Dylan* (Hodder, 2007)

Dylan, Bob, *Chronicles Volume One* (Simon & Schuster, 2004)

Dylan, Bob, *Tarantula* (Panther, 1973)

Dylan, Bob, *Writings & Drawings* (Grafton, 1974)

Egan, Sean (ed), *The Mammoth Book Of Bob Dylan* (Constable & Robinson, 2011)

Gray, Michael, *The Bob Dylan Encyclopedia, Revised* (Continuum, 2008)

Gray, Michael; Bauldie, John (ed), *All Across The Telegraph* (Sidgwick & Jackson, 1987)

Herdman, John, *Voice Without Restraint* (Paul Harris, 1982)

Heylin, Clinton, *Bob Dylan Day-By-Day 1941–1995* (Music Sales, 1996)

Heylin, Clinton, *Behind The Shades* (Penguin, 2001)

Heylin, Clinton, *Revolution In The Air* (Constable & Robinson, 2010)

Heylin, Clinton, *Still On The Road* (Constable & Robinson, 2010)

Heylin, Clinton, *The Double Life Of Bob Dylan Vol. 1: A Restless Hungry Feeling: 1941–1966* (Vintage, 2022)

Humphries, Patrick, *Complete Guide To The Music Of Bob Dylan* (Omnibus Press, 1995)

Irwin, Colin, *Legendary Sessions: Highway 61 Revisited* (Flame Tree, 2008)

McGregor, Craig (ed), *Dylan: A Retrospective* (Angus & Robertson, 1980)

Marcus, Greil, *Like A Rolling Stone* (Faber and Faber, 2005)

Polizzotti, Mark, *Bob Dylan's Highway 61 Revisited* (Continuum, 2006)

Rotolo, Suze, *A Freewheelin' Time: A Memoir Of Greenwich Village In The Sixties* (Aurum, 2009)

Scaduto, Anthony, *Bob Dylan* (Abacus, 1973)

Shelton, Robert, *No Direction Home: The Life And Music Of Bob Dylan* (Da Capo, 1997)

Sounes, Howard, *Down The Highway: The Life Of Bob Dylan* (Doubleday, 2001)

Thomson, Elizabeth M. (ed), *Conclusions On The Wall: New Essays On Bob Dylan* (Thin Man, 1980)

Thompson, Toby, *Positively Main Street* (Coward–McCann, 1971)

Trager, Oliver, *Keys To The Rain: The Definitive Bob Dylan Encyclopedia* (Billboard, 2004)

Wald, Elijah, *Dylan Goes Electric!: Newport, Seeger, Dylan, and the Night That Split The Sixties* (Dey Street, 2015)

Williams, Chris, *Bob Dylan: In His Own Words* (Omnibus, 1993)

Williams, Paul, *Bob Dylan: Watching The River Flow* (Omnibus, 1996)

Williamson, Nigel, *The Rough Guide To Bob Dylan* (Rough Guides, 2006)

bjorner.com/bob.htm
bobdylan.com
expectingrain.com
punkhart.com/dylan
searchingforagem.com
secondhandsongs.com

'The Futuristic Sounds Of The Factory Foreman' by Sean Casey, *Shindig!* issue 159, January 2025

Grateful thanks to Richie Unterberger for help with queries.

Index

Index

Index

269

Also available
from Jawbone Press